AF328383

# ROADSIDE BRITAIN

Text by Sam Mellish
Contributions by Max Houghton & Joe Moran
Photography by Sam Mellish © 2008-2012
Designed by diesel books & Butterdesigns

**diesel books**

**Web:**     www.dieselbooks.co.uk
**e-mail:**  info@dieselbooks.co.uk
**Tel:**     0044 (0) 780 787 0695
**Post:**    deisel books
             3 Sawyers Close
             Capel St Mary
             Ipswich
             Suffolk
             IP9 2HE

British Library Cataloguing-in-Publication Data
A catalogue record for this book is available from the British Library



ISBN: 978-0-9566928-1-8

Printed and bound in China by C&C Offset Printing Co. Ltd.

The imagery from page 47 - 113 was supported by the National Lottery through Arts Council England and first exhibited at the Babylon Gallery, Ely.

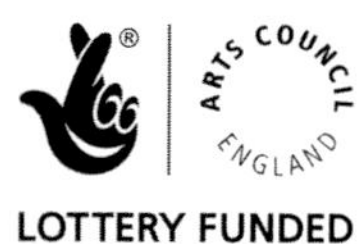

# ROADSIDE BRITAIN

## Sam Mellish

### Introduced by Max Houghton and Joe Moran

diesel books

# Contents

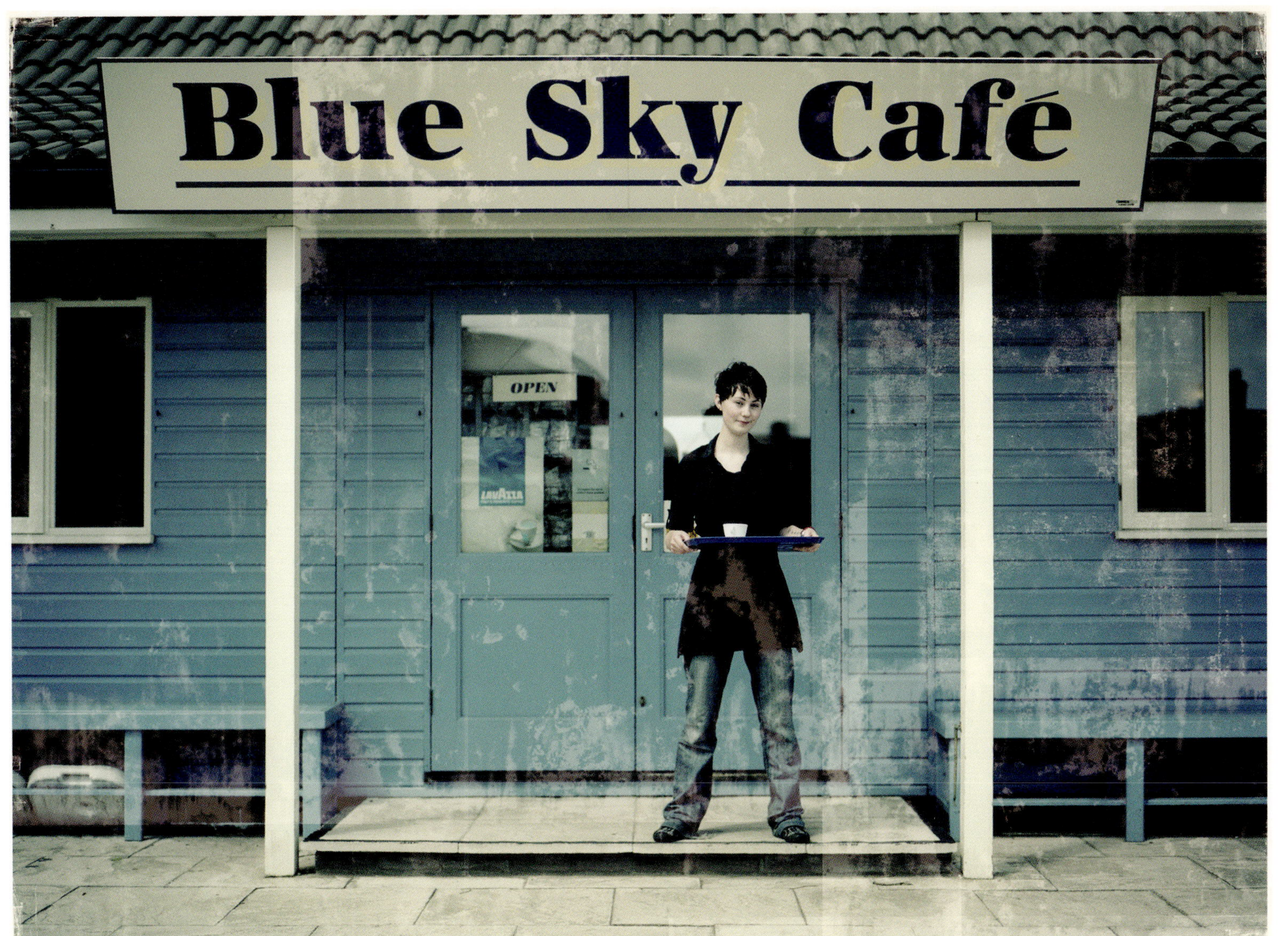

Blue Sky Café
OPEN
LAVAZZA

# Introduction
## by Max Houghton

**S**everal days before the deadline for writing this introductory text for Roadside Britain, I was walking along Upper Street in Islington, wasting time before a talk on photography. It was a clear, bright day, as forgiving as January can muster. A cyclist, sunglasses wrapped around his face, skidded to a halt beside me, calling my name. An unpeeling of various layers of black thermal wear revealed Sam, on his way back, he told me, from reshooting the cover for this book. With a magician's flourish, he pulled a cream paper napkin from his pocket, inscribed in blue biro with our names.

This kind of coincidental encounter happens rarely in a sprawling city like London, and points towards a kind of hidden order, an unfolding pattern that gives meaning to our random lives. Moreover, Upper Street, Sam later told me, is in fact the A1, the starting point for this book, and, to follow an important photographic lineage, for Paul Graham's work from 1981/82, *A1: The Great North Road*. There is certainly a sense that this project developed according to its own logic, fuelled by the thrill of the open road, meandering off in unexpected directions, and even photographic styles, in order to capture the spirit of the roadside café, bastions of anti-corporatism and purveyors of a full English and a proper cup of tea.

Paul Graham, who received an honorary doctorate from the University of Westminster a couple of years after Sam graduated with a Masters in Photojournalism, starts his photographic journey along the Great North Road with an oblique statement of political intent. It's an image that invokes the blue spectre of Margaret Thatcher, taken where the journey from south to north begins, on the A1 outside the Bank of England. Sam begins in another place entirely, making us question the very nature of his storytelling venture from the outset.

The photograph of a waitress outside the Blue Sky Café, shot on ultra-vivid colour film, has a kind of wash over it, making it look more like a poster that might be pasted onto a city wall, graffiti-style (in fact it was used as the invitation to one of Sam's exhibitions of this work in progress). The next image is simply trees on the roadside. Or is it? The trees are confounding nature, perfectly symmetrical. In fact, Sam created a mirror image from the original, a technique he also uses later on (page 62-3) with trees in Thetford Forest. With great journalistic thoroughness, coupled with a wanderer's curiosity, Sam spent time at shacks, huts, burger vans, cafes, diners and laybys the length and breadth of the country, and photographed the people and scenes that moved him. Where Paul Graham was showing us a country downtrodden by a ruling party that decreed 'There's no such thing as society', thirty years later, Sam's work reveals otherwise, seeking out moments of warmth and comfort.

Roads were created to bring us closer to each other (mainly to trade, of course) yet travelling along them for long periods can bring about a profound sense of loneliness and dislocation. Nowhere is this sense of unease more exacerbated than at a motorway service station, featuring the same understaffed, overpriced coffee chain, whose smallest cupsize must translate as Italian for 'bucket'. What Sam has observed in dozens of roadside cafes across the country is individuality, personal commitment, a lack of conformity to the latest trends, and most of all, a powerful sense of authenticity. It's right there in the food, in the bacon, egg and beans. It is celebrated in basic English eating habits that predate the mozzarella panini. It's found at Maz's Munchies, Daisy's Catering and Lucky Charms, where work looks like an extension of family life, not the other way around.

While these photographs celebrate an authentic sense of Britishness, there is also a debt to the American road trip, as it has been immortalized through photography, most notably that of Robert Frank. Hollywood Legends Diner in Swaffham, Norfolk, or the Stadium Diner in Colsterworth, Lincolnshire, each nestle into the English countryside like a small slice of 1950s America. If what was being served up there then was freedom, perhaps its UK incarnation offers a more stoic kind of hope.

Photography is often employed to record evidence, to capture things before they disappear. As the recession hits hard in high streets all over Britain, the survival of independent retailers becomes ever more parlous. This leaves us with a question that will only be answered by time itself: is this photographic ode to Roadside Britain a eulogy?

**Max Houghton, Brighton, February 2012**

# Roadside Cultures
## by Joe Moran

In his recently published memoir, *I, Partridge*, the North Norfolk digital radio presenter and former BBC chat show host Alan Partridge writes that one of the programme ideas he once unsuccessfully pitched to the BBC was 'Motorway Rambles': walking the hard shoulders of British trunk roads with special permission from the Transport Police.

Everyone immediately understands the joke, because spending any more time by the British roadside than you have to is supposed to be an inherently absurd activity. The roadside has long fed into resilient British narratives of nostalgia, loss and self-depreciation. The roadside verge is a hybrid place, neither urban nor rural, in which elegists can contemplate the natural world and lament its encroachment by modern abominations. These anxieties date back to the interwar period, when the rise of the motor car and the arrival of the National Grid meant that houses and factories tended to be built along roads rather than near coalfields. Many observers saw in Britain's new roadside topography the symptoms of moral degeneration and social crisis. Throughout J.B. Priestley's *English Journey* (1934), the roadside serves as a metaphor for cultural change, an augury of a future England made up of Tudor-style chain pubs, lock-up shops and redbrick villas where 'everything and everybody is being rushed down and swept into one dusty arterial road of cheap mass production and standardized living'.

Before the M1 opened in 1959, there were no service stations and roadside variety reigned. Well-to-do motorists, the so-called 'gin and jag' brigade, frequented the road houses, like the Clock at Welwyn on the Great North Road or the Ace of Spaces on the Kingston bypass: lavish hostelries with swimming pools, ballrooms and even polo fields attached. Lorry drivers, meanwhile, swore by the greasy spoon transport caffs, like Kate's Kabin on the A1 or Bert's on the A30, fondly known as 'Bert's Gone Mad', after he celebrated 20 years in business in the early 1950s by slashing the price of a cuppa to a penny.

When they first opened, the motorway service stations were stylish places to which young people would drive at high speeds to play pinball and drink Cona coffee, as a more alluring alternative to the only other all-night venue, the launderette. Bridge restaurants were built over the motorways, so that patrons could practise what now seems a strange form of sightseeing: watching speeding traffic. You could even buy postcards from vending machines, and send your loved ones a souvenir of your trip to Newport Pagnell.

By the mid-1960s, though, habit had worn a hole in the service station's allure. The operators began to cut their overheads, and the service station became a notorious land of unswept floors, sticky tabletops and congealed food slowly expiring under hot lamps. Its awfulness became part of our national mythology, a metaphor for the general malaise of economic and cultural decline. For a certain generation of motorist, the words 'Newport Pagnell' or 'Scratchwood' are like Proust's madeleine, instantly conjuring up a host of mental associations: our post-imperial, post-industrial identity crisis encapsulated in a gristly Scotch egg.

Margaret Thatcher tried to solve this with her very first privatisation scheme in 1979, selling off the motorway service area freeholds and allowing private franchises to invest in the sites. This deregulation of the industry got rid of much of the grottiness and transformed the service station into a super-bland corporate space, like a roadside shopping mall. The infamous cafeterias gave way to 'food courts', open-plan spaces with communal seating surrounded by counters for McDonald's and Burger King. Nowadays the service stations are like quasi-airports: clean, efficient and expensive. Even the A roads, which used to be the last redoubt of the transport caff and the Little Chef – that peculiarly British fusion of neo-vernacular folksiness and American diner flashiness – are being colonised by chain-owned service stations, identical to those found on motorways. By the roadside, a corporate-owned monoculture increasingly rules.

But there are some parts of the British roadside that still resist the relentless pull of sameness and blandness, and these improvised roadside shacks are the subject of Sam Mellish's ongoing photographic project, On the Road. In this he joins an emerging but increasingly distinguished tradition. It was probably Paul Graham who began it all with his photographic project on the A1 (the 'Great North Road') conducted during 1981 and 1982, a subject returned to by Jon Nicholson in his 2004 book *A1: Portrait of a Road*. Until the 1960s, the A1 was the main road connecting the north and south of Britain, but it has now been superseded by the M1 and other motorways, so both Graham and Nicholson seek to represent a partially dying world. It is here that you see drivers sitting alone: lone bikers resting their helmets on tabletops or men in hangdog suits with vacant stares – the sort of sad roadside cafe people whom the philosopher Alain de Botton has compared to the lone figures in Edward Hopper paintings.

Others have joined the pilgrimage by the roadside: the Church of England vicar John Davies in his book *Walking the M62*; the artist Edward Chell, who combines oil paintings depicting motorway verges on the M6 with text pieces in the form of customised road signs; and the poets Paul Farley and Michael Symmons Roberts in their recent book Edgelands. Like these artists and writers, Sam Mellish demonstrates that spending time carefully observing and recording what goes on by the British roadside is not in fact a remotely Partridgesque activity. It is a worthwhile, enlightening and often touching one.

**Joe Moran, Liverpool, November 2011**
**Author of *On Roads: A Hidden History***

# A Brief History of Roadside Britain

We spend much of our lives on the road: commuting, working, making our way to friends or family, setting off on holiday, or just drifting and letting loose, enjoying a spontaneous road trip. Roads have become an intrinsic part of our culture. From Kerouac's seminal *On The Road* and the songs of Willy Nelson and Bobby Troup's *Route 66*, written in celebration of the American open road, to the more modern day and prosaic accounts of road-use in the UK by Morrissey and Billy Bragg (and not forgetting Chris Rea's *Road to Hell*, written during a hellish traffic jam on the M25), the concept of the road is ingrained in our vernacular.

The imagery which features in this book was created over three distinct periods. It was in 2008, while studying for a Master of Arts at the University of Westminster, that I first considered a documentation of traditional roadside services in the UK. Taking influence from Paul Graham, Martin Parr, Tony Ray Jones and, to my mind, the absolute master of 'On The Road' style photography, Robert Frank, I initially planned a trip from Land's End to John o'Groats. However it soon became clear that this journey was just too big to complete in the three-month time frame available, so I decided to concentrate on a London to Land's End leg for my final project, which was more achievable, given the time constraints.

Graduating with an MA in Photojournalism, and with the beginnings of a totally new style of photography, I decided to seek funding to complete my initial Land's End to John o'Groats plan. To my delight, help came in 2009 from the Arts Council of England; with support from ADeC (Arts Development in East Cambridgeshire) and the Babylon Gallery in Ely, I was awarded a Grant for the Arts. My initial application to capture material throughout the whole of the UK was denied, but not to be defeated, I made a second proposal to concentrate on the trunk roads of East Anglia (Suffolk being my birthplace), ending with a six week solo exhibition at the Babylon Gallery. In October 2009 my application was granted.

After nine months documenting roadside service culture on my home patch, ending with a well-received exhibition at the Babylon Gallery in August 2010, I paused to consider my next move. I did not have to wait for long. Having self-published my debut book, *On The Road: London to Land's End* as a limited run to complement the exhibition, the work was shortlisted as one of 20 street photography books created using the do-it-yourself book producer *Blurb*, to be exhibited at the Format International Photography Festival in Derby in 2011.

This gave me both the confidence and the means to once more broaden the scope of the project. From London to Land's End and the trunk roads of East Anglia, I decided to push the boundaries of the project not only to the north of Scotland, but into Wales and across the water into Ireland. By the middle of that year, after celebrating a second three month exhibition, this time at Ipswich Art School, I was able to self-fund the numerous trips in and out of London required to complete the series.

From the initial thought in 2008 to the resultant book in 2012, the creation of *Roadside Britain* has proved to be quite a journey, both in a figurative and literal sense. It's taken well over 6000 miles, well into 800 litres of petrol, hundreds of cups of tea and nearly as many bacon sandwiches. I hope you enjoy it.

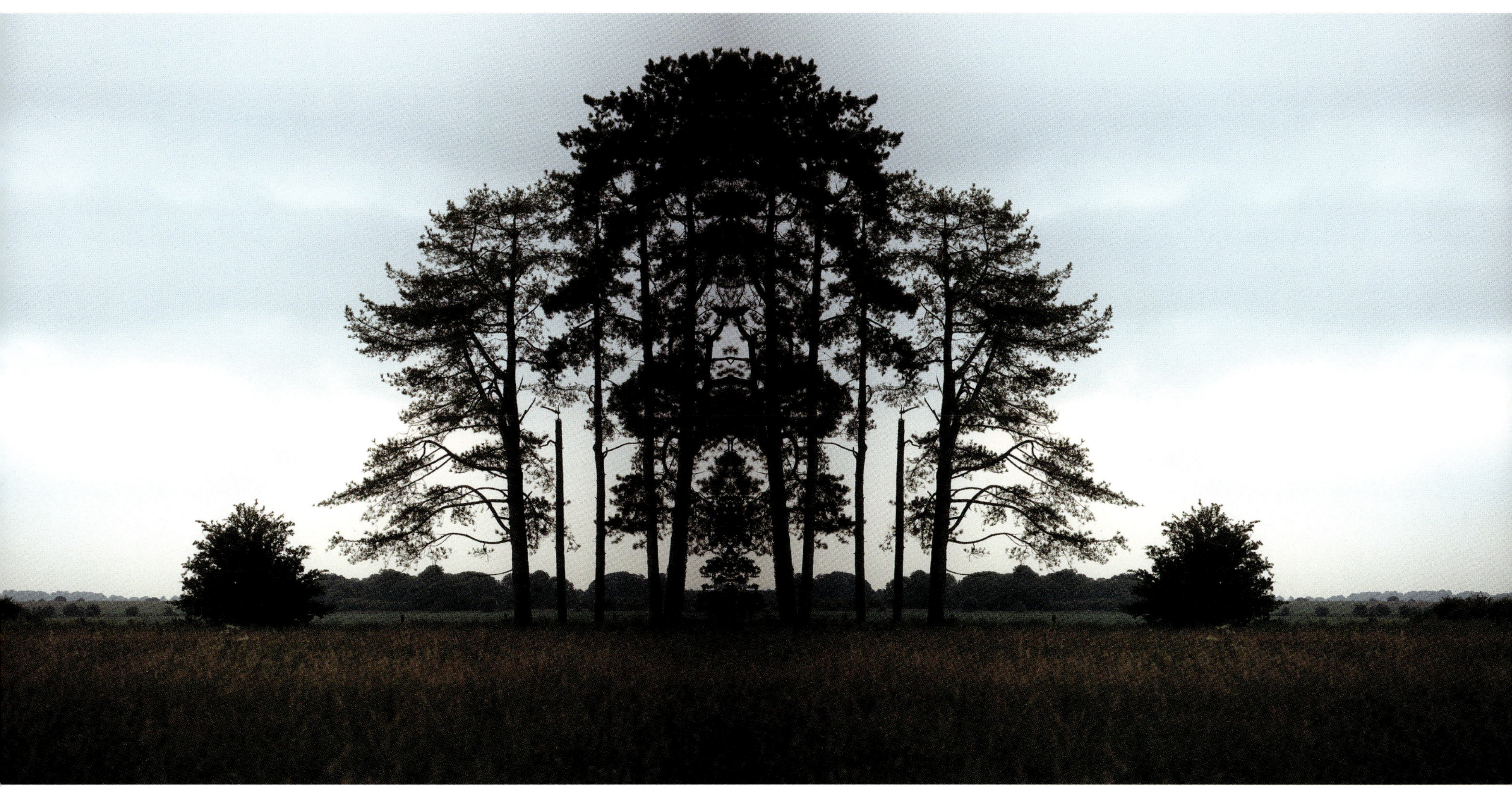

# A1: The Test Shoot

**B**efore I began this project back in 2008, I wanted to test both my equipment and what it would be like to shoot in the environment of a traditional roadside caff.

For some time I'd wanted a good reason to shoot on a proper medium format camera, having always been drawn to the dimensions of a square image as well as the grainy results that film delivers. I'd been shooting on a Woca 120G, ever since buying one of the unorthodox plastic medium format cameras on Sunset Boulevard in Los Angeles, following a winter in New Zealand in 2005. These pin-hole analogue toys became a fad with the rise of the Lomography worldwide community, but I wanted to up my game and use a traditional medium format camera, one that offered perfect results.

Incorporating both film and digital seemed to be the perfect combination for this project. At the time, I was shooting day to day on a Canon EOS5D, which was ideal for non-stop reportage, so I loaned a medium format Bronica 6x6 from the University of Westminster, which required a more composed and considered approach.

Back then I was living in Muswell Hill in North London. Before I set off on the 284-mile-long journey along the A30 to Land's End, I wanted to gauge the reaction of the subjects, and determine my shooting style. I also needed to familiarise myself with the Bronica viewfinder. Naturally I headed to Paul Graham's home turf, the A1 at Goswell Road, heading north past Holloway. Eschewing my digital camera, and only allowing myself one roll of 120mm film, I set off on my old-fashioned Raleigh three-speed bicycle. I spent much of this time in The Hope Workers Cafe, where Chris and Sue Anayiotou (the chef and waitress pictured opposite) allowed me a free rein to shoot. The results felt very organic and ultimately encouraging. A metaphoric green light was given for this project to take shape and by all accounts, I was rather excited.

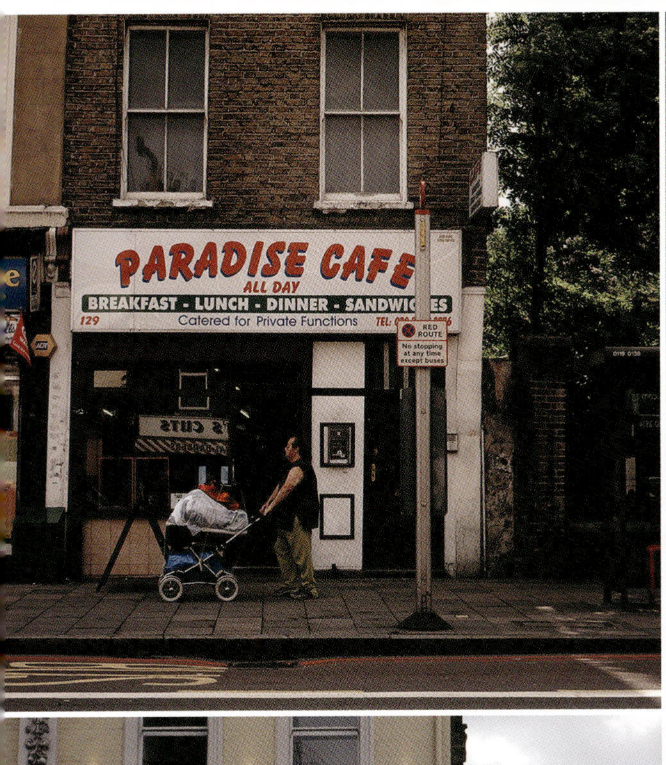

PARADISE CAFE
ALL DAY
BREAKFAST - LUNCH - DINNER - SANDWICHES
129
Catered for Private Functions
TEL:
RED ROUTE
No stopping at any time except buses


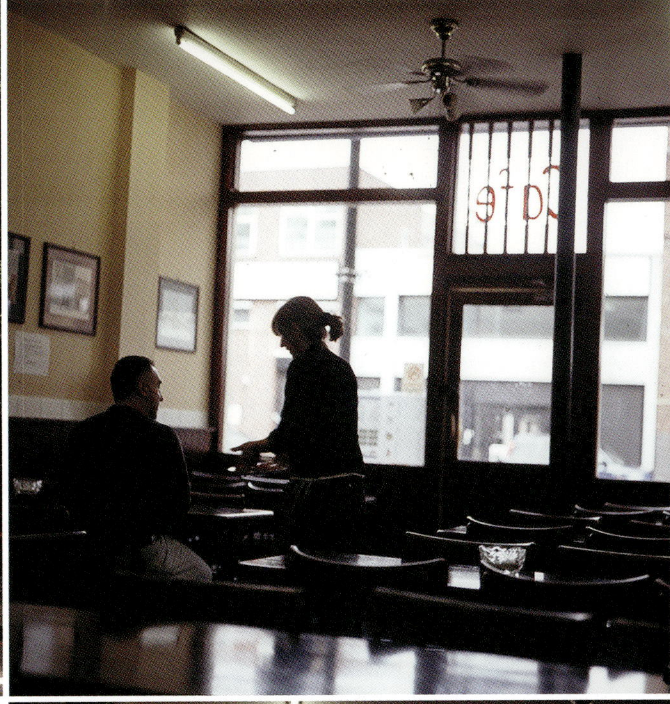

Cafe


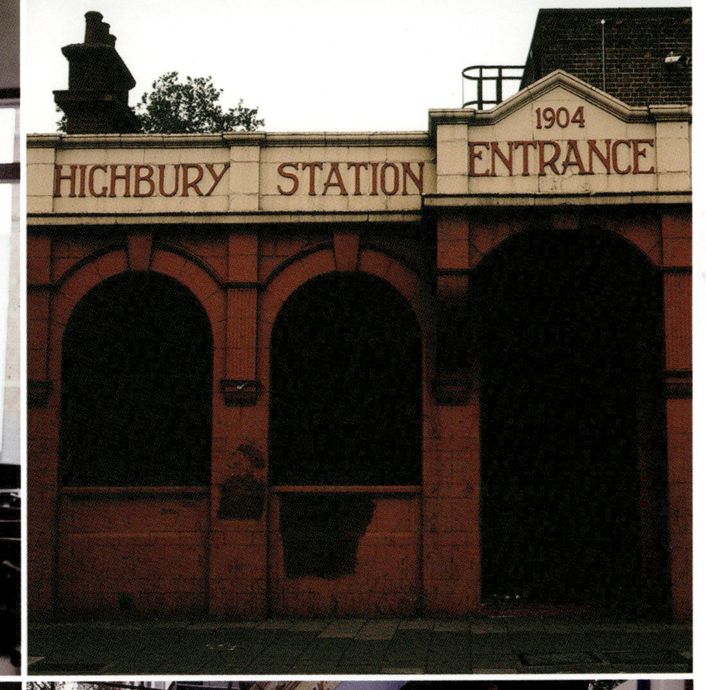

HIGHBURY STATION ENTRANCE
1904


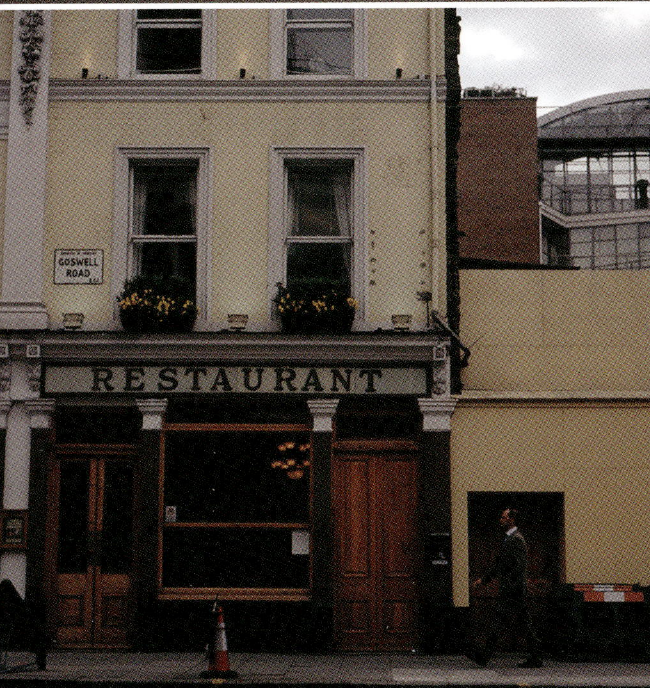

GOSWELL ROAD
RESTAURANT


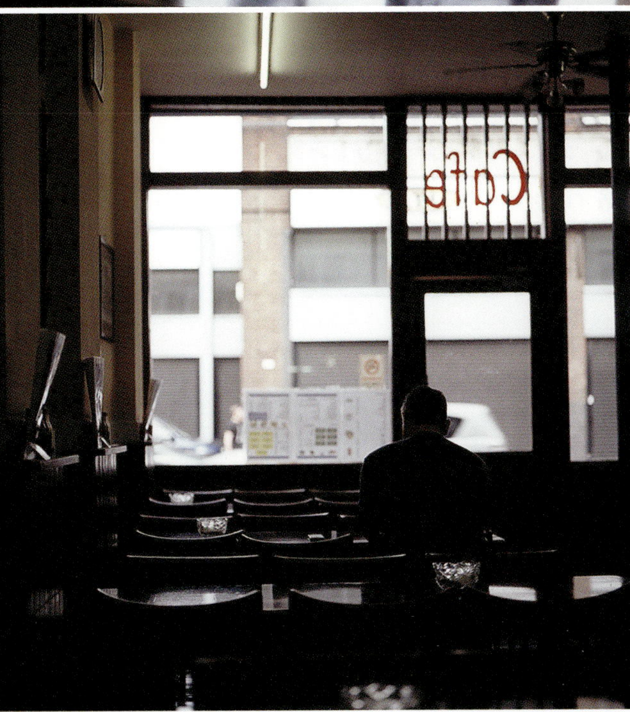

Cafe


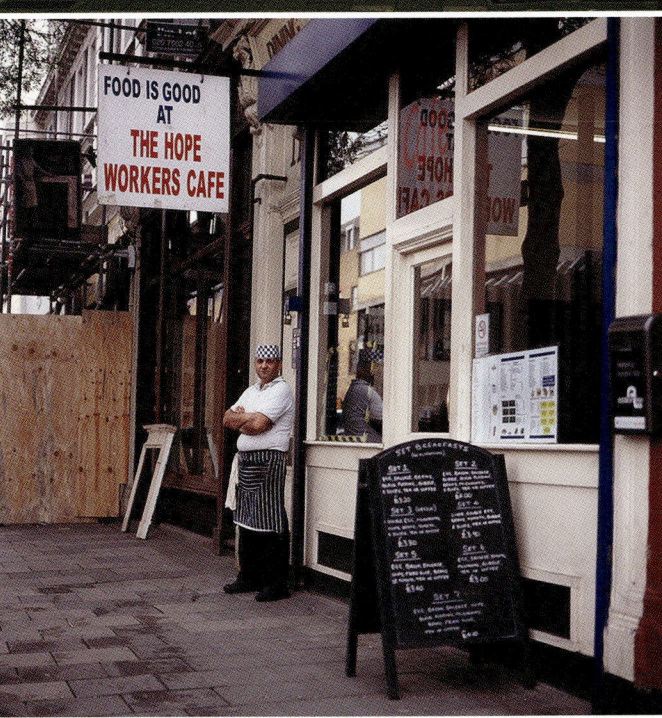

FOOD IS GOOD
AT
THE HOPE
WORKERS CAFE

# London To Land's End

London to Land's End, a sprint from commerce to coast, traverses spectacular countryside. The route's origins lie in the era when the Romans were in full pursuit of their conquest of Britain. The London to Exeter via Silchester route was one of the first roads in the country to lay its foundations. Stretching through eight counties, with 284 miles of tarmac ending at Lands End peninsular, the route became typically known as the Great South West Road, and has been a getaway route for many over the years.

Paul Graham's early work, *A1, The Great North Road* is essentially an observation of England and English society, using the road as a guise; a portrait of the North-South divide, as the A1 travels from an early 1980s Conservative London, to a bleak, recession-hit North. The images were a huge influence when I first began this work; notably that of a waitress at John's Cafe in Sandy, Bedfordshire, another showing blue boiler-suited lorry drivers discussing redundancies at the Morley Cafe in Markham Moor, and the image of the rain sodden Little Chef at St Neots. I was also hugely affected by Rupert Martin's introductory quote, used by Graham in the preface.

> *"The road is a no-man's land on the edge of society, and its inhabitants – the staff of cafés or hotels, the lorry drivers, salesmen and others who ply the road – are often imbued with a solitary stoicism, a kind of self-sufficient melancholy"* [1]

Taking inspiration from Martin's prose and Graham's imagery, I set about creating a body of work, which observes the way roadside cultures coincide. I asked myself: what do we look for when drifting? What eradicates the drudgery of getting from A to B? What contrasts the iconic Route 66 culture with Great Britain's trunk roads? As Joe Moran mentioned in his preface, *Roadside Cultures*, if it's such a chore to spend so much time on the road, why is the notion of a road trip so romanticised?

The A30 – the Great South West Road – was the perfect route to initially document. A single road joining the city with the sea, it has been the blight or delight of commuters since early history. I incorporated the A303 into this work as much of the A30's traffic was re-routed in the 1960s, after the need for rejuvenation and the demand for faster journey times. With a historic link to the A30, I found the characters along the A303 equally intriguing.

The imagery over the next 30 pages was completed over two ten-day trips in spring 2008. With my old Rover 216 laden with what seemed like masses of camera equipment, a borrowed tent and a sleeping bag, it was the beginning of an adventure that would last for the next four years as I trudged the length and breadth of the country to document, observe and converse with as many people as possible. Back in 2008, I was entirely naive about producing a project in this manner, and I think this was my biggest advantage. Unencumbered by expectation, I still consider these initial images to be some of the best in the whole series.

---

[1] *Rupert Martin: Written for A1: The Great North Road by Paul Graham, Grey Editions, 1983*

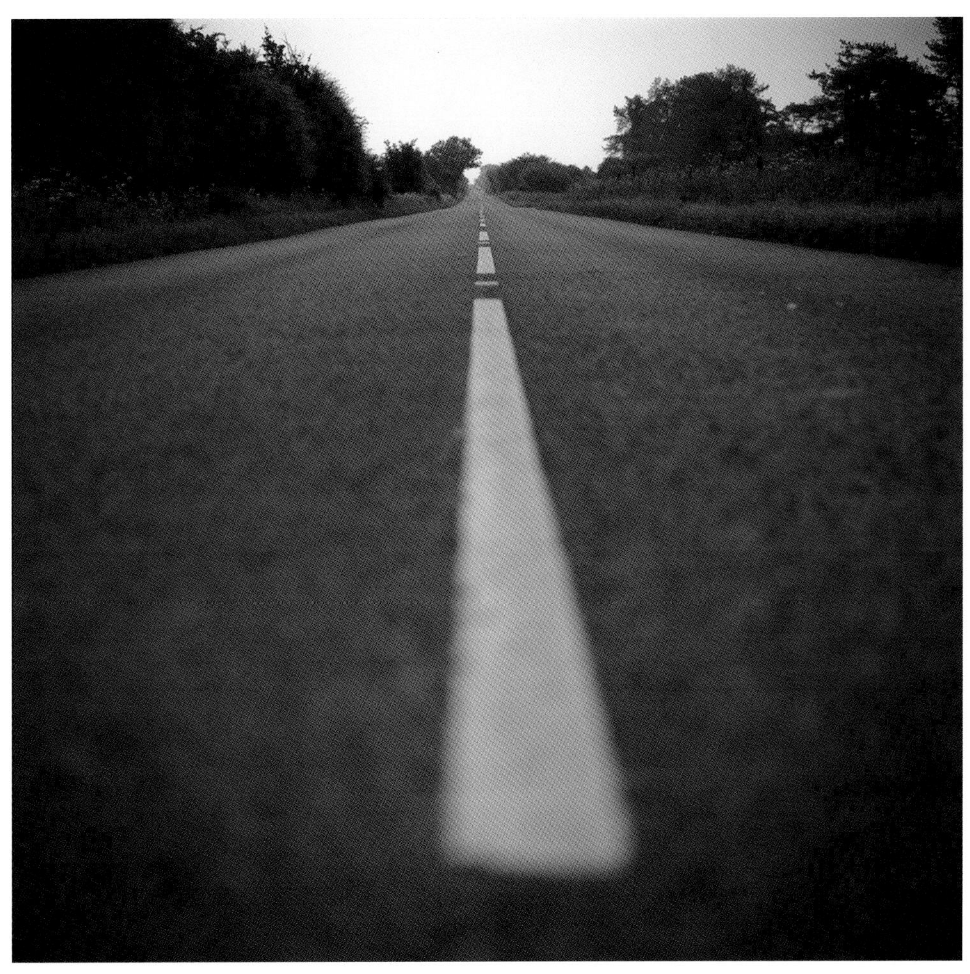

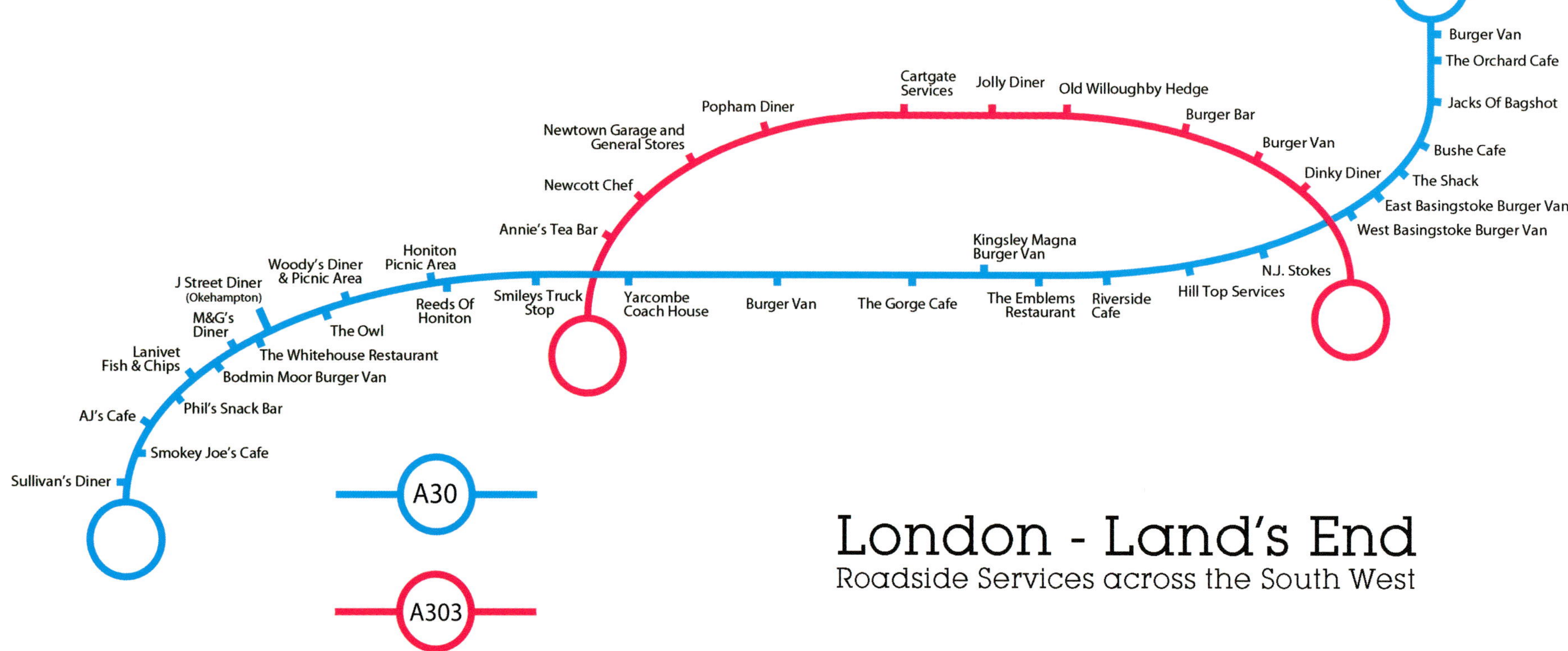


# London - Land's End
## Roadside Services across the South West

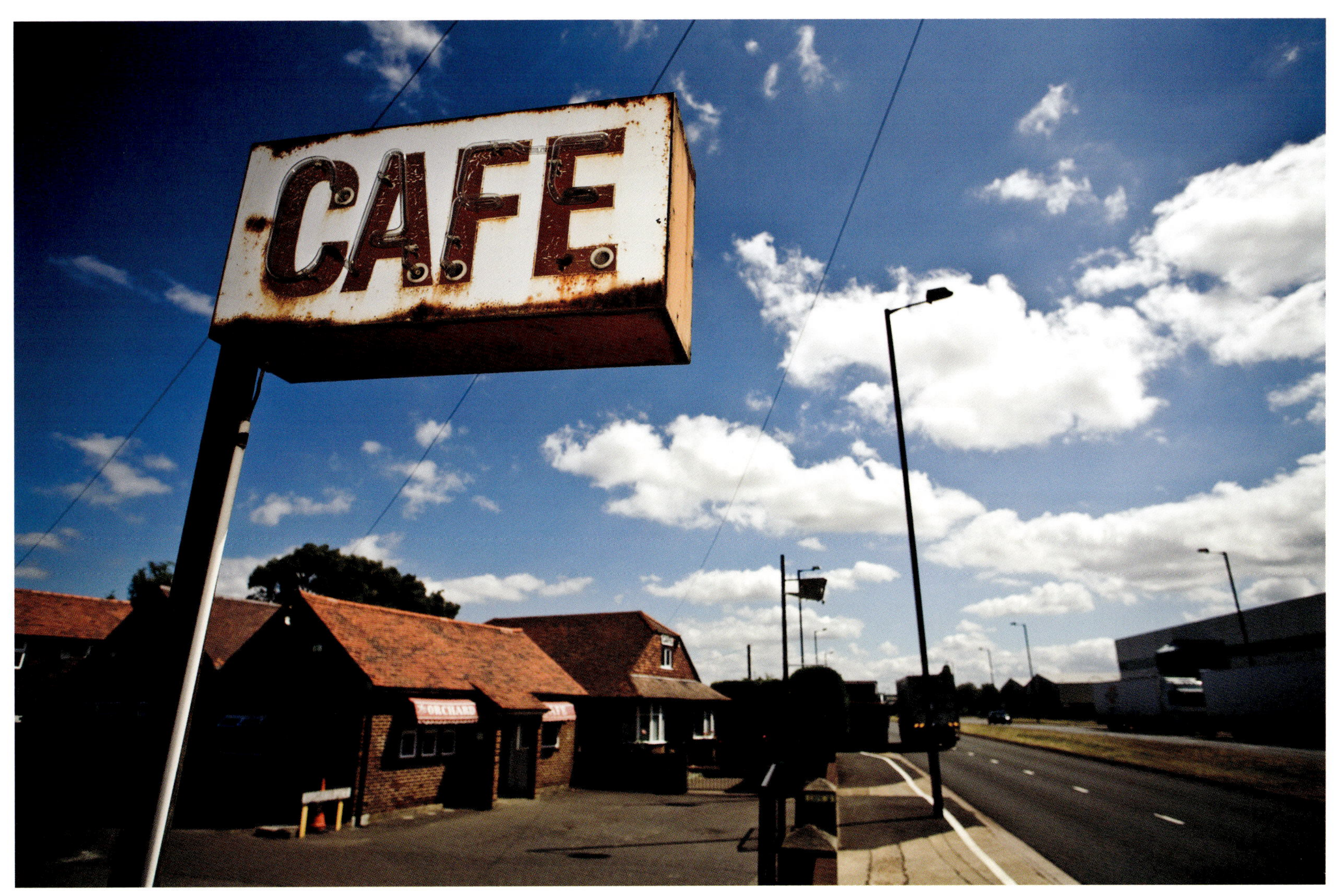


The Orchard Cafe – Staines Road – Hounslow – Greater London – A30

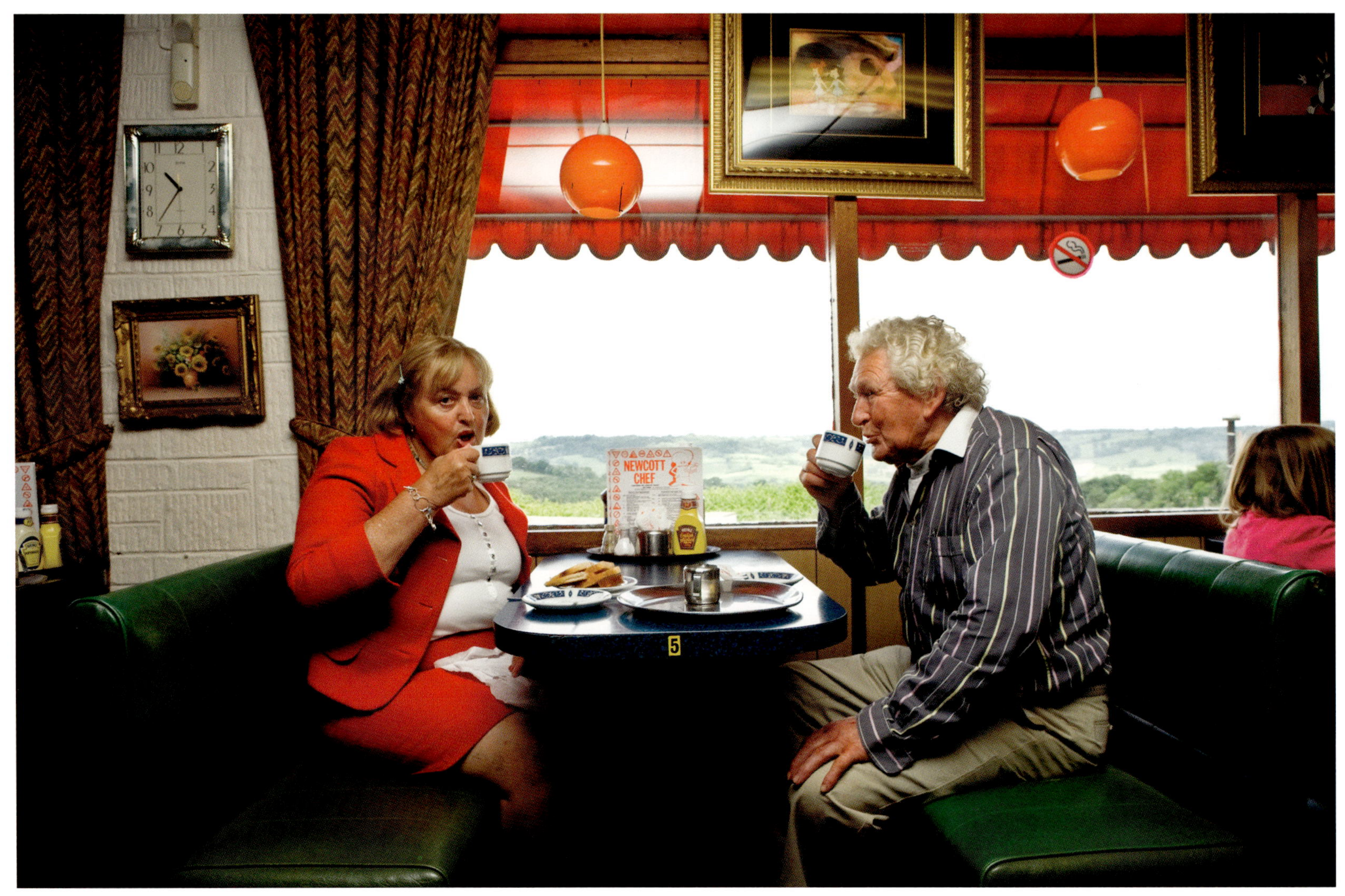

  Tea and Toast – Newcott Chef – Yarcombe – Devon – A303

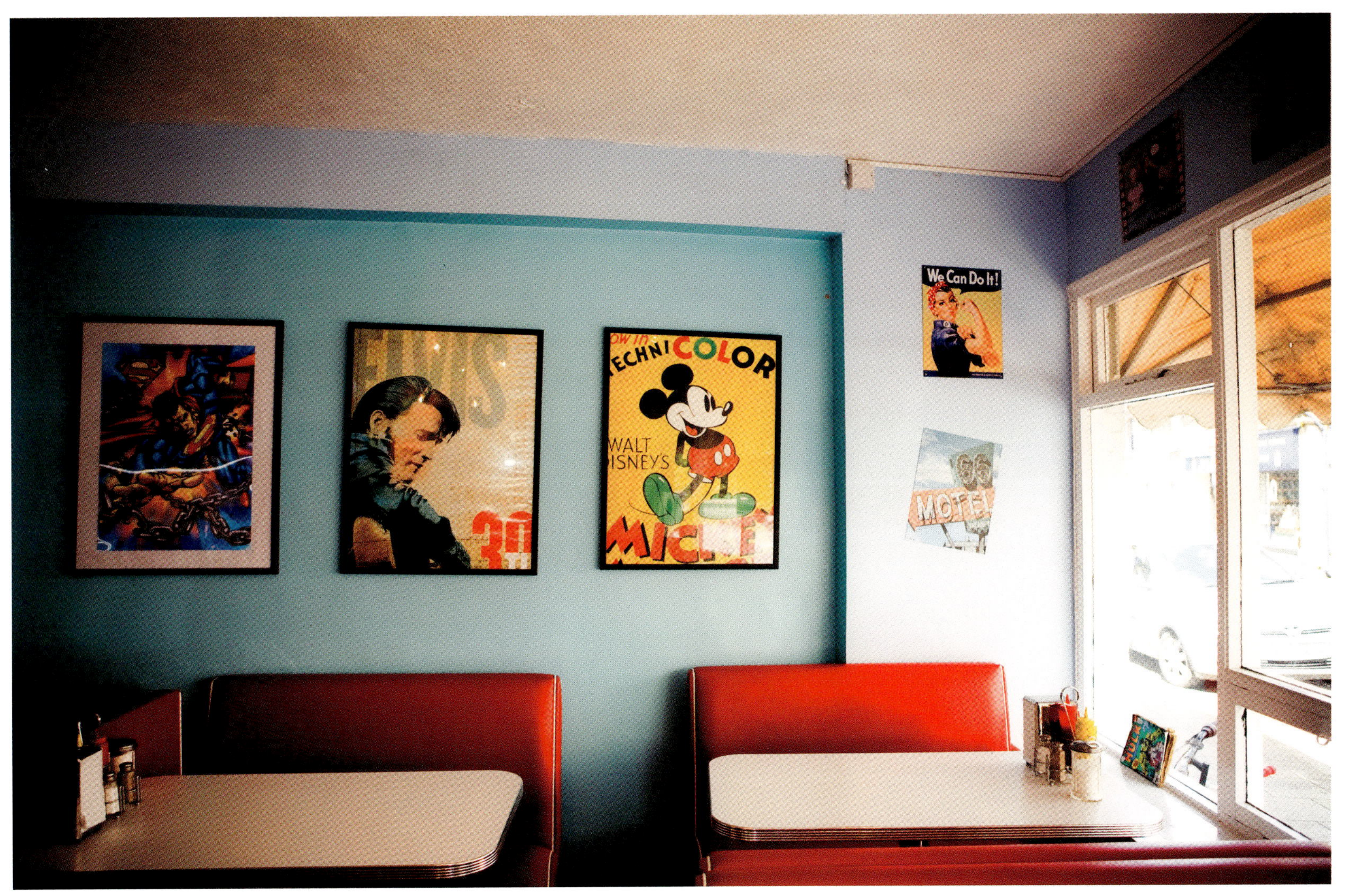


J Street Diner – Okehampton – Devon – Off the A30      19

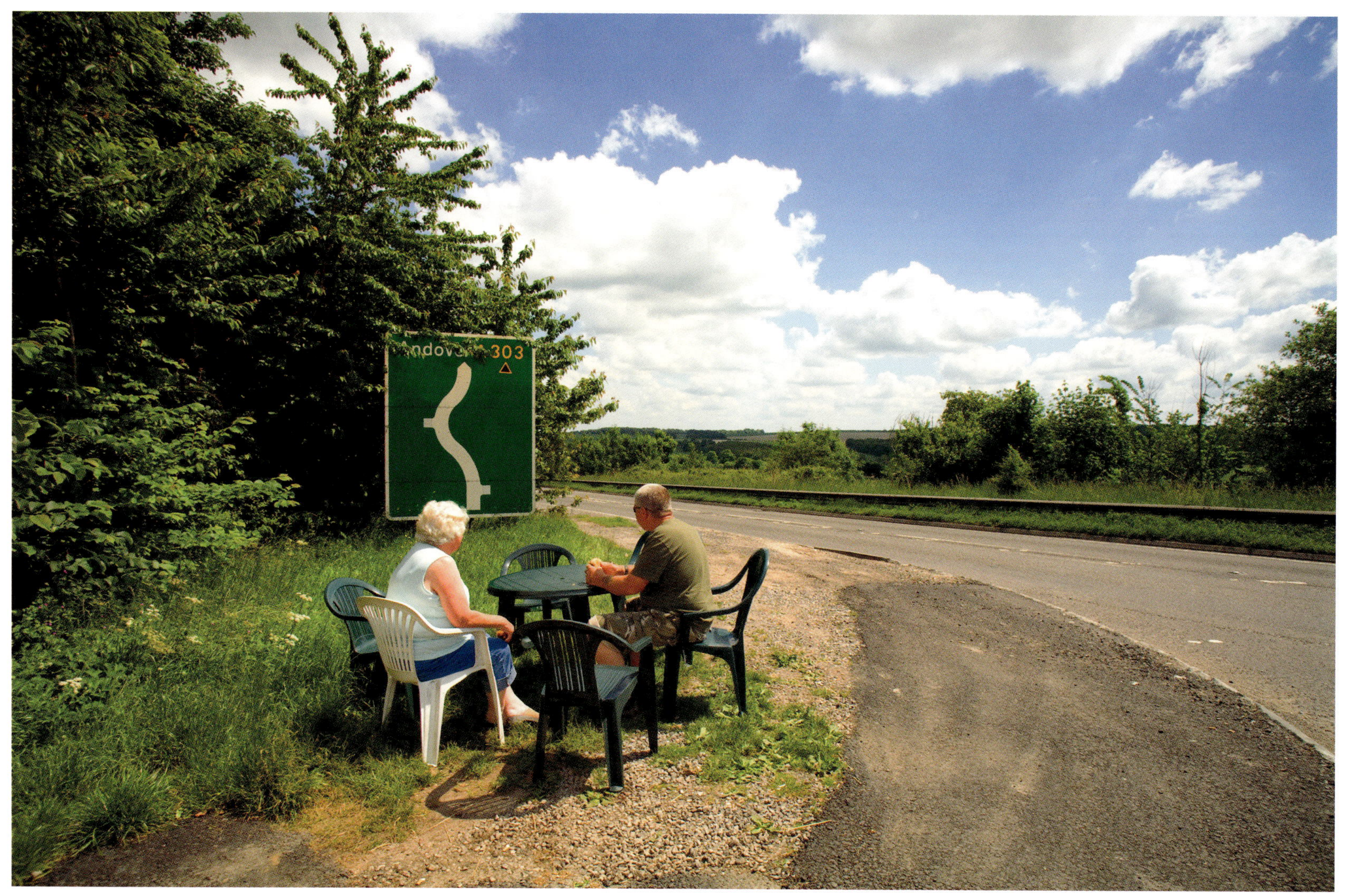


 Lunch with a View – Winterbourne Stoke – Wiltshire – A303

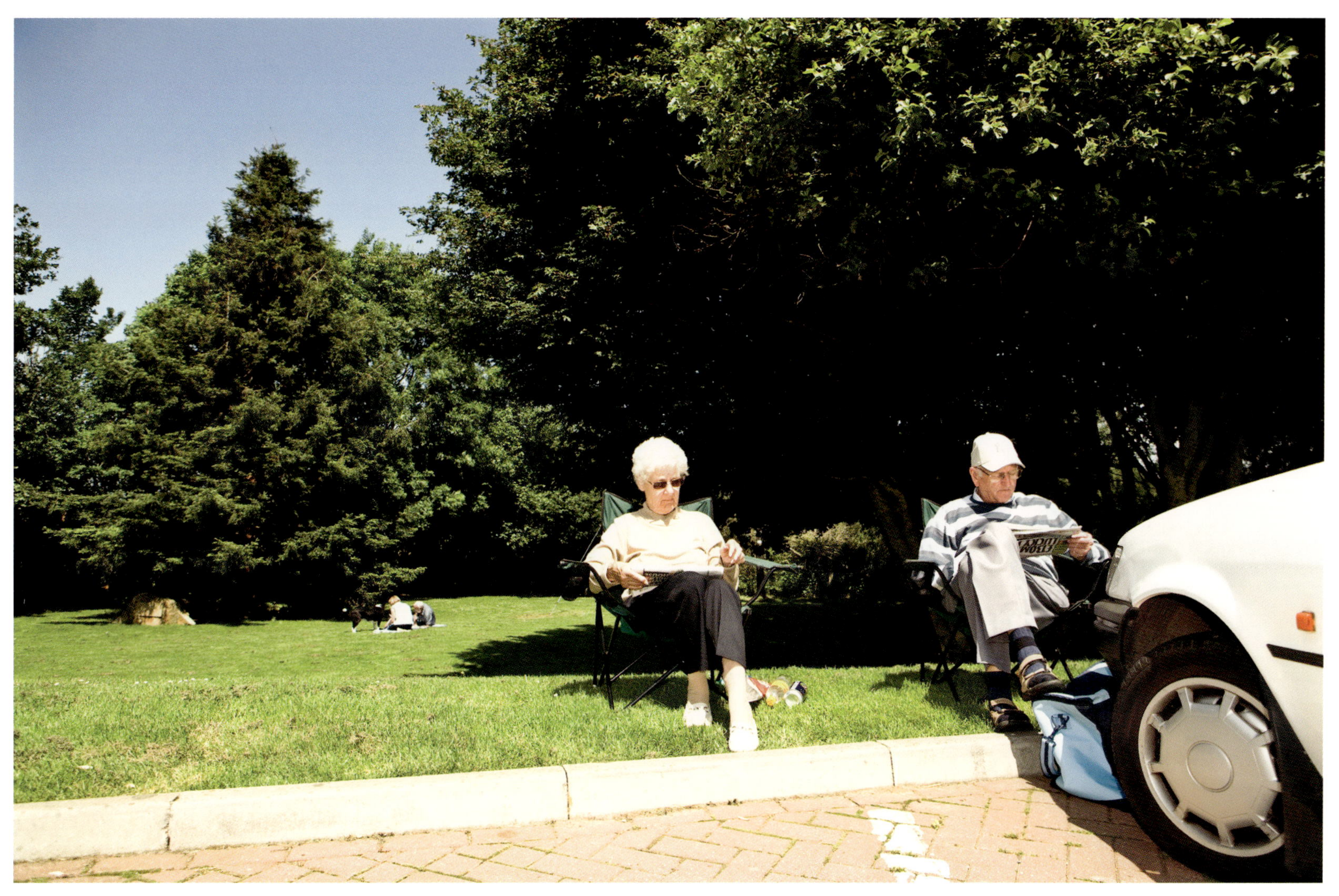

Boycotting the Mainstream – Cartgate Services – Devon – A303    21

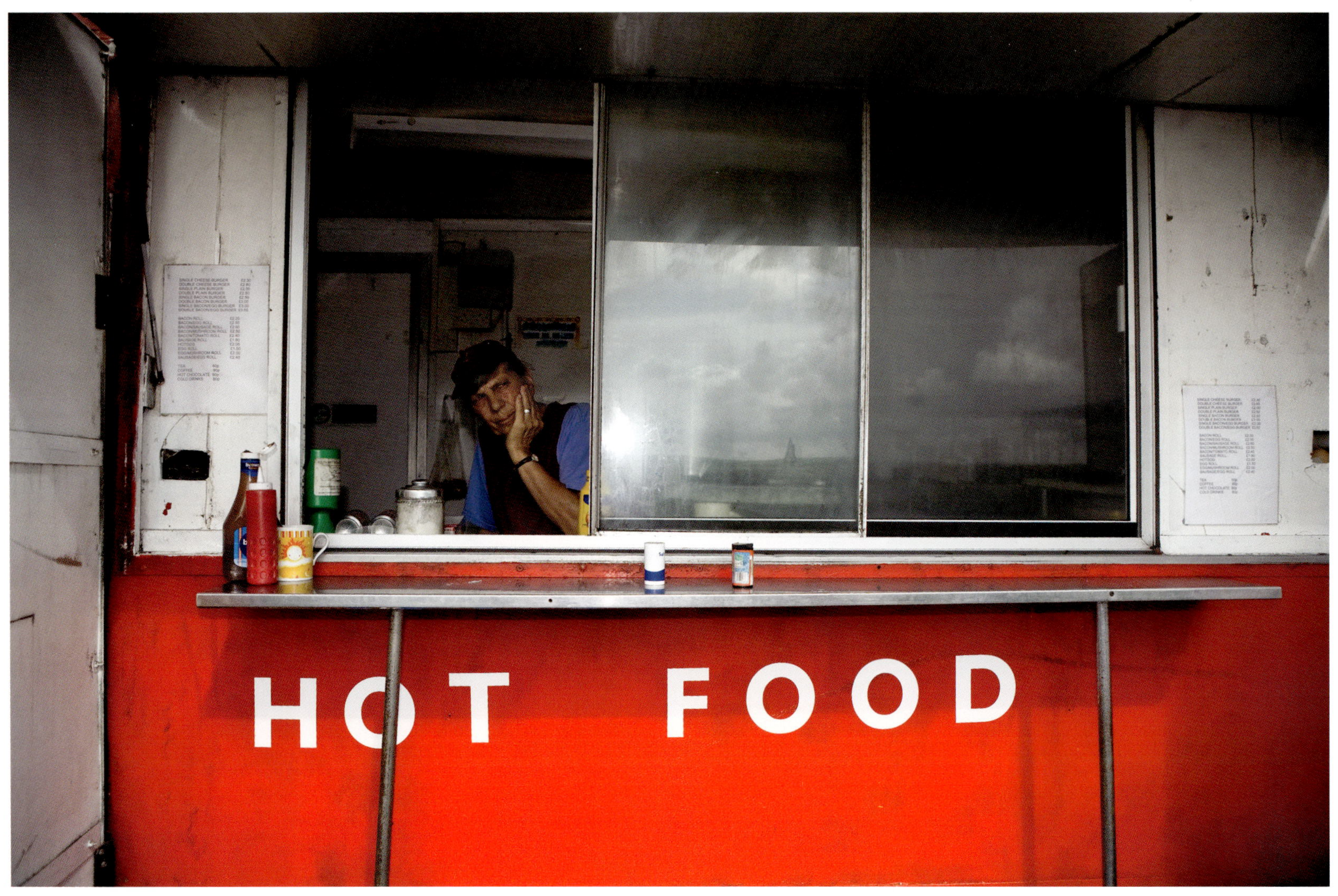



 Between Services – Bodmin Moor Burger Van – Cornwall – A30

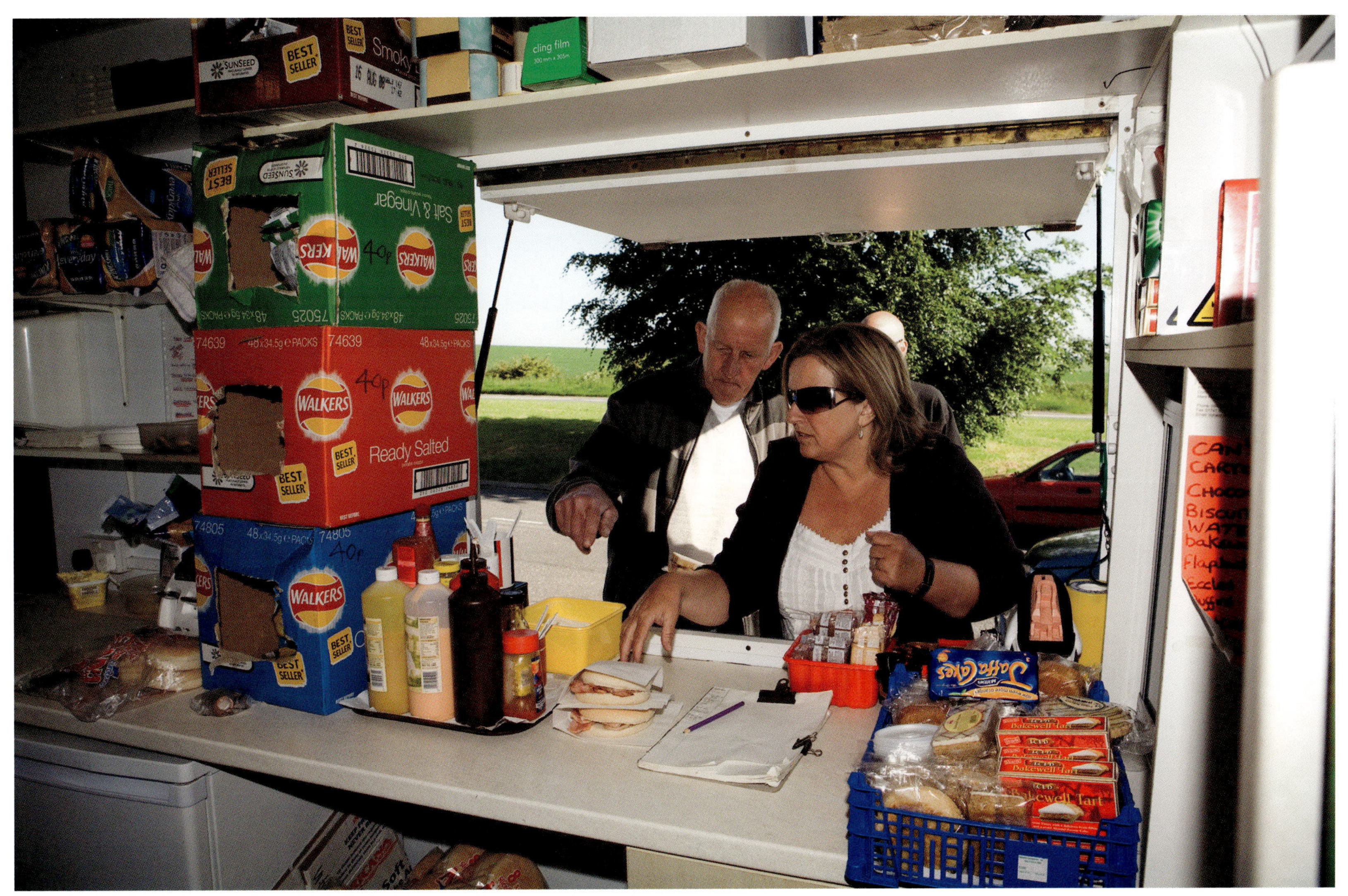



Mid Morning Rush – Old Willoughby Hedge Cafe – West Knoyle – Wiltshire – A303    23

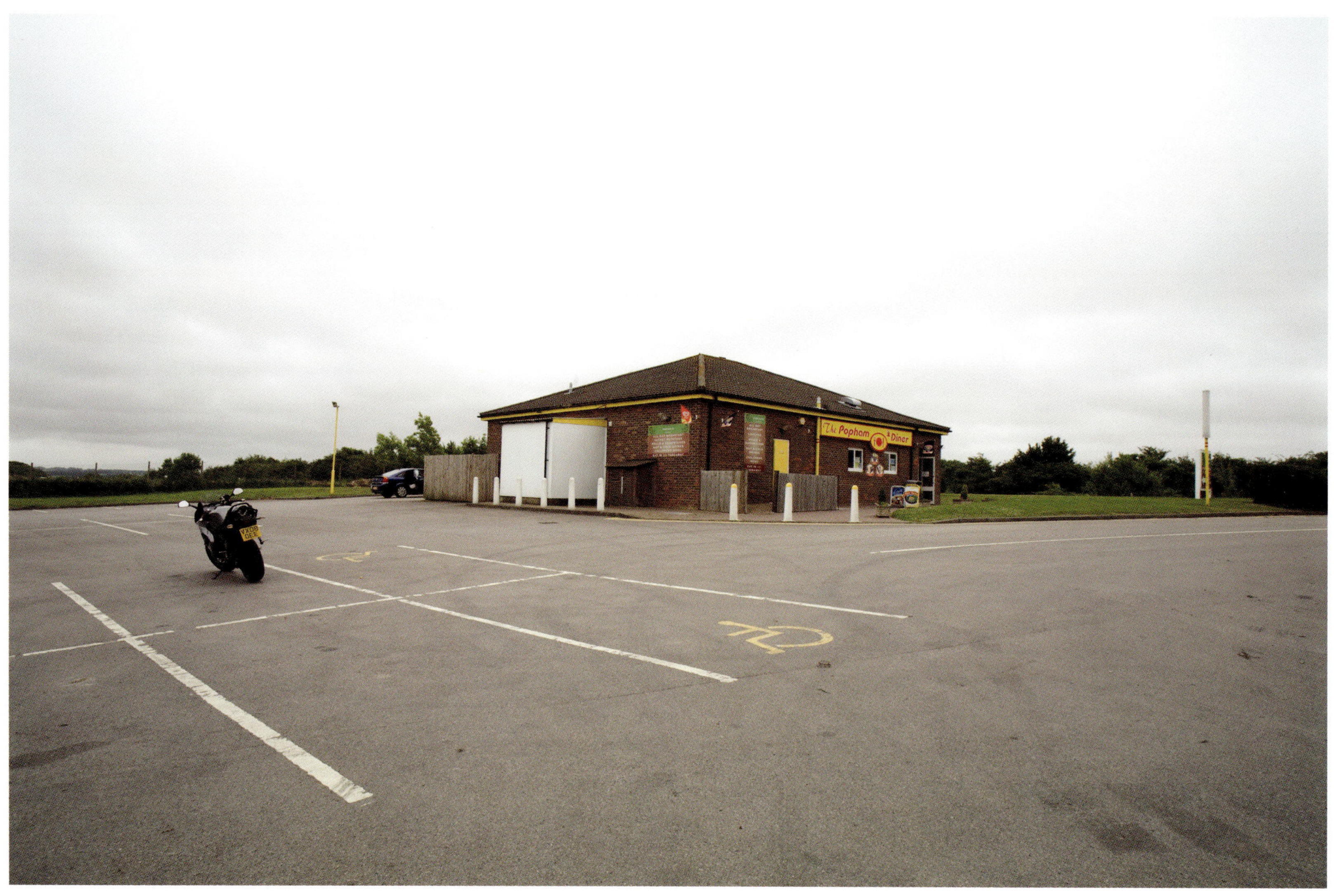

  The Popham Diner – Popham – Hampshire – A303

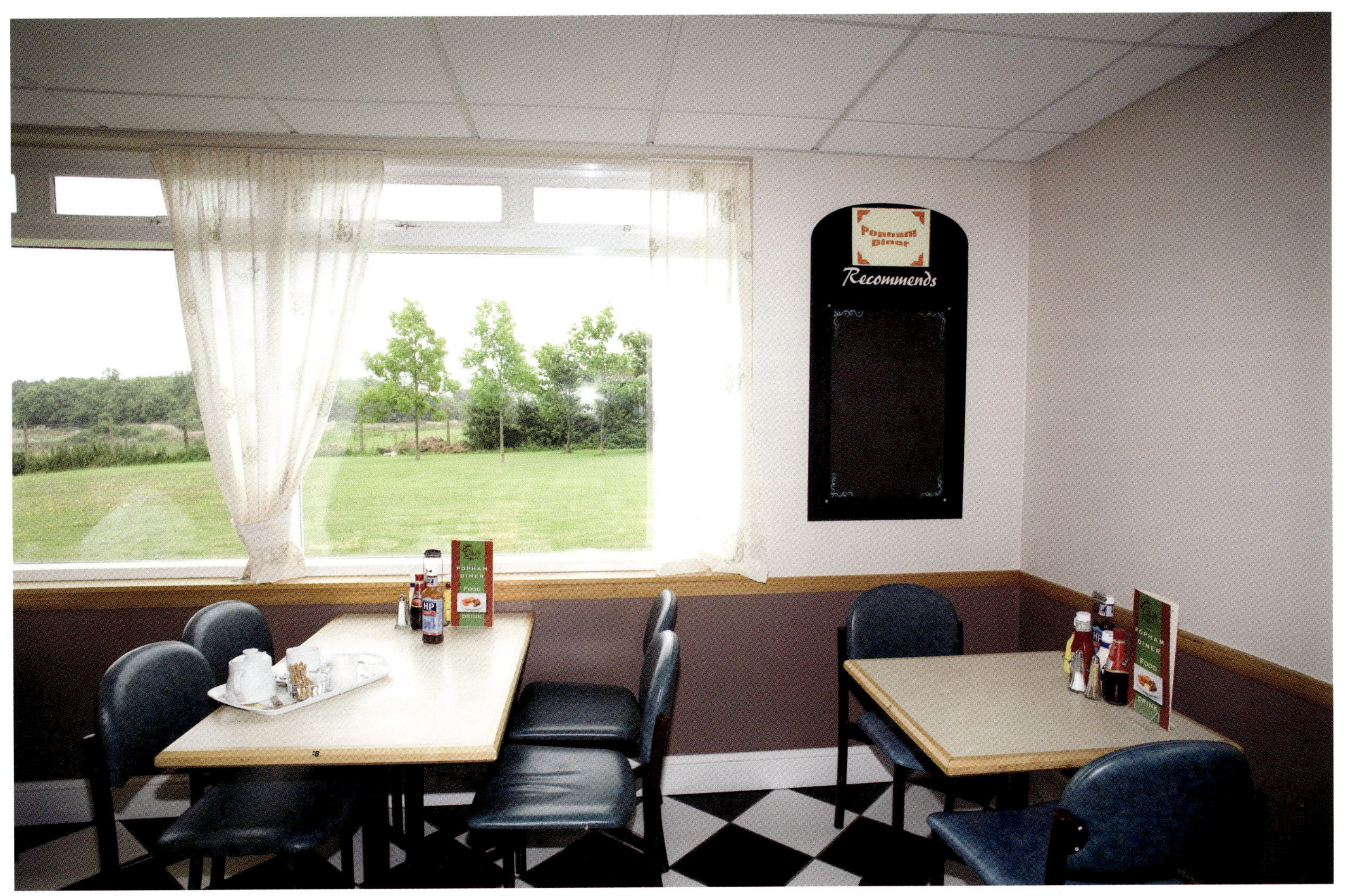

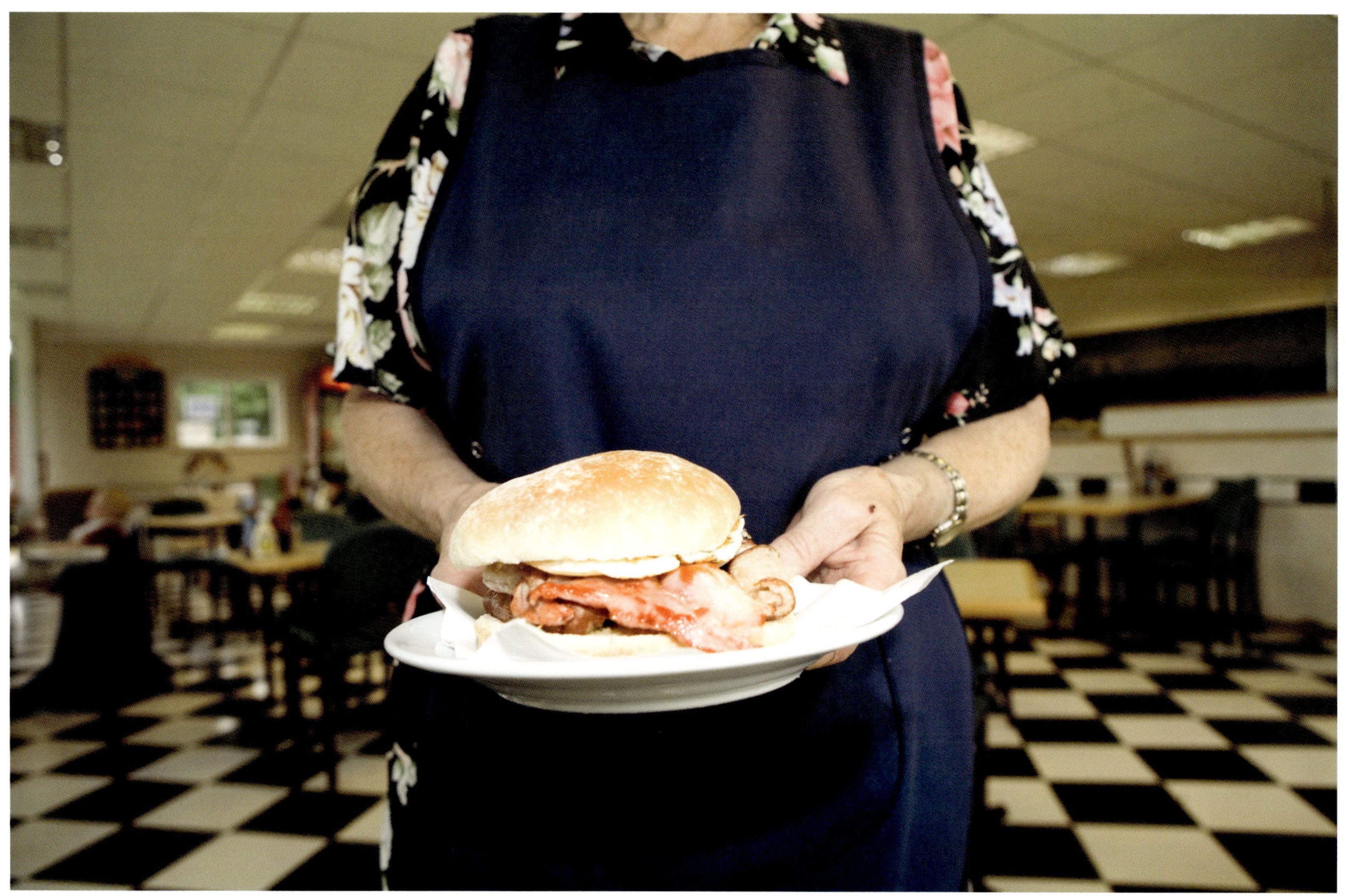

26    The Popham Diner – Popham – Hampshire – A303

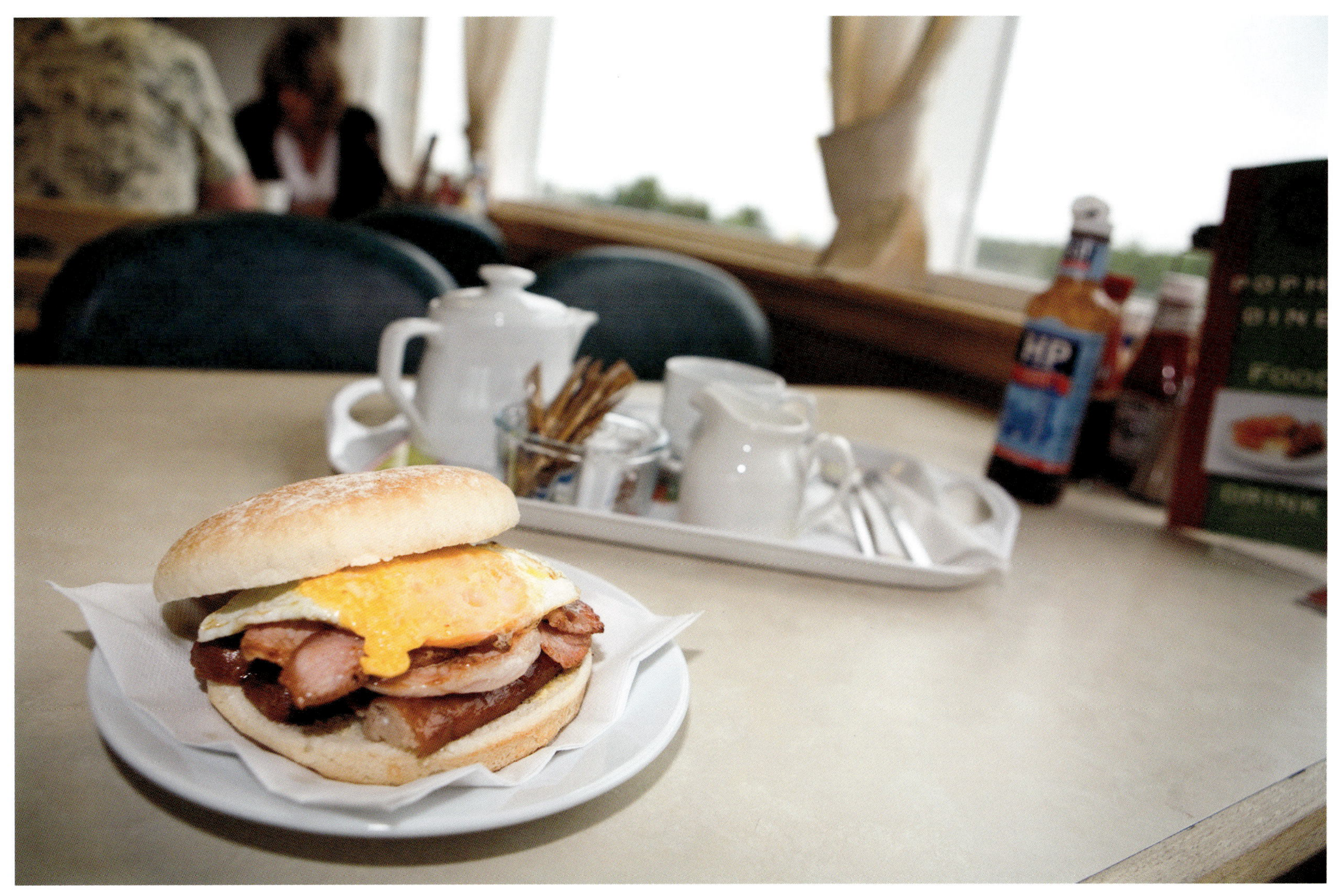



The Popham Diner – Popham – Hampshire – A303

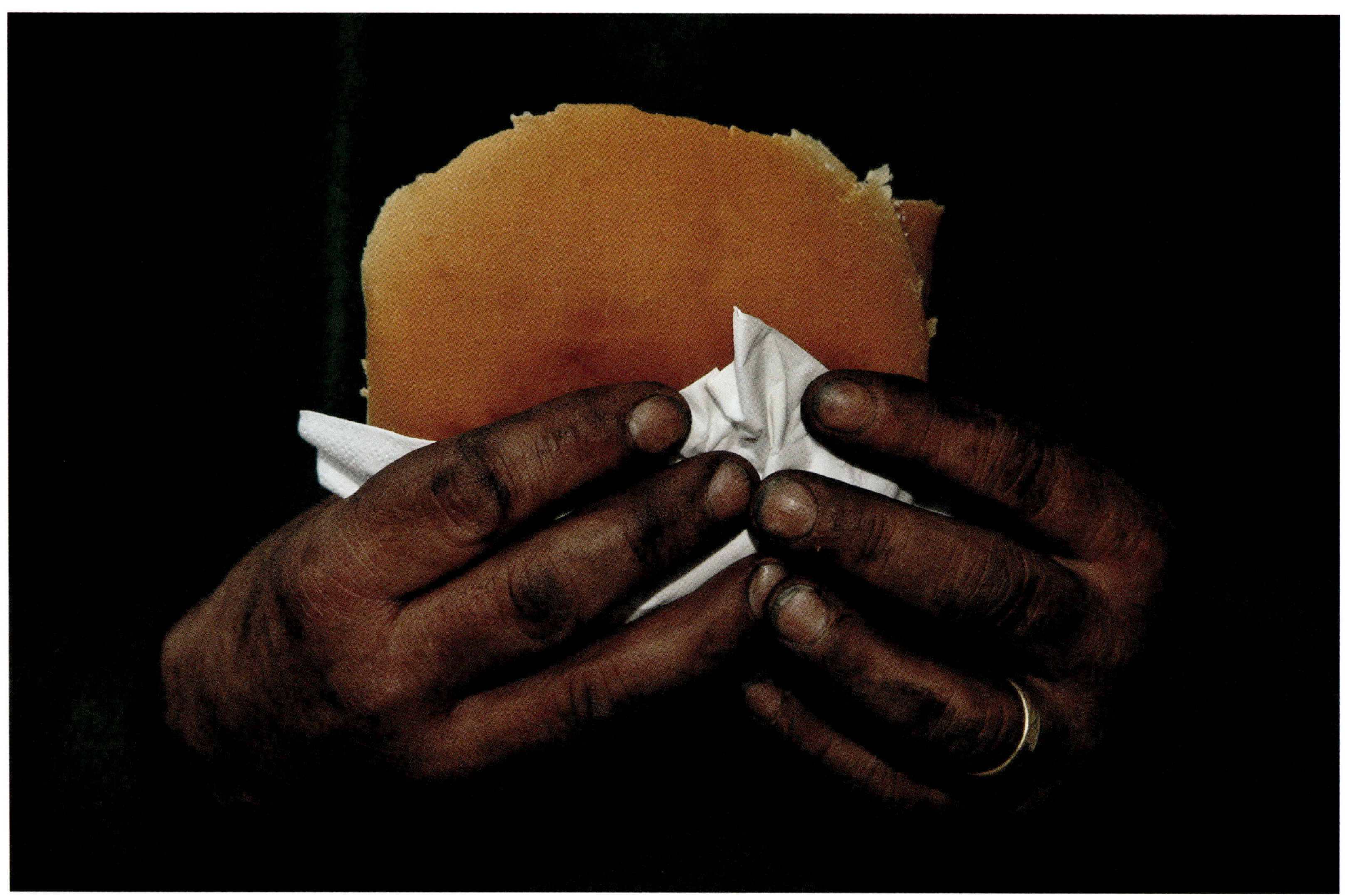

 Roadside Burger Van – Somerset – A30

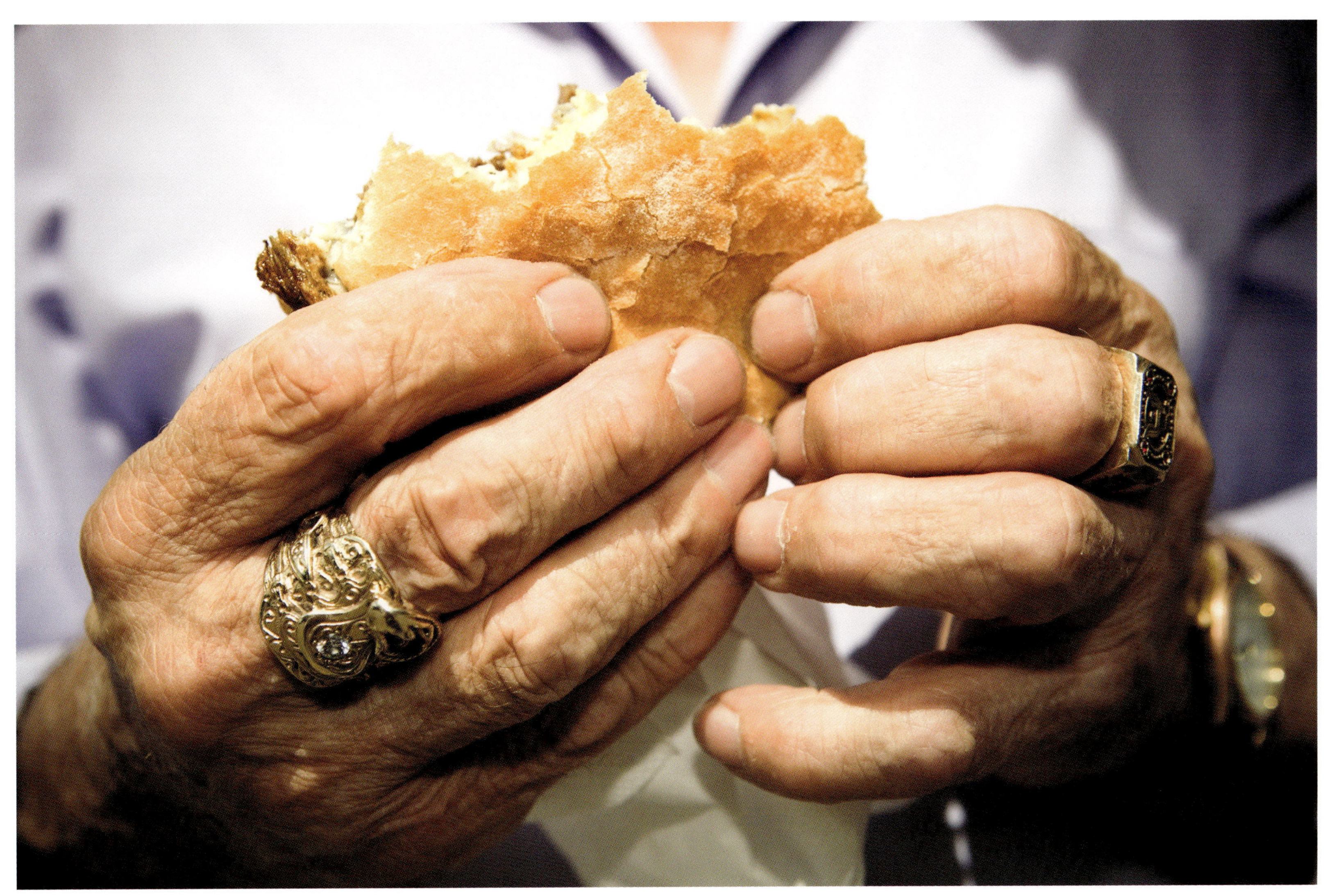

Roadside Burger Van – Kingsley Magna – Dorset – A30     29

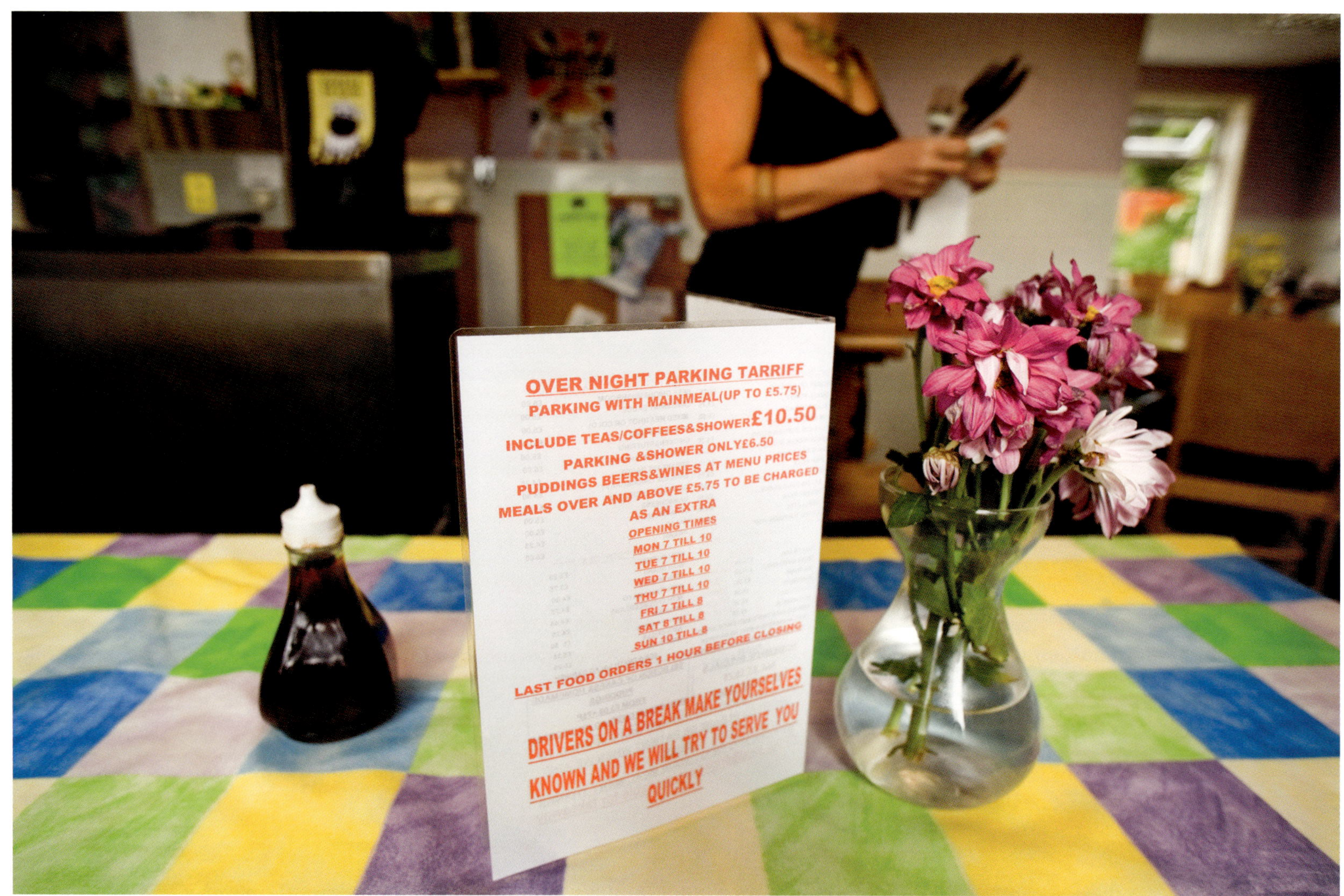




Smokey Joe's Cafe – Blackwater – Cornwall – Old A30

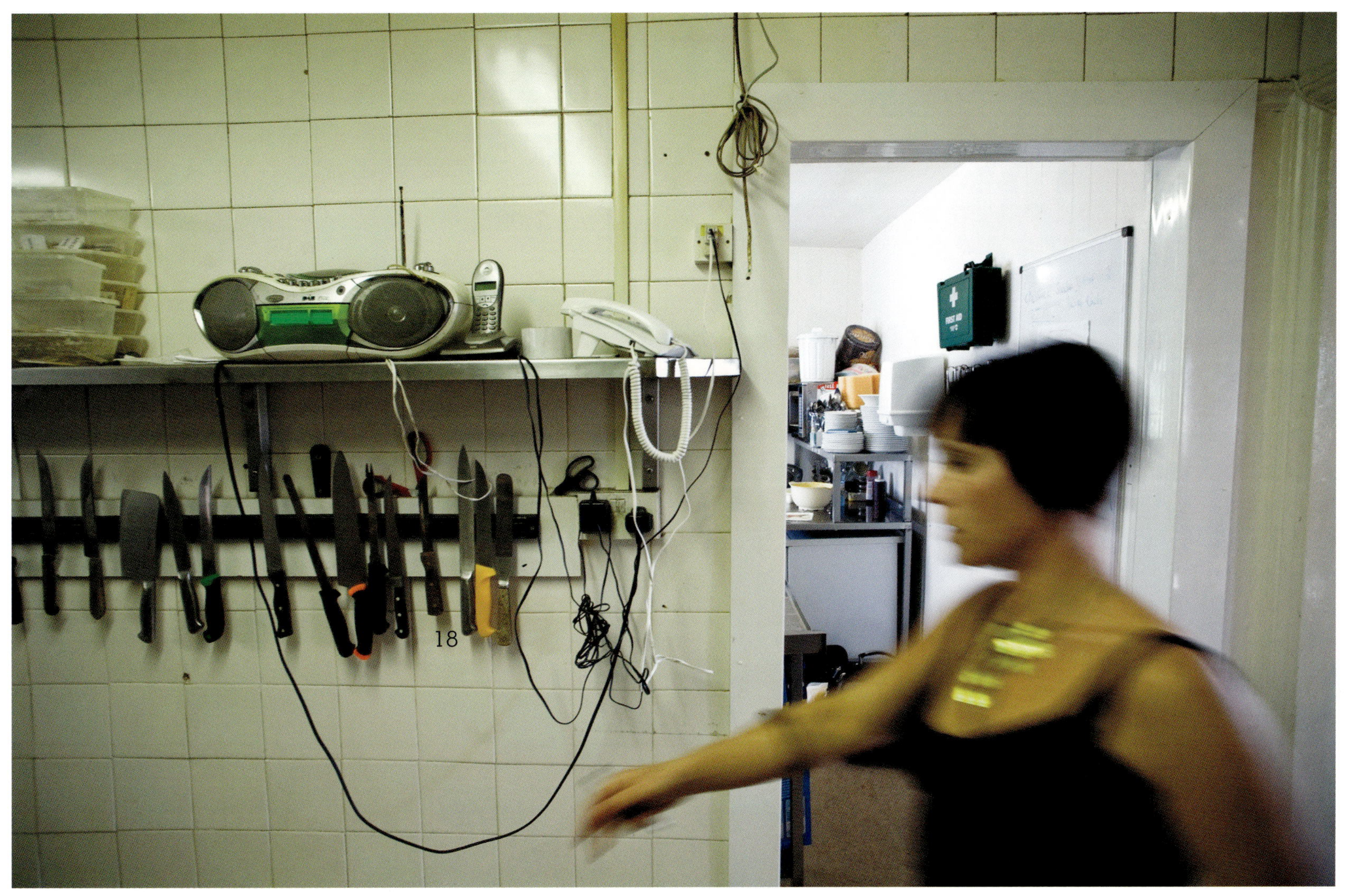

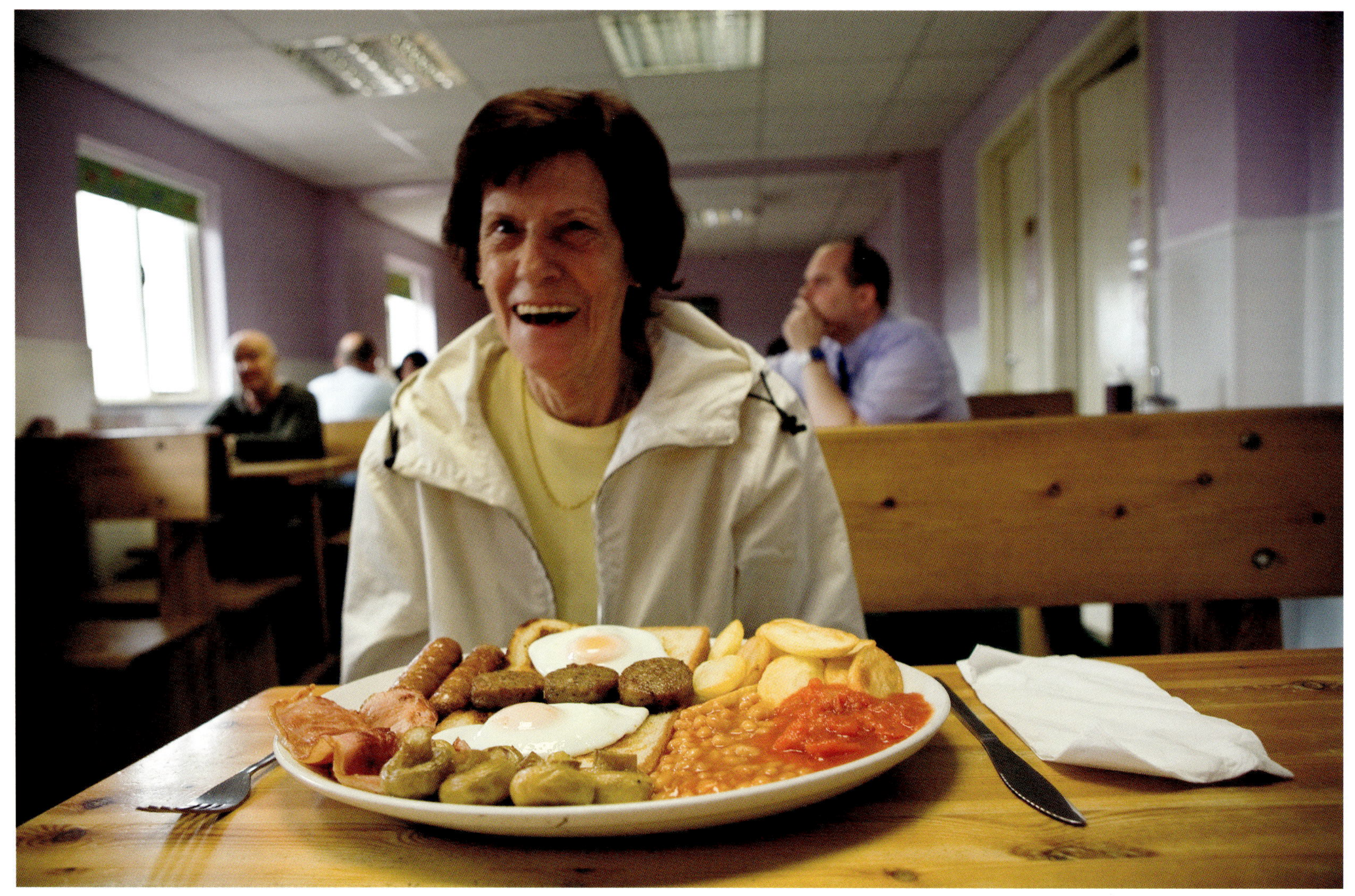

32    Pat – Smokey Joe's Cafe – Blackwater  – Cornwall – Old A30

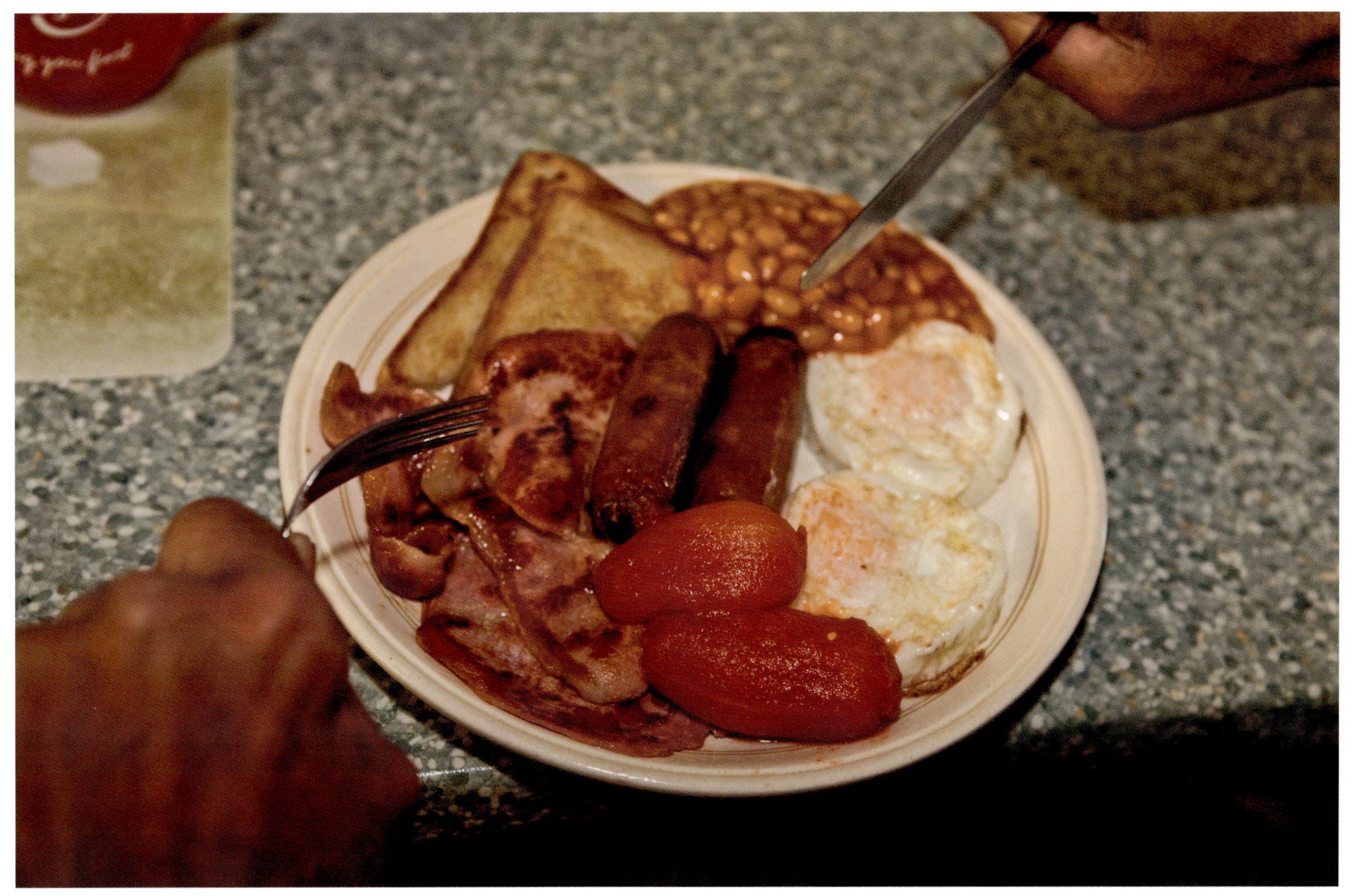

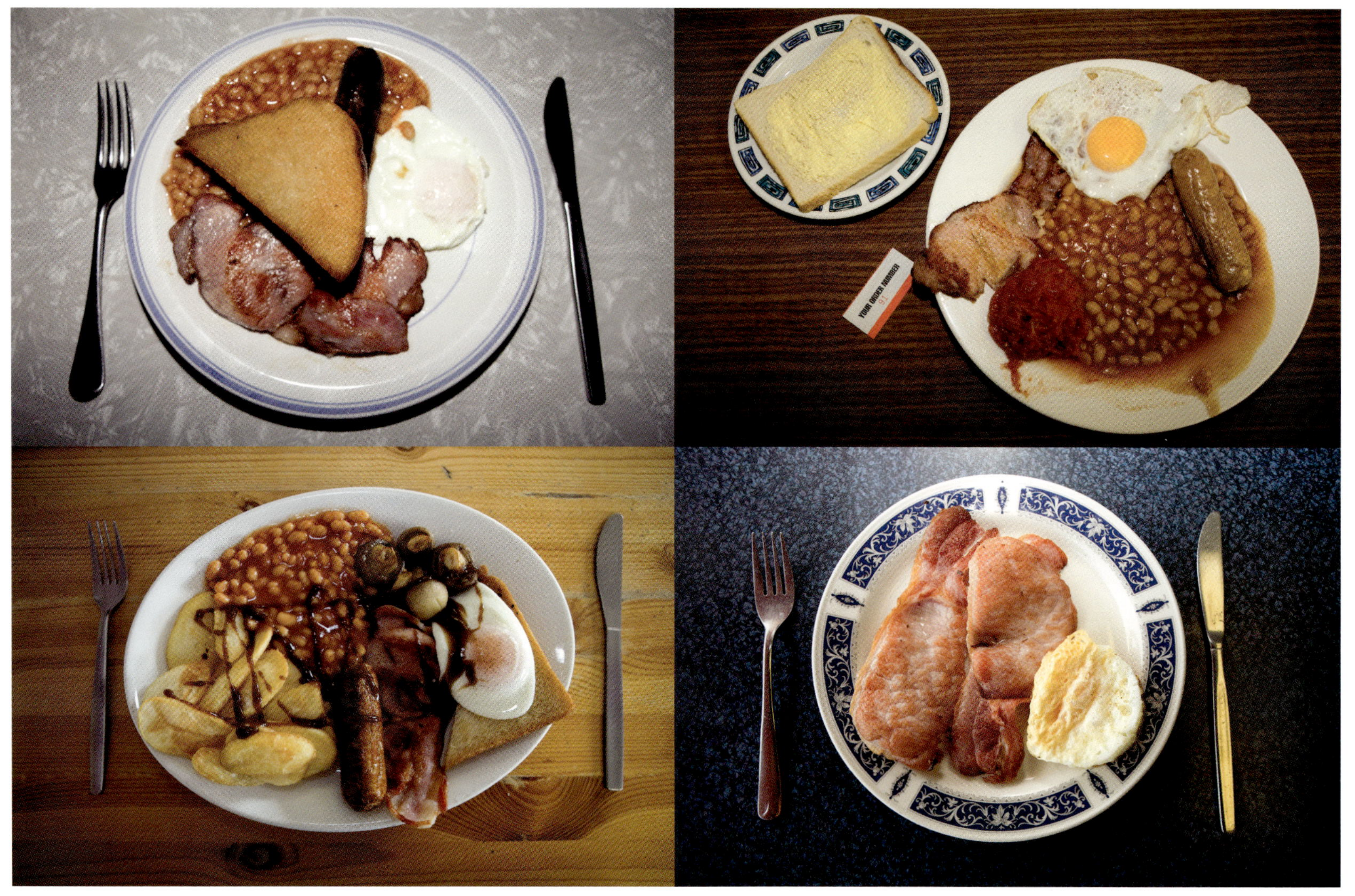

   All Day Breakfasts along the A30 & A303

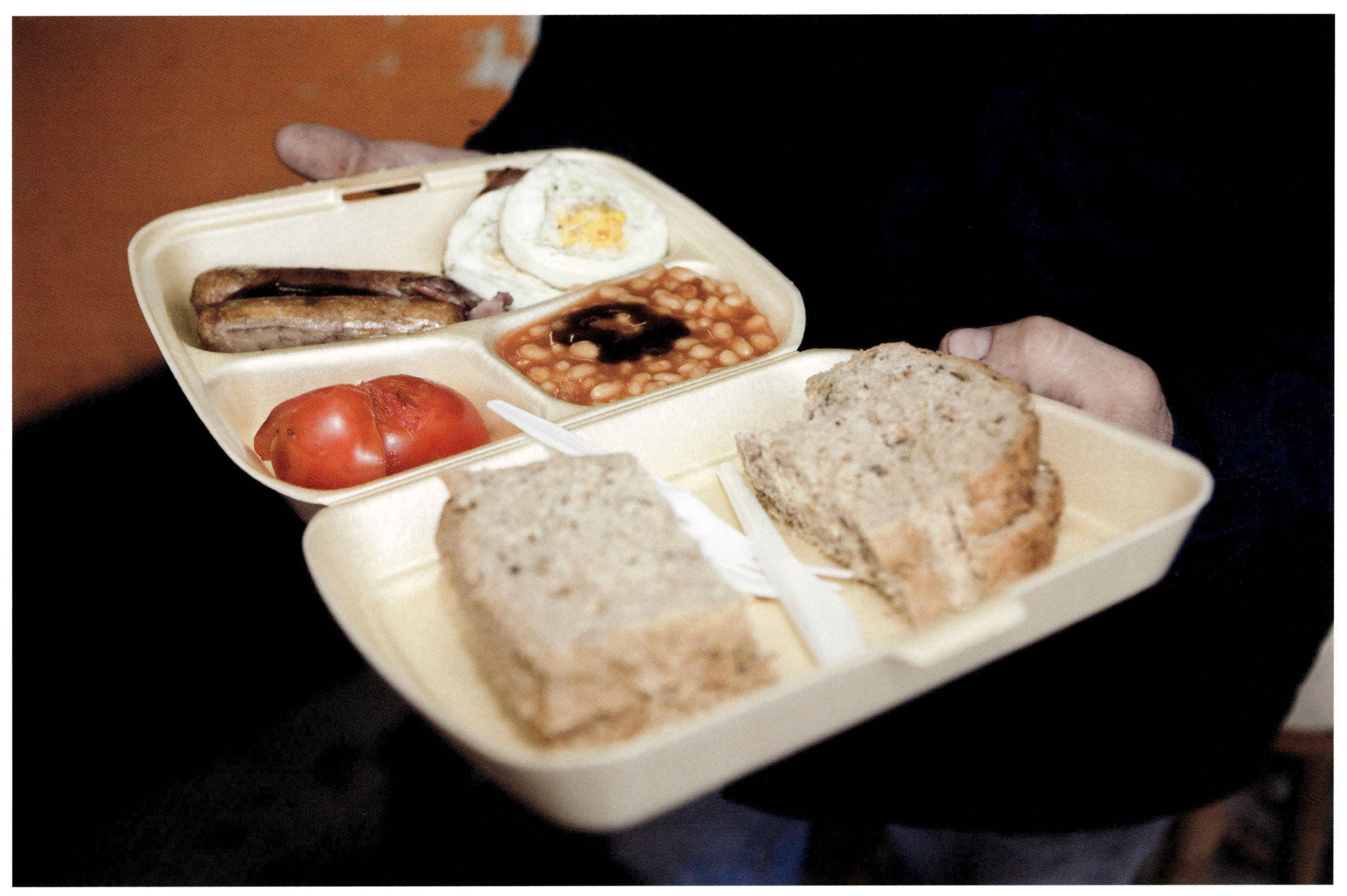

All Day Breakfast Take-Away – Phil's Snack Bar – Victoria – Cornwall – A30    35

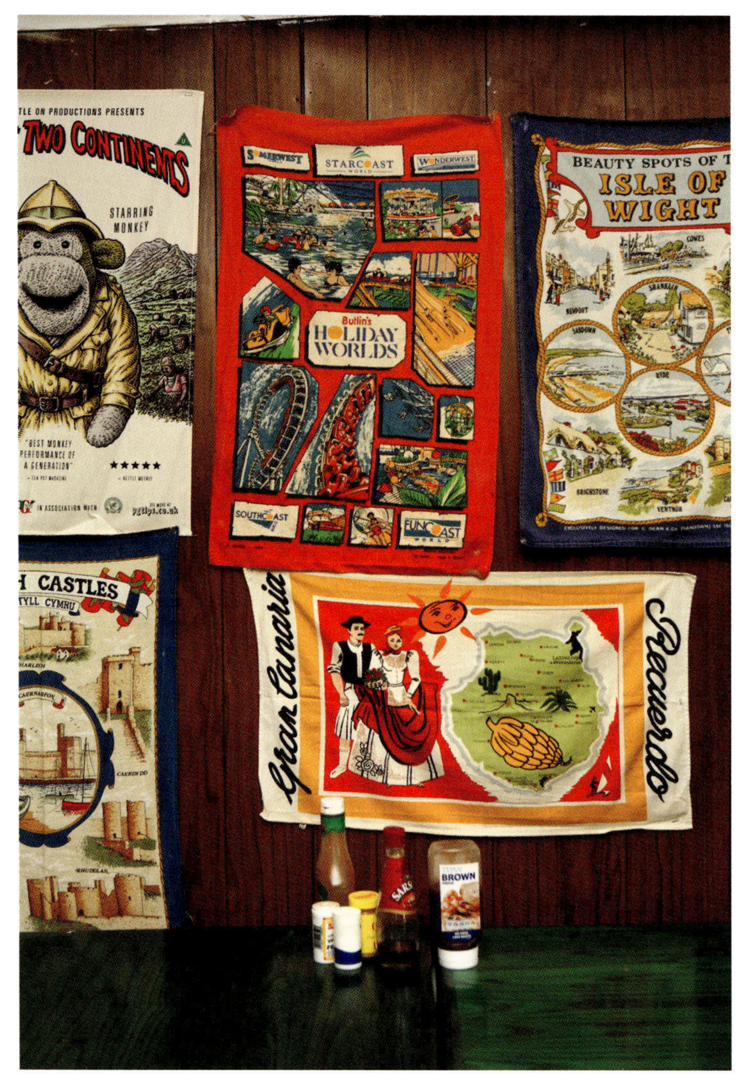
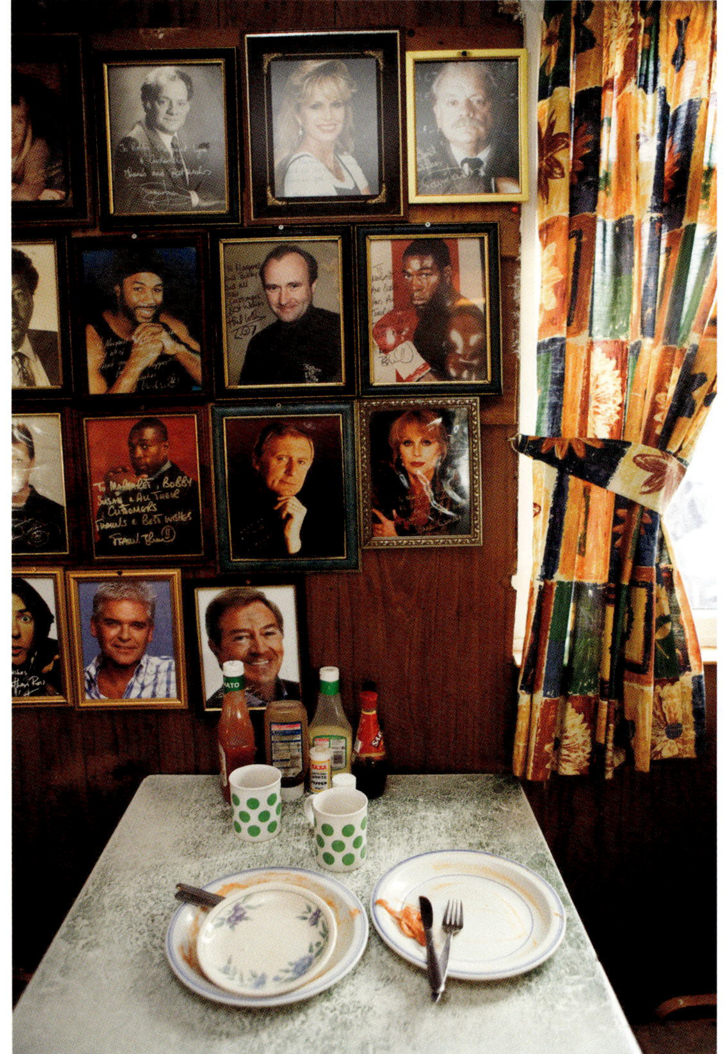

Above & near right: The Shack – Hook – Hampshire – A30
Far right: The Gorge Cafe – Yeovil – Somerset – A30

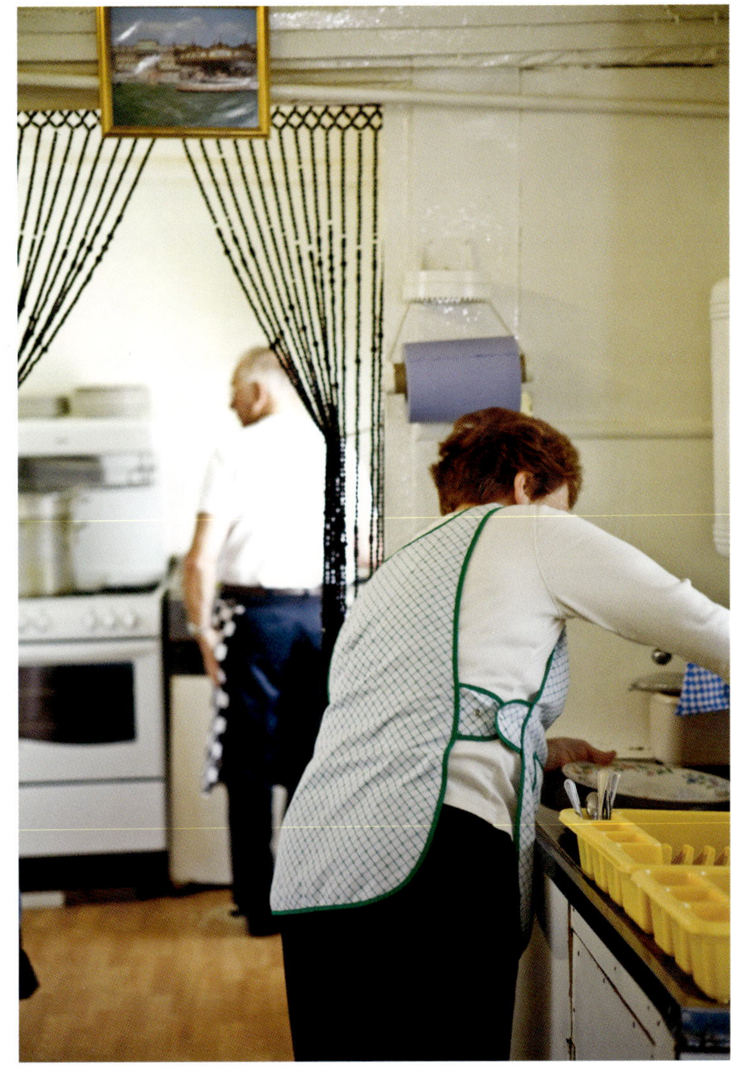

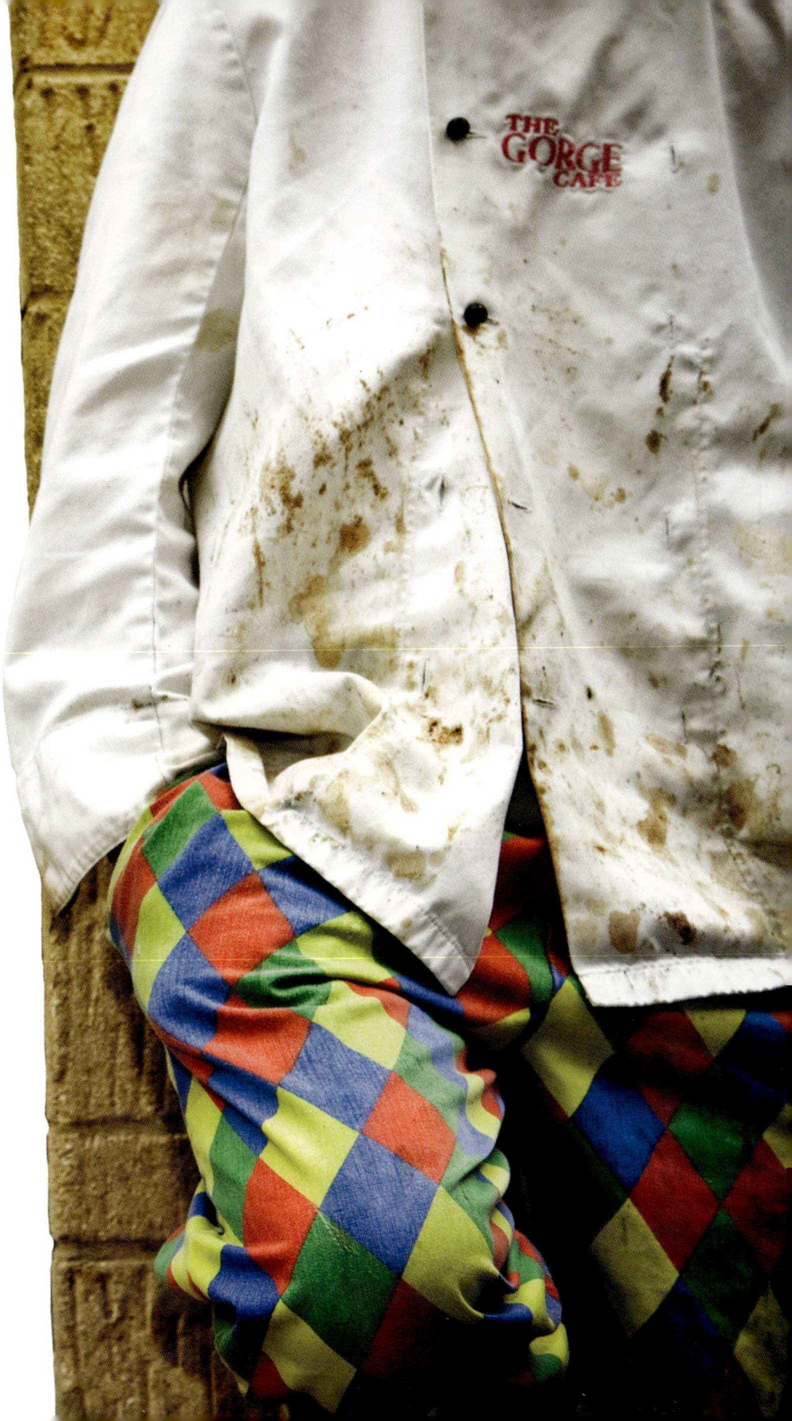

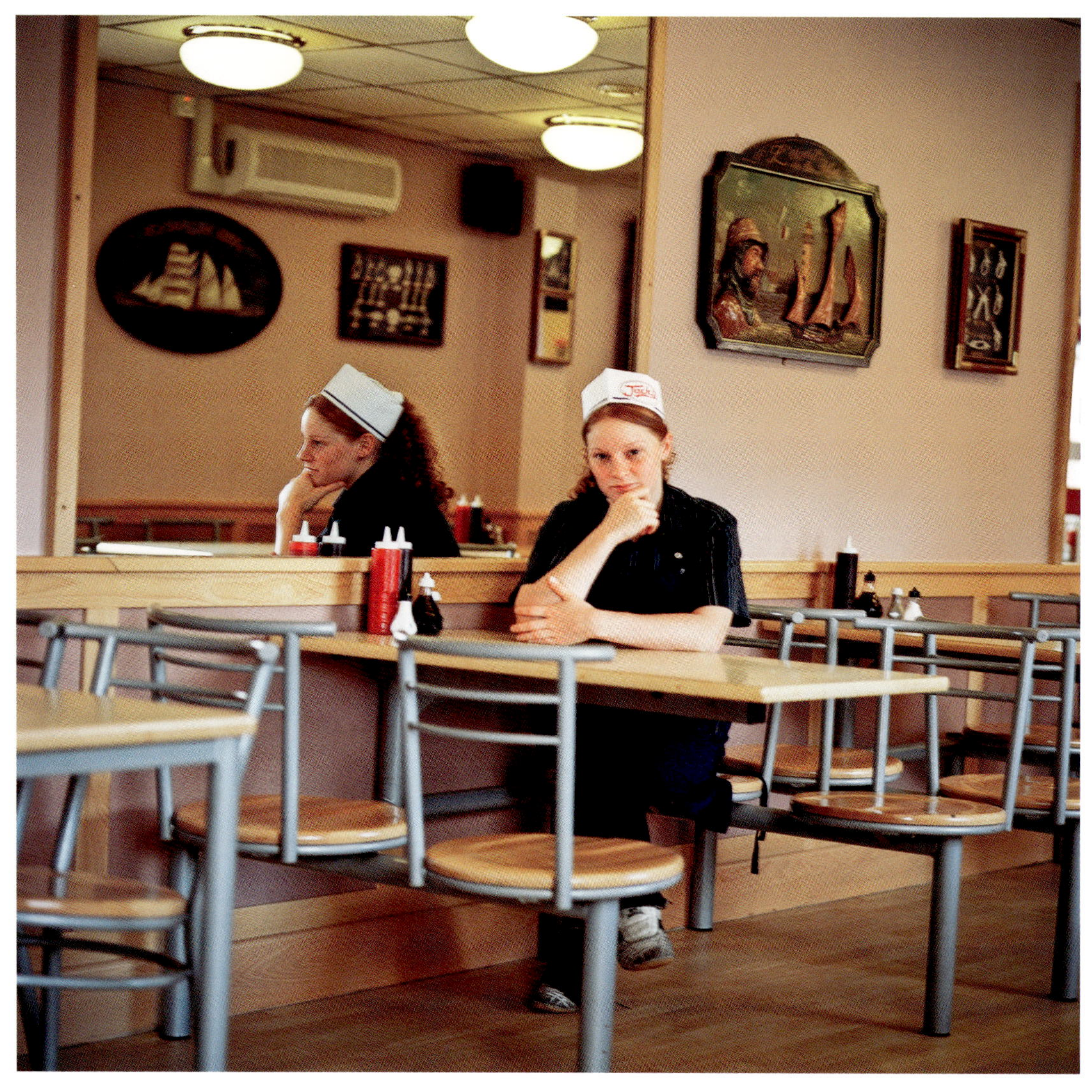

38   Lizzie – *Jack's of Bagshot* – Bagshot – Surrey – A30

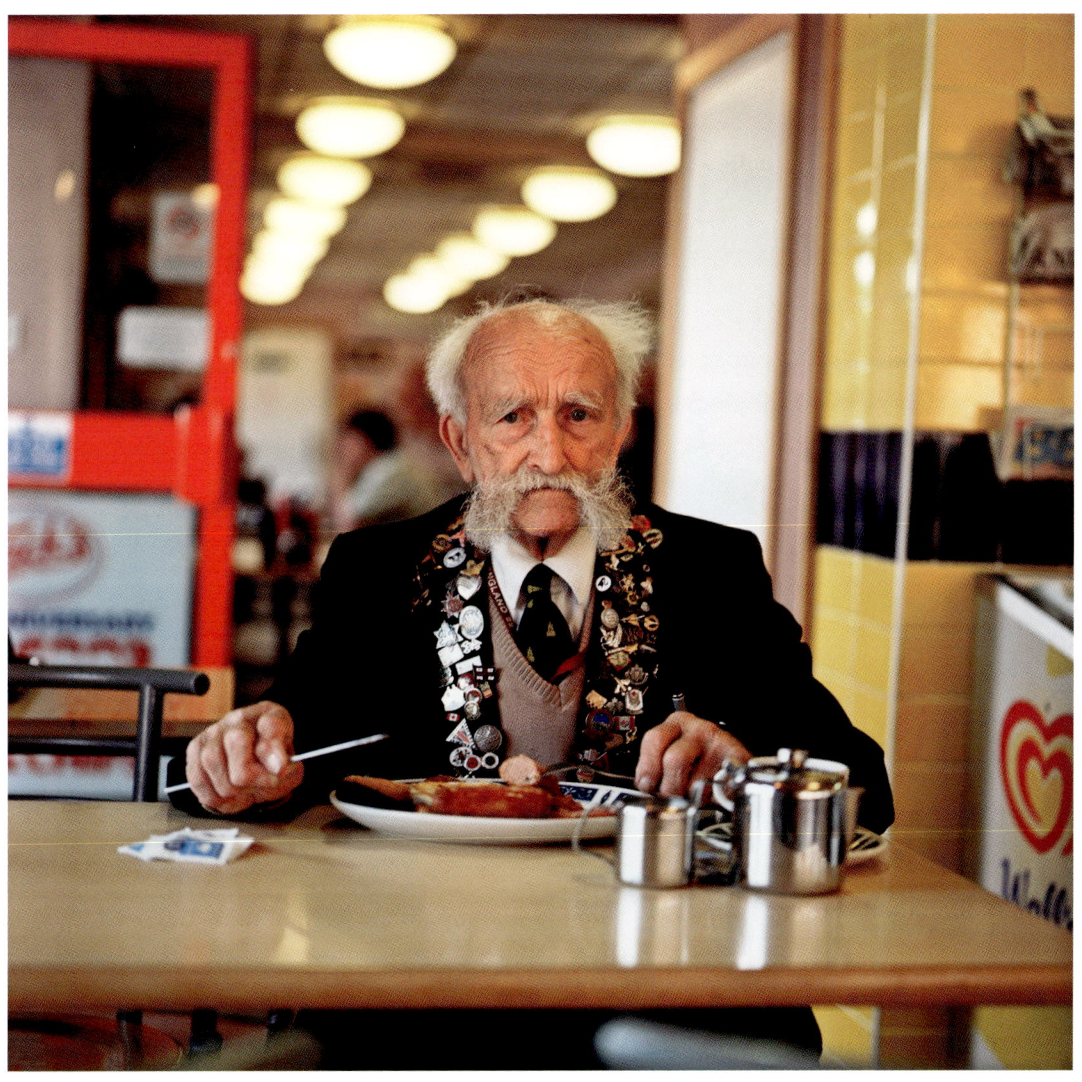

# Portraits On The Road

In one of the many notebooks I kept throughout this project, I've written "*the current 'Jack's of Bagshot' was once the infamous 'Bert's Gone Mad', notorious for giving truckers slashed prices on food and drink*". Memories of the cafe's existence, regardless of name or owner, stretch back to the 1930s.

When I walked into Jack's and saw the large, wall mounted mirrors and all-in-one tables and chairs, I was instantly inspired to re-create my favourite of Paul Graham's images – that of the waitress at John's Cafe in Sandy. I asked Lizzie, (page 38) a part-time waitress who was studying for her A-levels, if she'd sit for me. She did, and the result is one of my favourite images of the entire project.

Another of the most important characters that I met as part of this project was Pat (page 39), an ex-employee and now regular patron of Jack's. Chatting with Pat for well over an hour, as the waitresses asked if I wanted refills of coffee, Pat opened his heart, recounting how, since the sad passing of his wife, the cafe provides him with daily meals as a token of appreciation for all the hard work he'd put in during his time working there. Pat grew up working on farms around Norfolk. He later served in the army, and wears his medals and military badges with justifiable pride.

Heading further west along the A30 I came across Stockbridge, a picturesque hamlet on the banks of the River Test, a small stream that passes through the main street, with eels and trout glistening in the daylight. Locals told me how N.J. Stoke Garage in the village was once a brothel and in it's heyday, girls would parade along the balconies advertising their wares. It all seemed so very Wild West, and hard to now imagine amidst the quaintness of the village. The old-fashioned swing pumps of the garage were still a little incongruous amongst the pristine houses.

I waited all day for John Stoke, pictured opposite, to show up. Walking-stick in hand, a roll of twenties almost falling out of his breast pocket, he was only too happy to pose for a portrait. I neither told him where to stand or what to do; instinctively he leant against his stick and placed himself in front of his swing pumps. I may have asked him to tiptoe left or right a touch, but he had all the moves. I very much liked John and what he stood for, and how, out of the whole village, with it's neatly capped flowerpots and wood stained shutters, his garage kept it's rustic edge. I was sad to think that his garage and petrol pumps would inevitably be up-rooted and cleaned up.

The following pages show Yarcombe Coach House Garage and Services. This was another place that jumped out, as I turned the corner along the A30 and saw the entire yard spilling out in front of me. With the rolling hills parading as the backdrop, I captured a few images of the petrol pumps, using the Bronica and the natural light available. While the mechanic (page 43) was working away on a new Land Rover, I asked if he'd mind having his picture taken. He didn't of course, and despite his rather menacing expression, he was very charming.

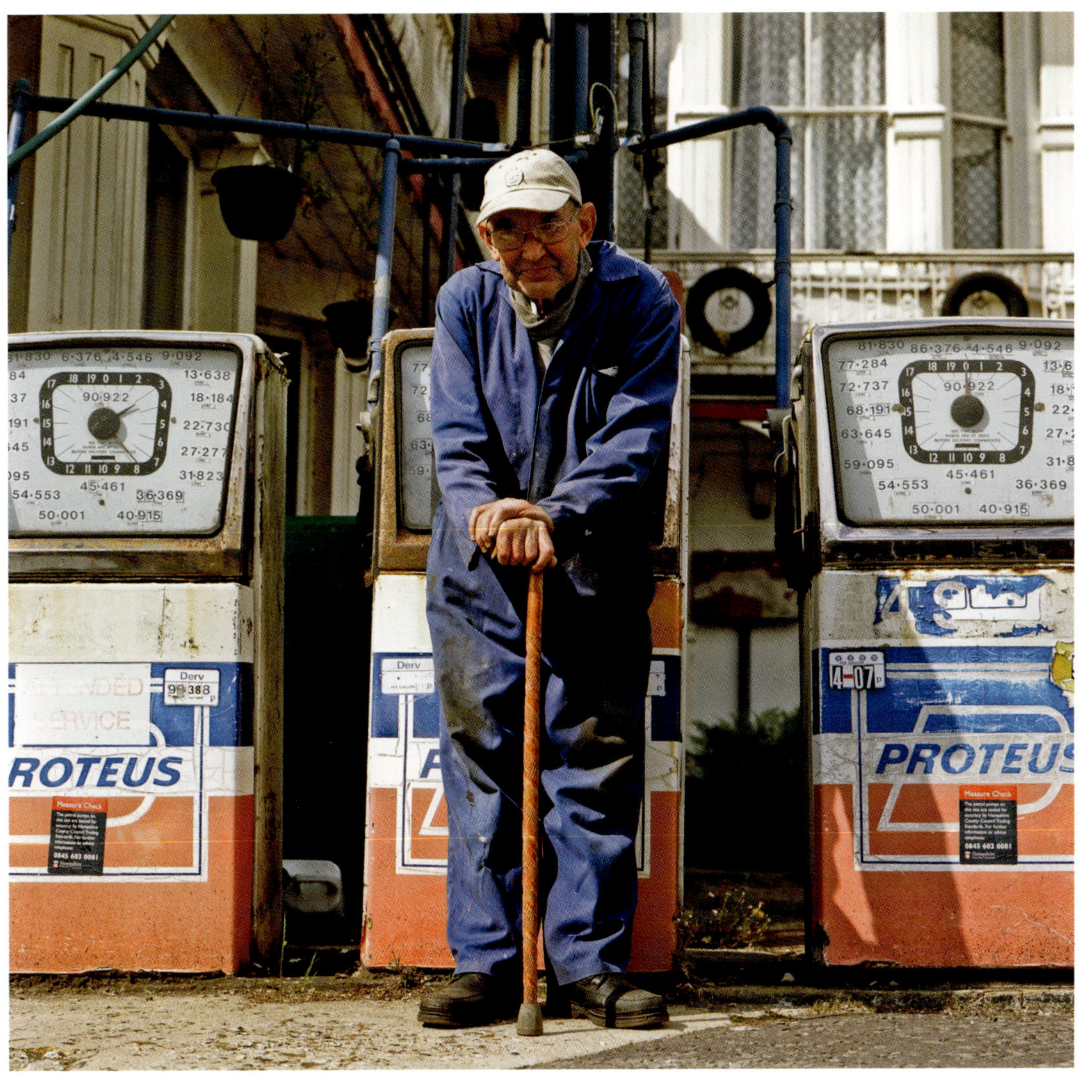

John – NJ Stokes – Stockbridge – Hamphsire – A30    41

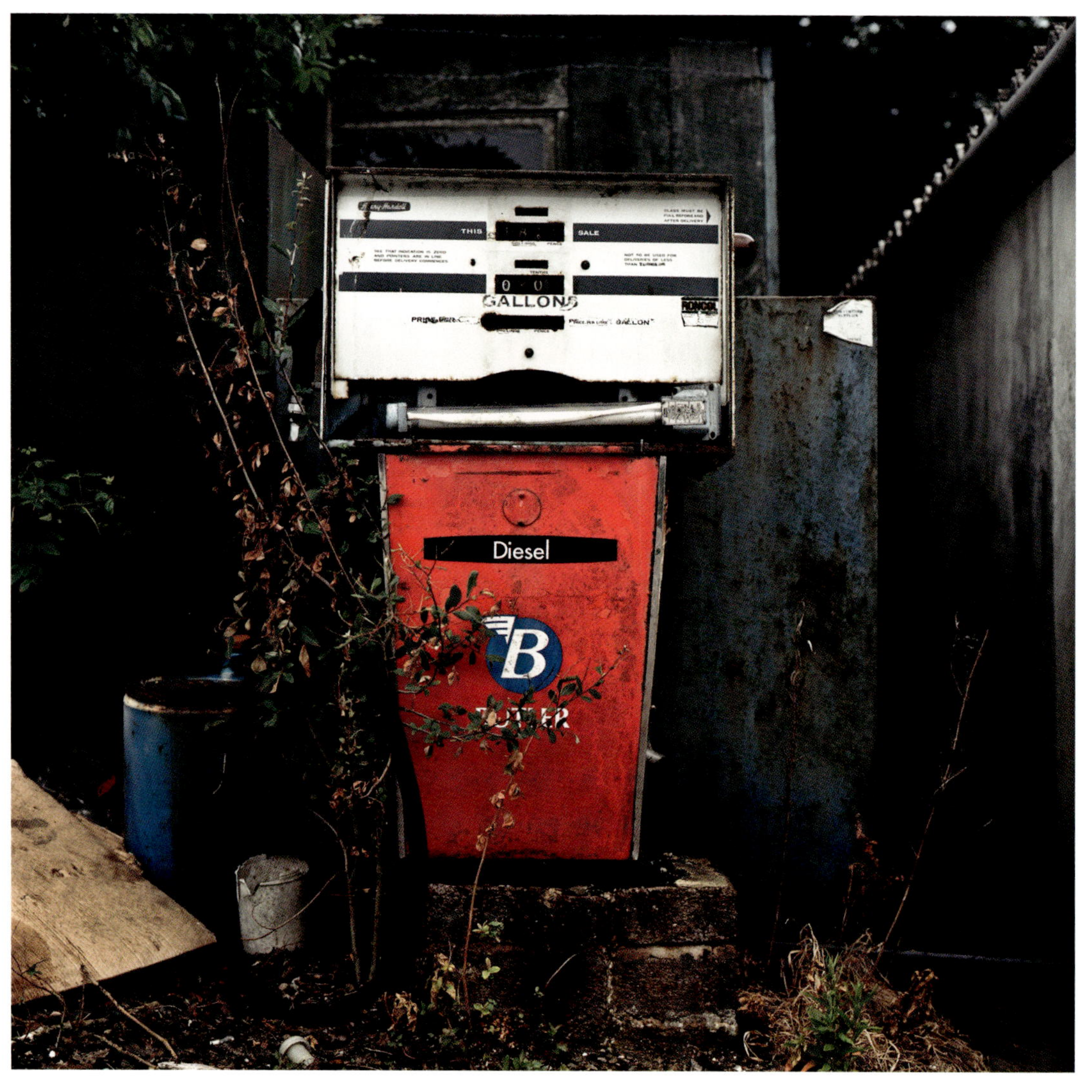



   Yarcombe Services – Yarcombe – Devon – A30

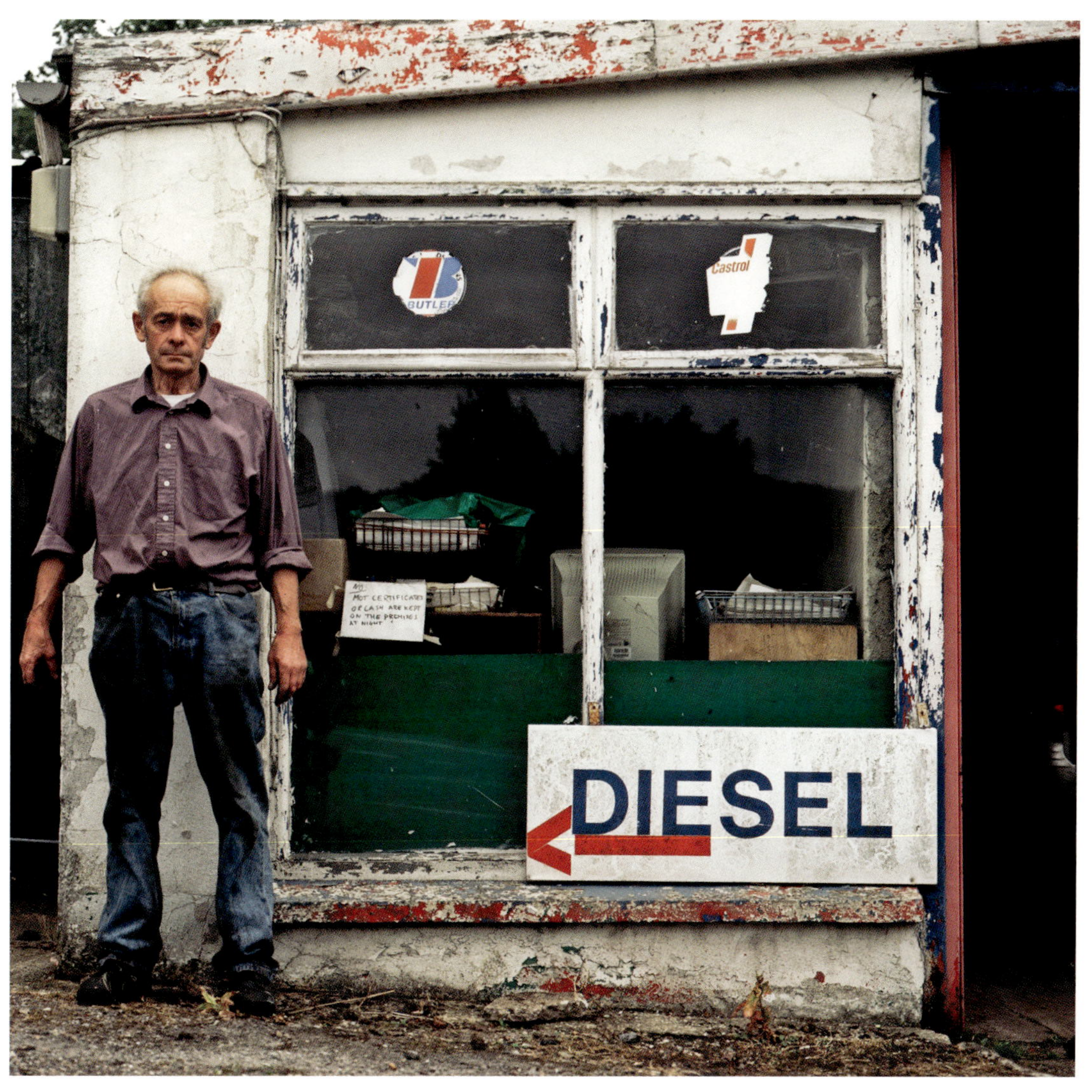



The Mechanic – Yarcombe Services – Yarcombe – Devon – A30 43

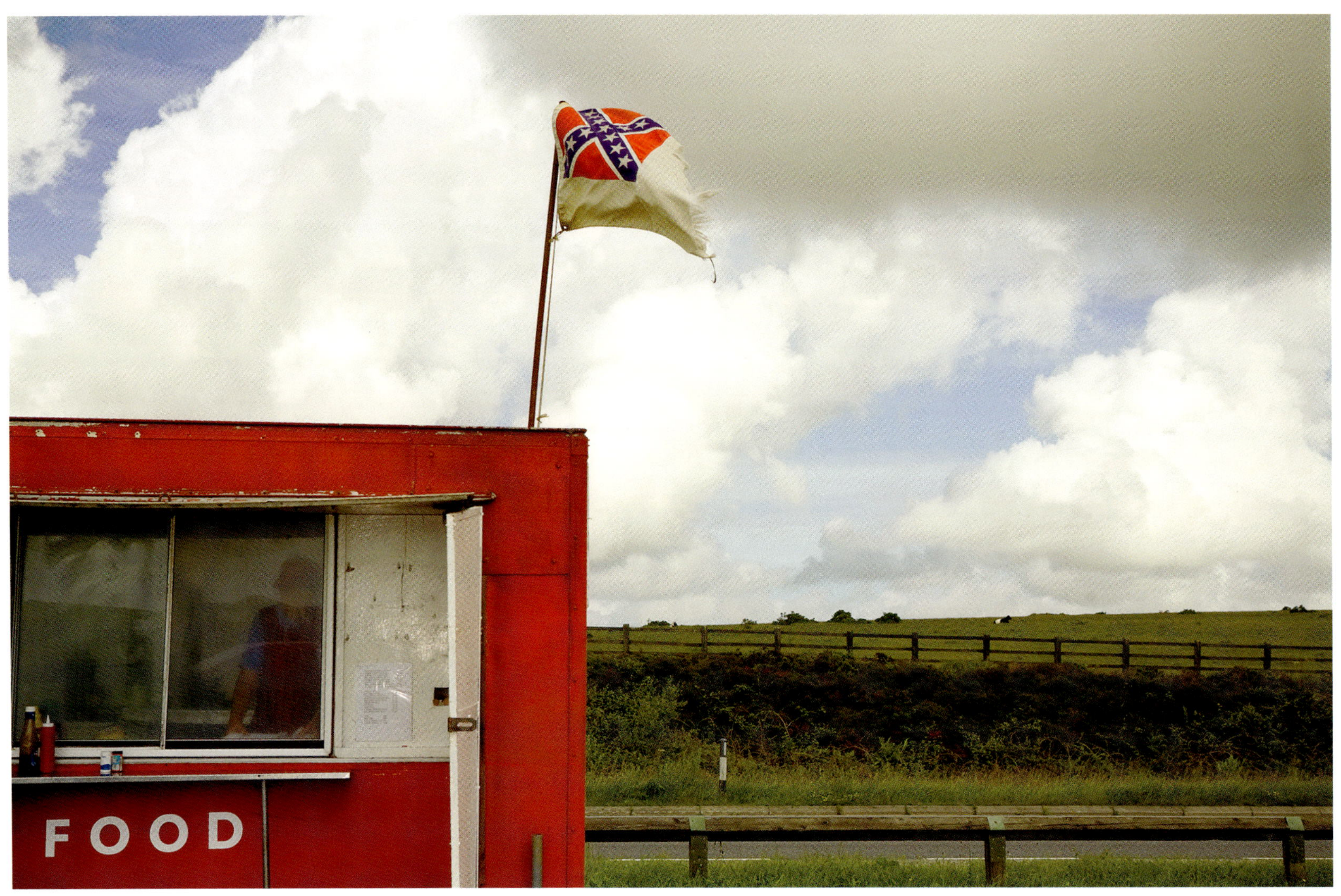



44     Bodmin Moor Burger Van – Bodmin Moor – Cornwall – A30

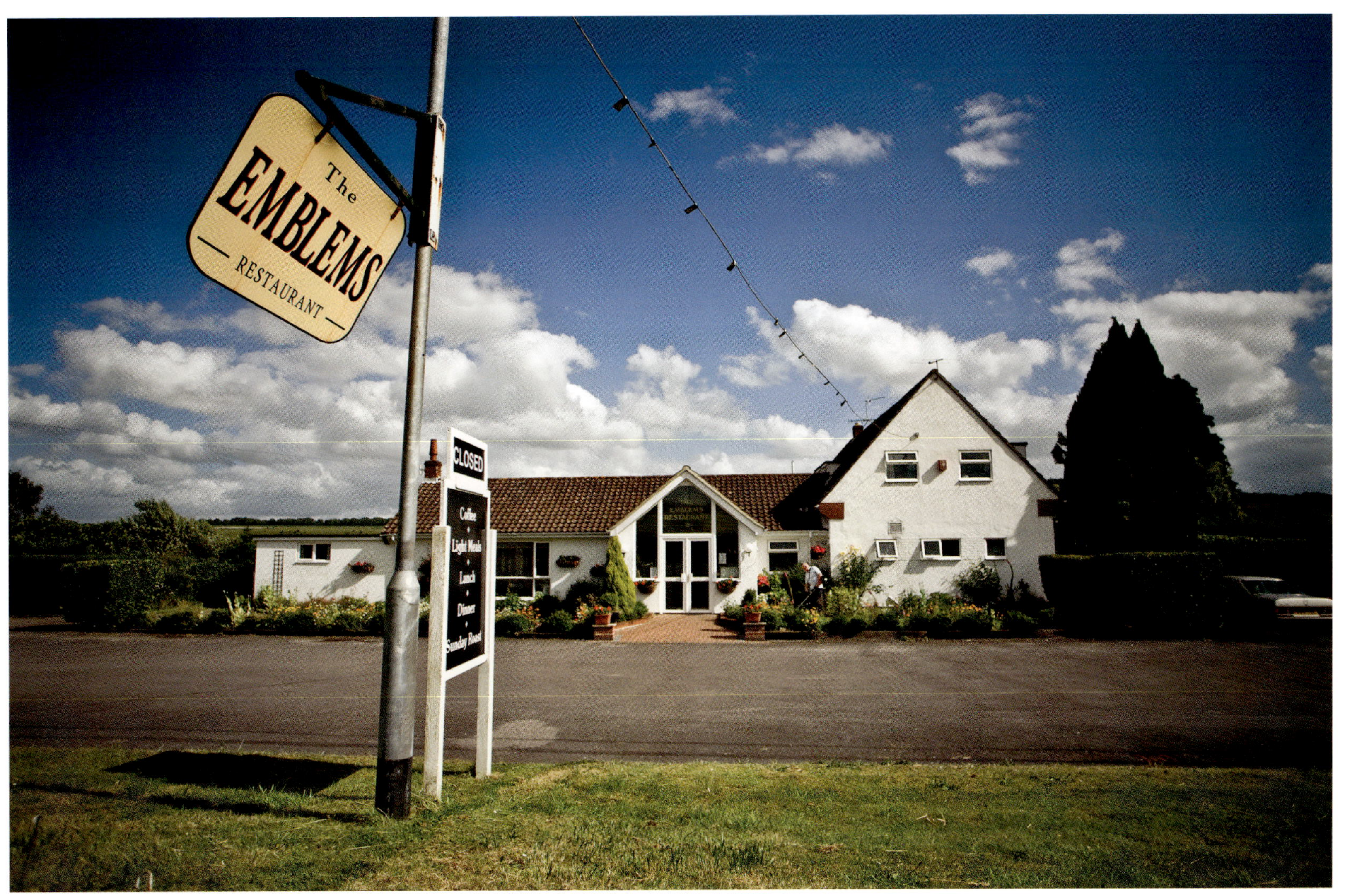


The Emblems Restaurant – Refurbished Truck Stop – Fovant – Wiltshire – A30

# East Anglia

When I was growing up my experiences of roadside cafes didn't get much more exciting than a Little Chef, or a Happy Eater. As is the way when you're young, I was reliant on my parents' choice of places to eat. Meals at independent greasy spoons were seen as rare treats, but I knew they were inherently more attractive and interesting than the two well-branded and well-known household names I was used to.

Boss Hoggs on the old A12 was something of an urban legend to me. Only a stone's throw away from the village near Ipswich where I was brought up, my friends would recount stories of mountainous plates of food, fry-ups fit for kings, and portions only a well-rounded trucker could ever finish. I never made it there, even though looking back I could have gone at any point after the age of 13 or 14 without my parents. But by then I was spending my pocket money on the latest music and computer games, with little left over for gut-busting fry-ups that left you temporarily paralysed.

Shooting in the East, which I began doing in 2009, gave me great pleasure. At the age of about 18, I'd left Suffolk in search of a more adventurous lifestyle, and over the next ten years lived and worked throughout Europe and Australasia and volunteered as a project photographer in Africa and Asia, so it felt good to be back home creating work in the area of my upbringing.

As a child, I'd explored coastal Suffolk on family outings along the A12, heading to seaside towns with names like Walberswick, Southwold and Aldeburgh, where in 2003 local resident Maggi Hambling displayed her celebrated Scallop sculpture. Having had images of Hambling's Scallop published in a local magazine, as part of a coastal Suffolk photo-essay, I was always intensely attracted to her raw style. I'll never forget a photograph of Hambling I once saw in the East Anglia Daily Times; she stood cigarette in hand, clothed in black, clutching an ornate whisky glass.

Exploring East Anglia really helped me understand more about the region I grew up in. I noticed, for example, that the landscape of the Wash in North Norfolk is reminiscent of the imagery from the American Farm Security Administration survey of the 1930s, as the bustling A17 slashes through the flat and bleak countryside. In many ways like stepping back to yesteryear, as families on outings and tourist loaded buses flock along this route in pursuit of coastal excursions, it's a unique stretch of road.

During this time, I was working part-time as a chef at a tapas bar in Ipswich, and although I had received Arts Council Funding for this part of the trip, hotels or guesthouses were luxuries not afforded to me. Therefore, on occasions when I needed somewhere convenient to bunk down, if no-one was watching, in particular farmers or the like, I'd often set up my tent near the entrance to a field, shaded by hedgerow, adjacent to a road. If not, it was the backseat of the car listening to Radcliffe and Maconie on Radio 2 in laybys, carparks or wherever I found. It wasn't comfortable, but it worked. I must have spent about 50 nights either 'adventure camping' or sleeping in my car from October 09 to June 2010.

The work created throughout East Anglia was kindly supported by The National Lottery through the Arts Council of England and exhibited at Babylon Gallery, Ely, 2010. The following year, the work was exhibited during a three-month exhibition at Ipswich Art School, Suffolk.

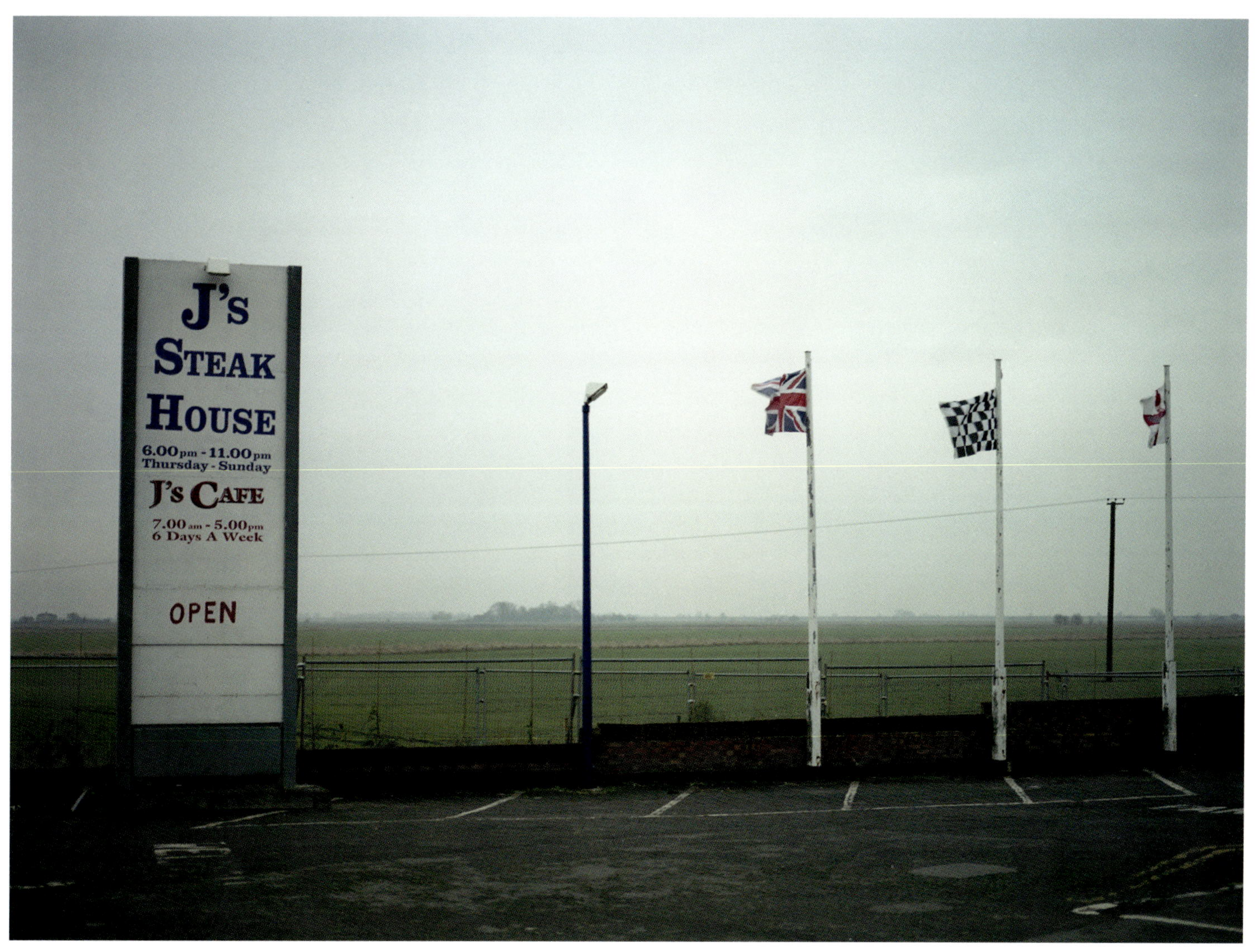


J's Steak House – Thorney Toll – Cambridgeshire – A47

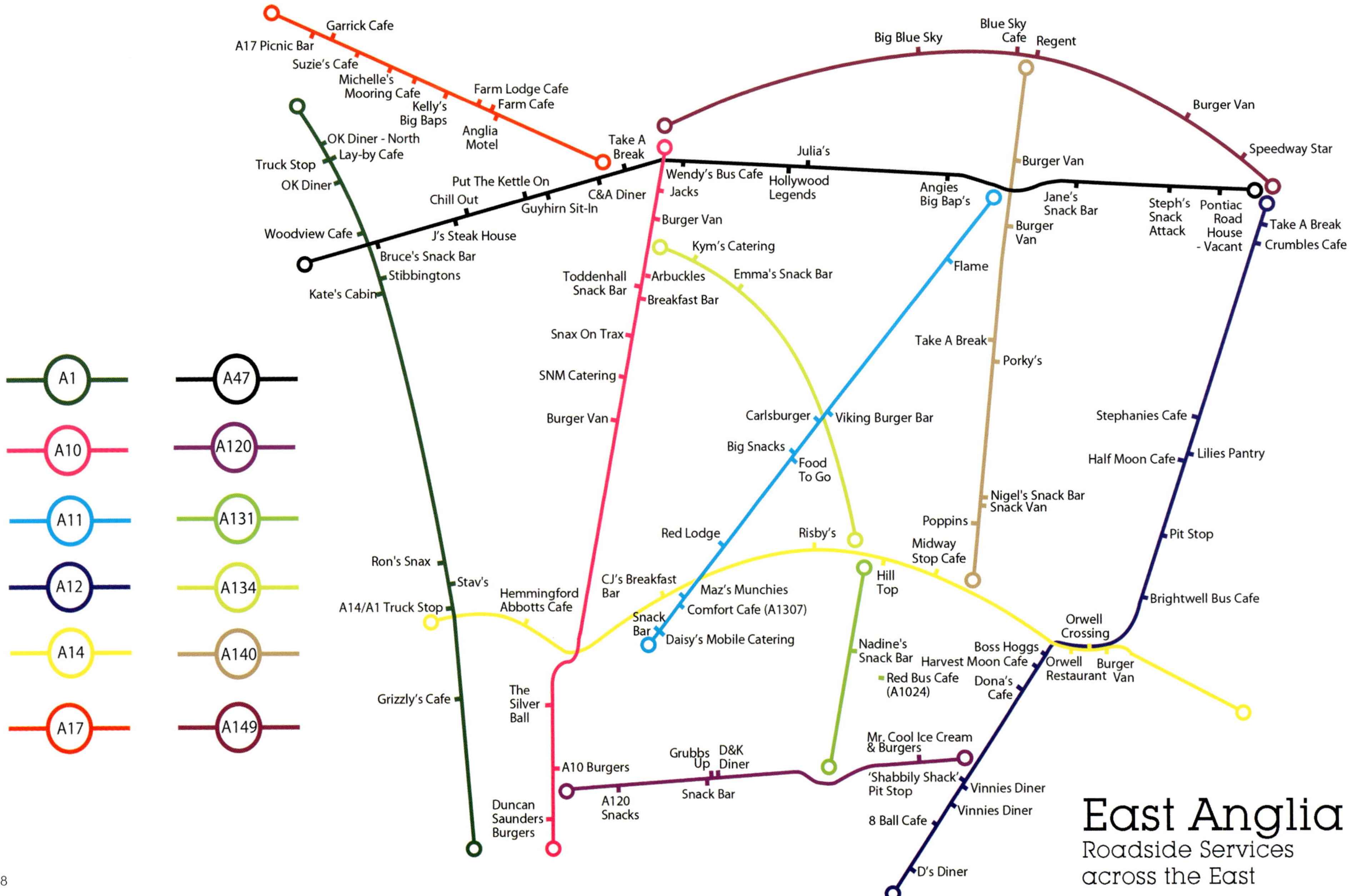

A1
A10
A11
A12
A14
A17
A47
A120
A131
A134
A140
A149

Garrick Cafe
A17 Picnic Bar
Suzie's Cafe
Michelle's
Mooring Cafe
Kelly's
Big Baps
OK Diner - North
Lay-by Cafe
Truck Stop
OK Diner
Woodview Cafe
Kate's Cabin
Farm Lodge Cafe
Farm Cafe
Anglia
Motel
Put The Kettle On
Chill Out
Guyhirn Sit-In
J's Steak House
Bruce's Snack Bar
Stibbingtons
Take A Break
C&A Diner
Wendy's Bus Cafe
Jacks
Julia's
Hollywood
Legends
Burger Van
Kym's Catering
Arbuckles
Emma's Snack Bar
Toddenhall
Snack Bar
Breakfast Bar
Snax On Trax
SNM Catering
Burger Van
Big Blue Sky
Blue Sky
Cafe
Regent
Burger Van
Speedway Star
Angies
Big Bap's
Burger Van
Jane's
Snack Bar
Steph's
Snack
Attack
Pontiac
Road
House
- Vacant
Take A Break
Crumbles Cafe
Flame
Take A Break
Porky's
Carlsburger
Viking Burger Bar
Big Snacks
Food
To Go
Red Lodge
Risby's
Nigel's Snack Bar
Snack Van
Poppins
Midway
Stop Cafe
Stephanies Cafe
Half Moon Cafe
Lilies Pantry
Pit Stop
Ron's Snax
Stav's
Hemmingford
Abbotts Cafe
CJ's Breakfast
Bar
Maz's Munchies
Comfort Cafe (A1307)
A14/A1 Truck Stop
Snack
Bar
Daisy's Mobile Catering
Hill
Top
Brightwell Bus Cafe
Orwell
Crossing
Grizzly's Cafe
The
Silver
Ball
Nadine's
Snack Bar
Boss Hoggs
Harvest Moon Cafe
Dona's
Cafe
Orwell
Restaurant
Burger
Van
Red Bus Cafe
(A1024)
Duncan
Saunders
Burgers
A10 Burgers
A120
Snacks
Grubbs
Up
D&K
Diner
Snack Bar
Mr. Cool Ice Cream
& Burgers
'Shabbily Shack'
Pit Stop
8 Ball Cafe
Vinnies Diner
Vinnies Diner
D's Diner
East Anglia
Roadside Services
across the East

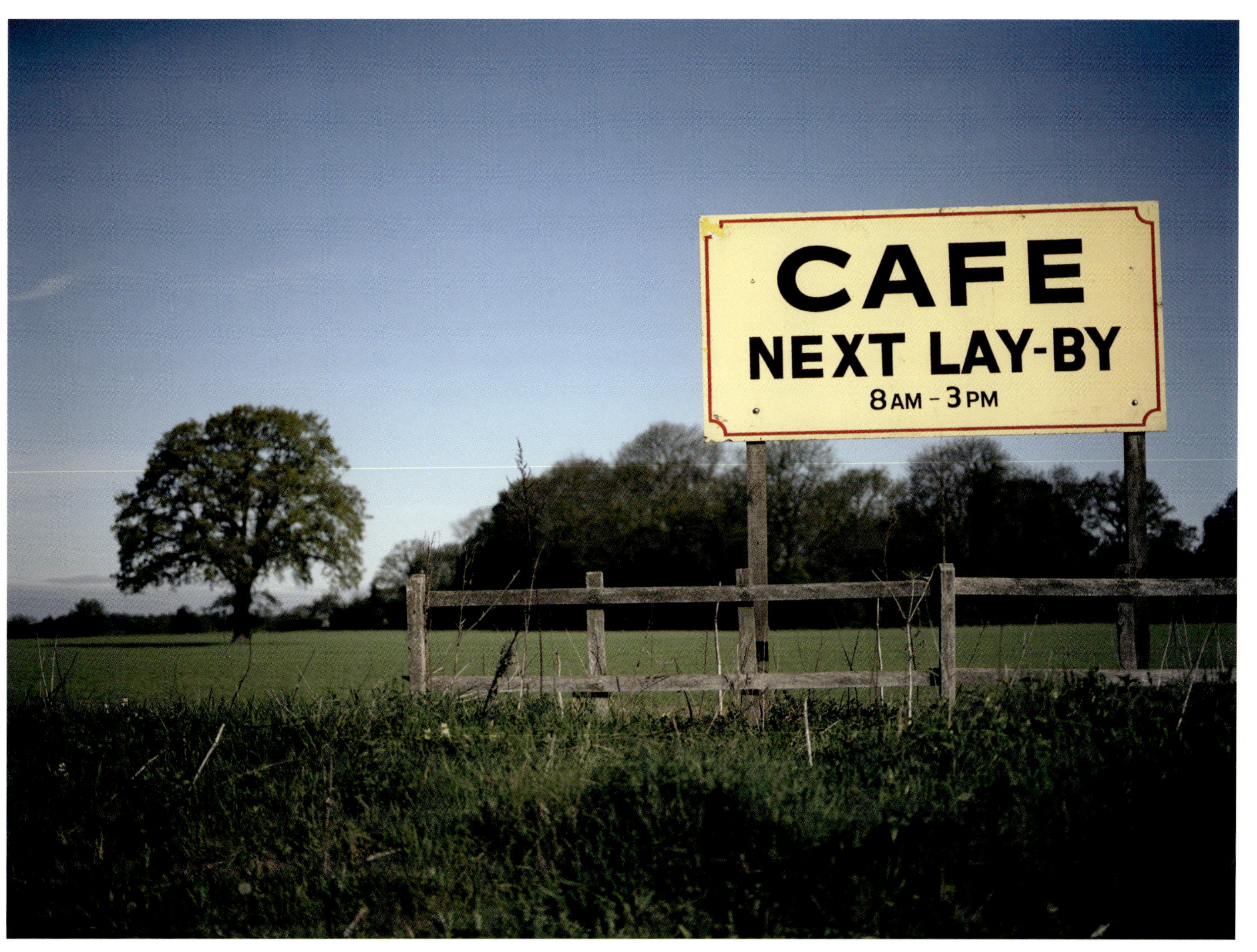


Dona's Cafe – Stratford St Mary – Suffolk – A12

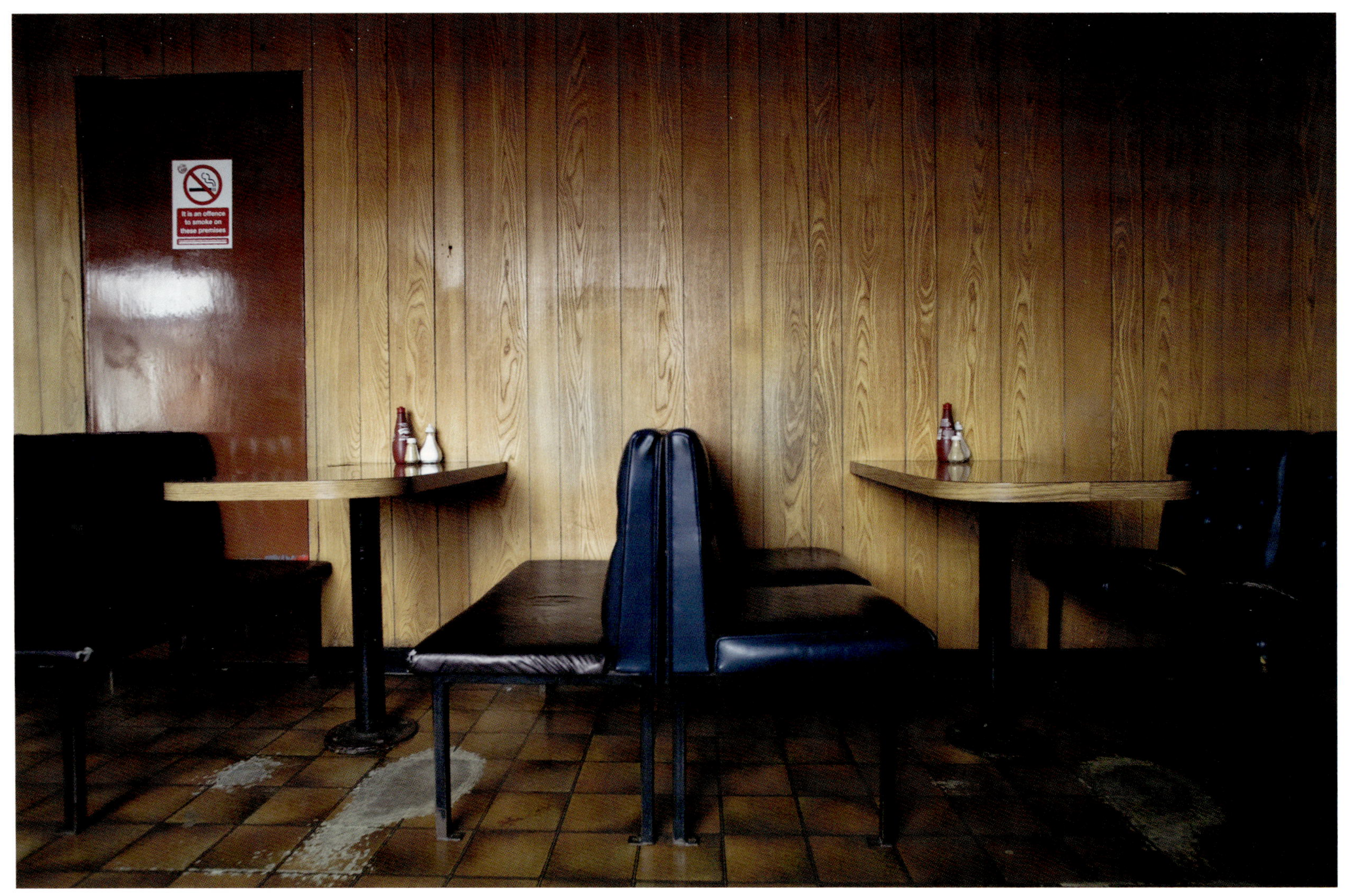

50   Boss Hoggs – Capel St Mary – Ipswich – Suffolk – Old A12

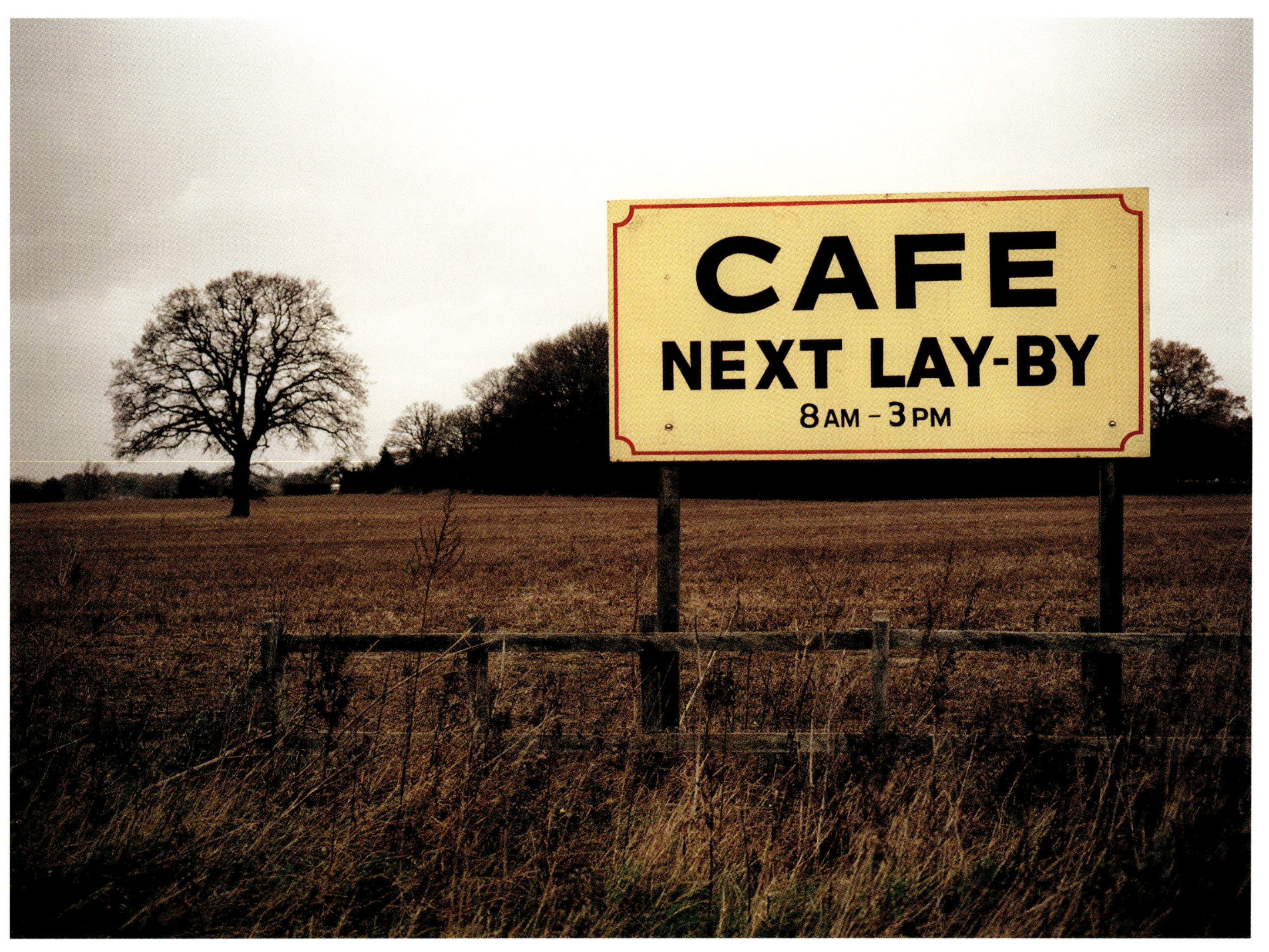


Dona's Cafe – Stratford St Mary – Suffolk – A12

# Dona's cafe

**I**n many ways, Dona's cafe (pictured opposite) prompted the idea for this series and led to four years of work. Dona's Cafe has been in business for well over 40 years. Situated on the fringes of Stratford St Mary in Suffolk, where the beginning of an incline towards East Bergholt slows the pace of passing lorries and commuters, it's on a great stretch of road. On winter mornings, the views over Dedham Vale are worth their weight in gold, while the pastoral summer sunsets are worthy of any of local hero John Constable's paintings. I used to bike along the A12 as a youngster, when I worked as 'un plongeur', as Orwell would describe a kitchen porter, at the nearby Le Talbooth Restaurant. This part-time vocation kindled my love for food and photography. The cuisine at Le Talbooth is among the best in the region, while photo-based food books such as *White Heat* by Marco Pierre White inspired me, both with the avant-garde recipes featured, but also with the raw reportage imagery of White and his team captured by the late Bob Carlos Clarke. Owned by the Milsom family, Le Talbooth gained excellent recognition and won countless awards including a Michelin star. Delia Smith came into the kitchen once when I was mopping the floor, and I remember thinking how short she was. On my way to work I'd bike past Dona's Cafe. I once accidentally took the keys for the huge walk-in fridge home with me after a day shift – I made the 12-mile round-trip twice that day. Using my bike to return the keys certainly earned me some kudos with the head chef, despite the fact I'd taken them in the first place. I'd always wonder at the significance of this lonesome cafe, closed up after hours. Leaving the realms of silver service dining, bow ties and black suits, this place of solitary mysticism seemed a world apart. I was fascinated. I knew it was important, yet, I would never have expected Dona's Cafe would be the inspiration for starting this project ten years down the line.



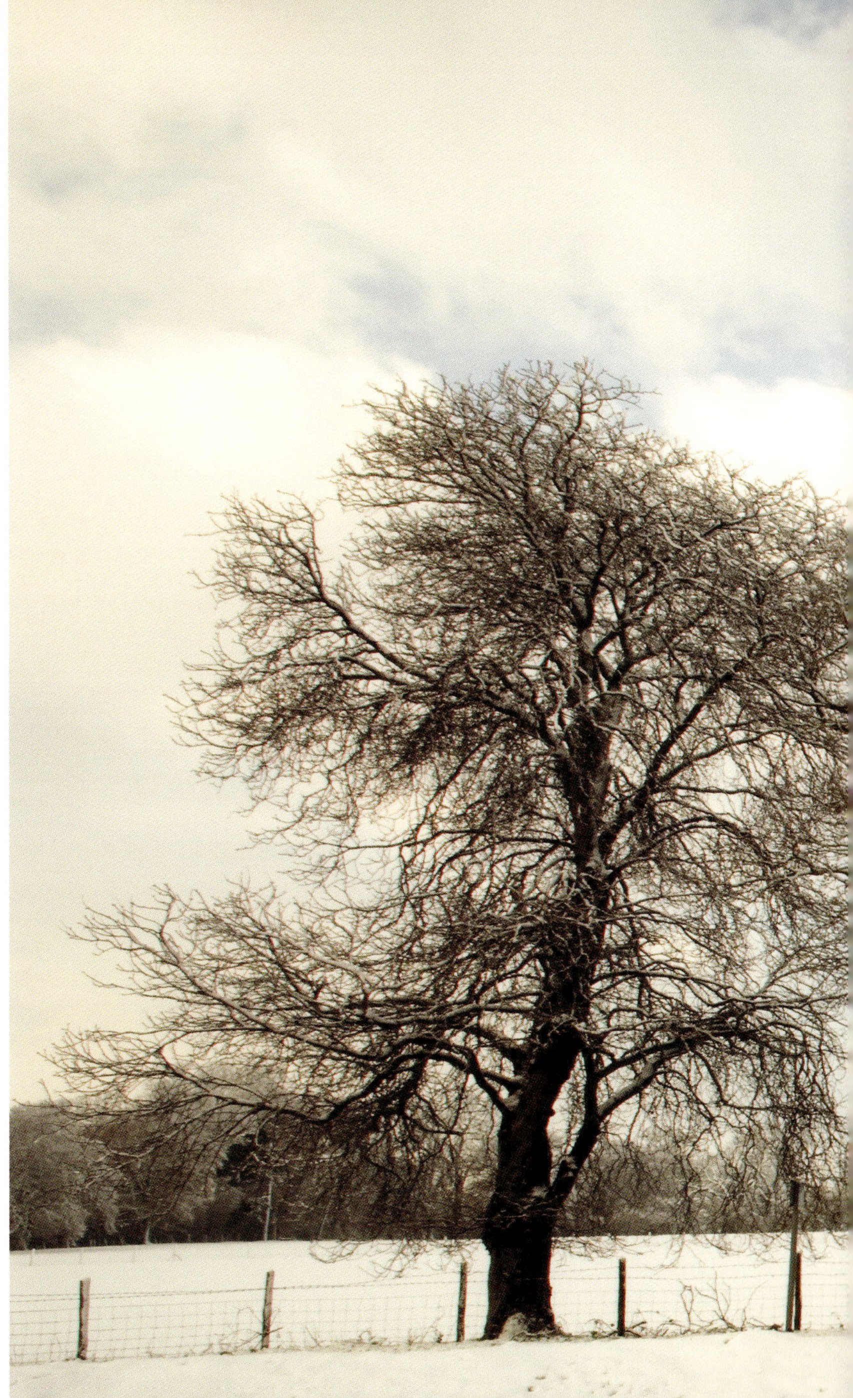

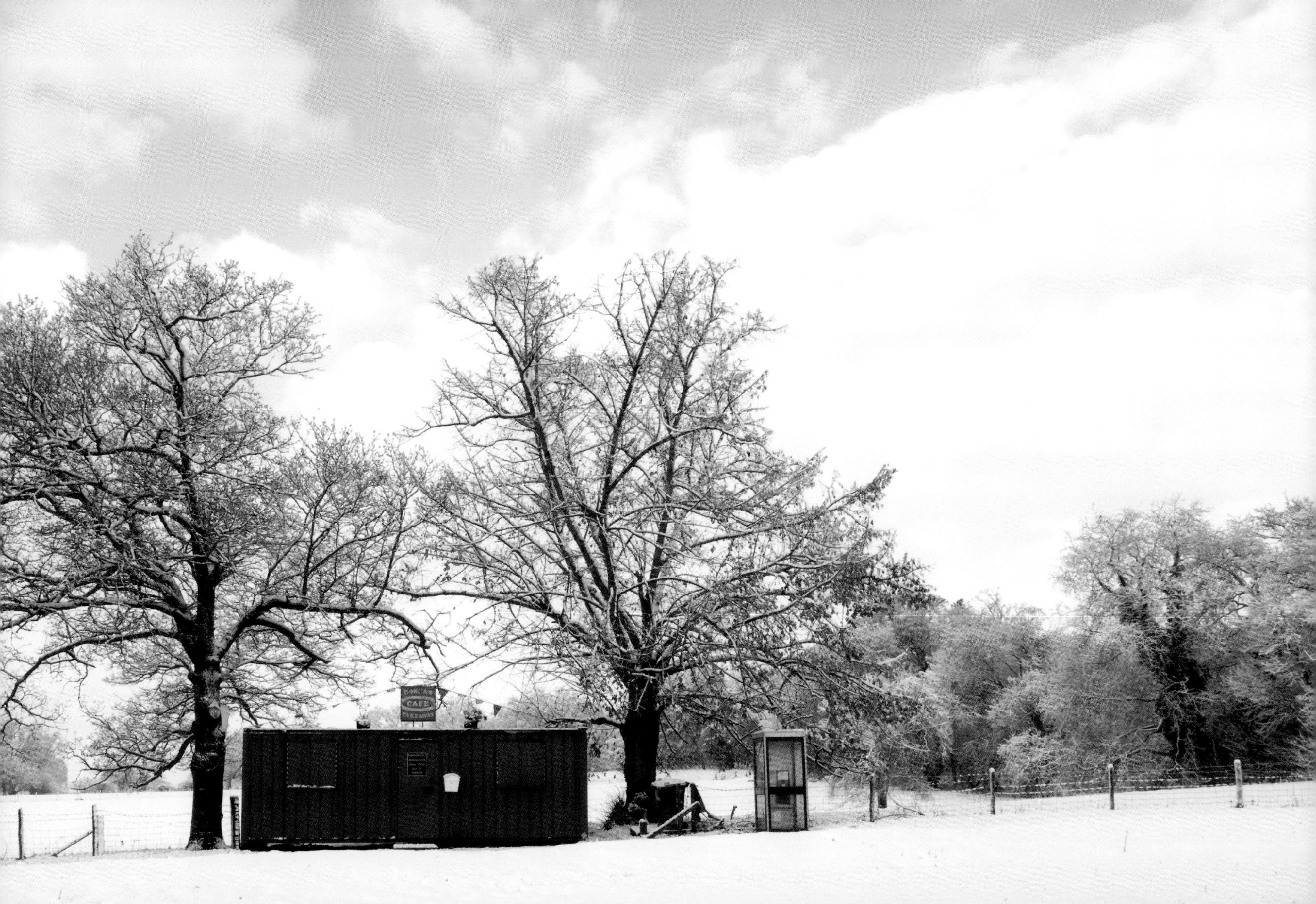
DONIA'S
CAFE
TAKEAWAY

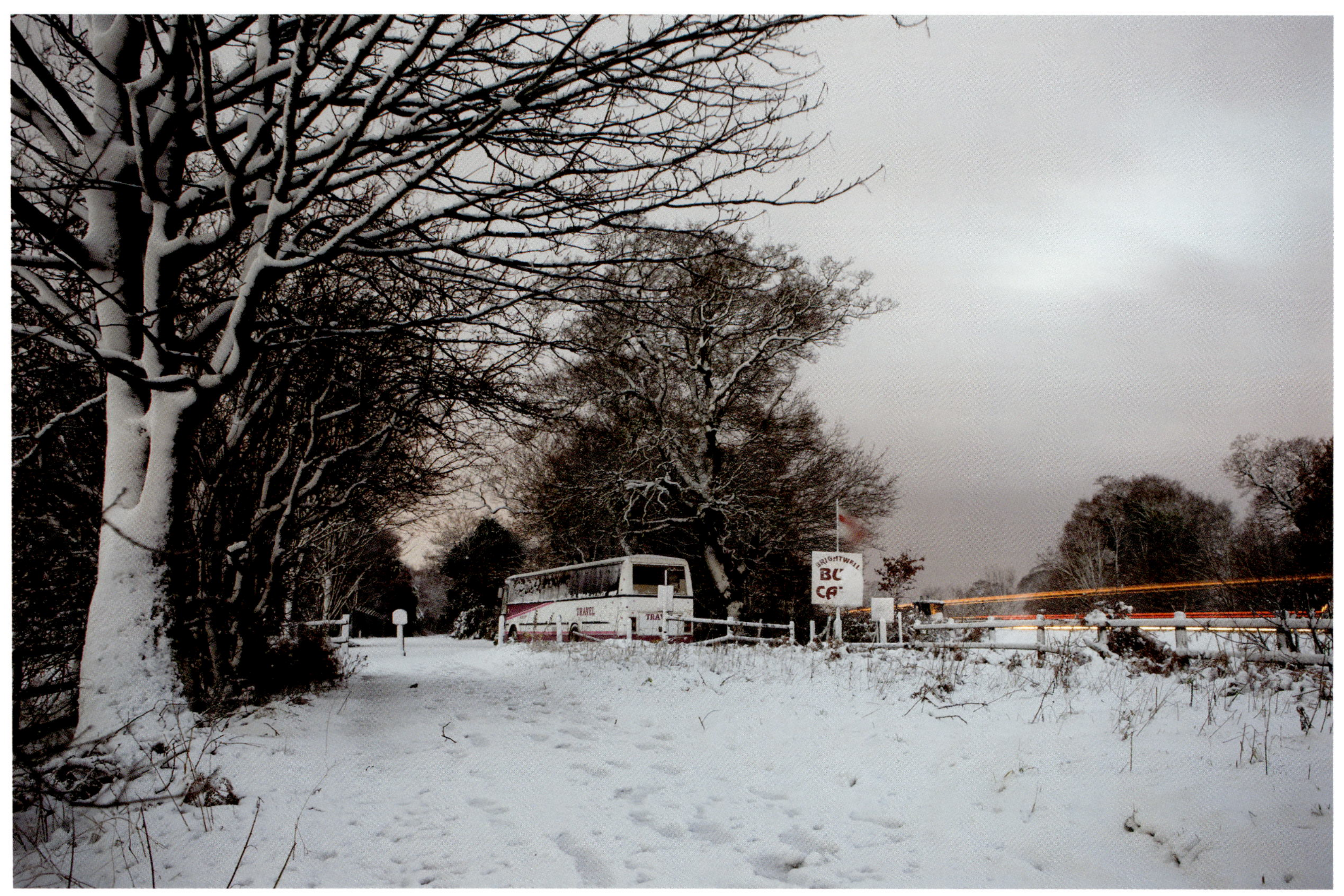

Brightwell
BU
CA
TRAVEL

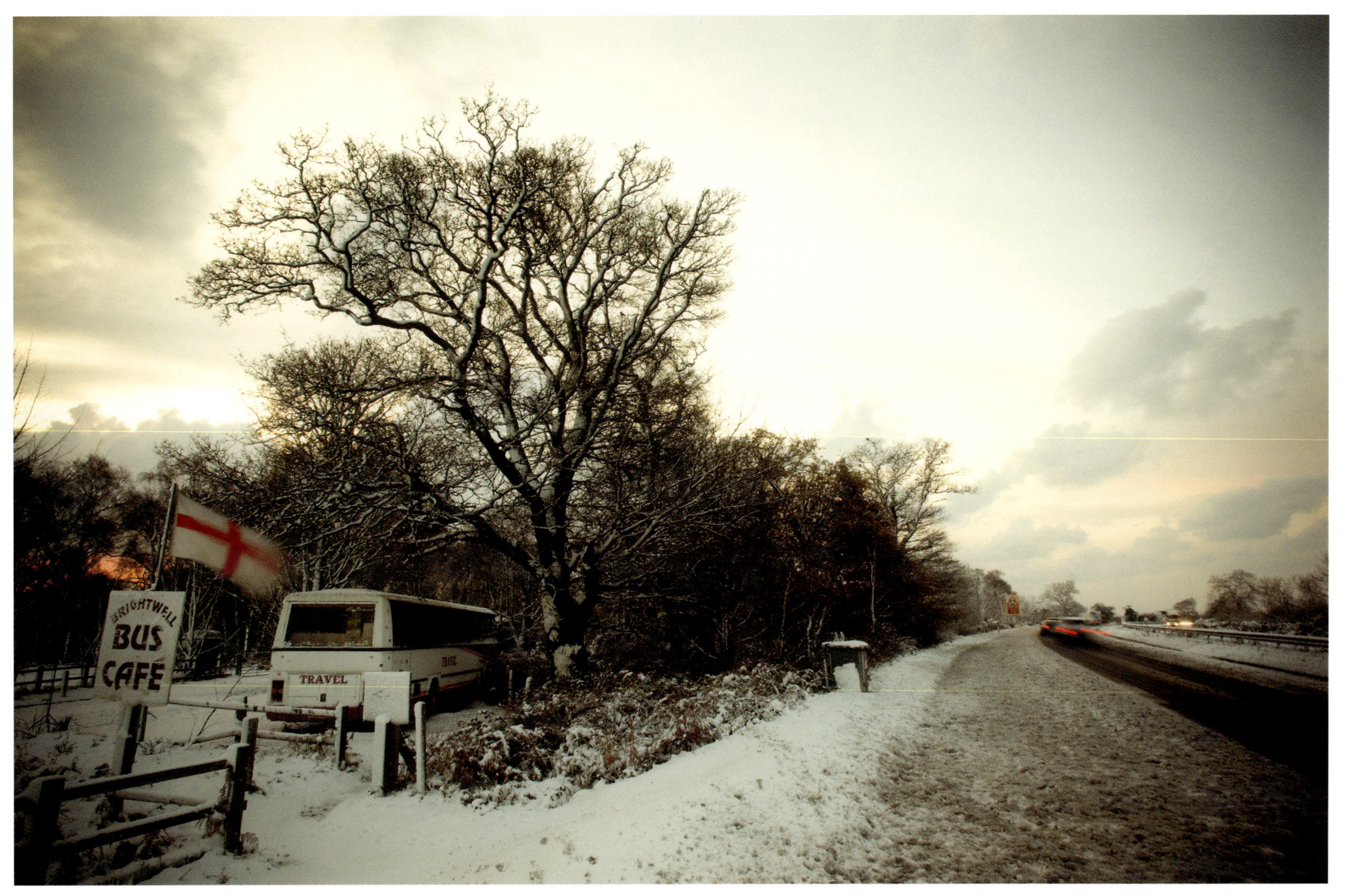

Brightwell Bus Cafe – Brightwell – Suffolk – A12    55

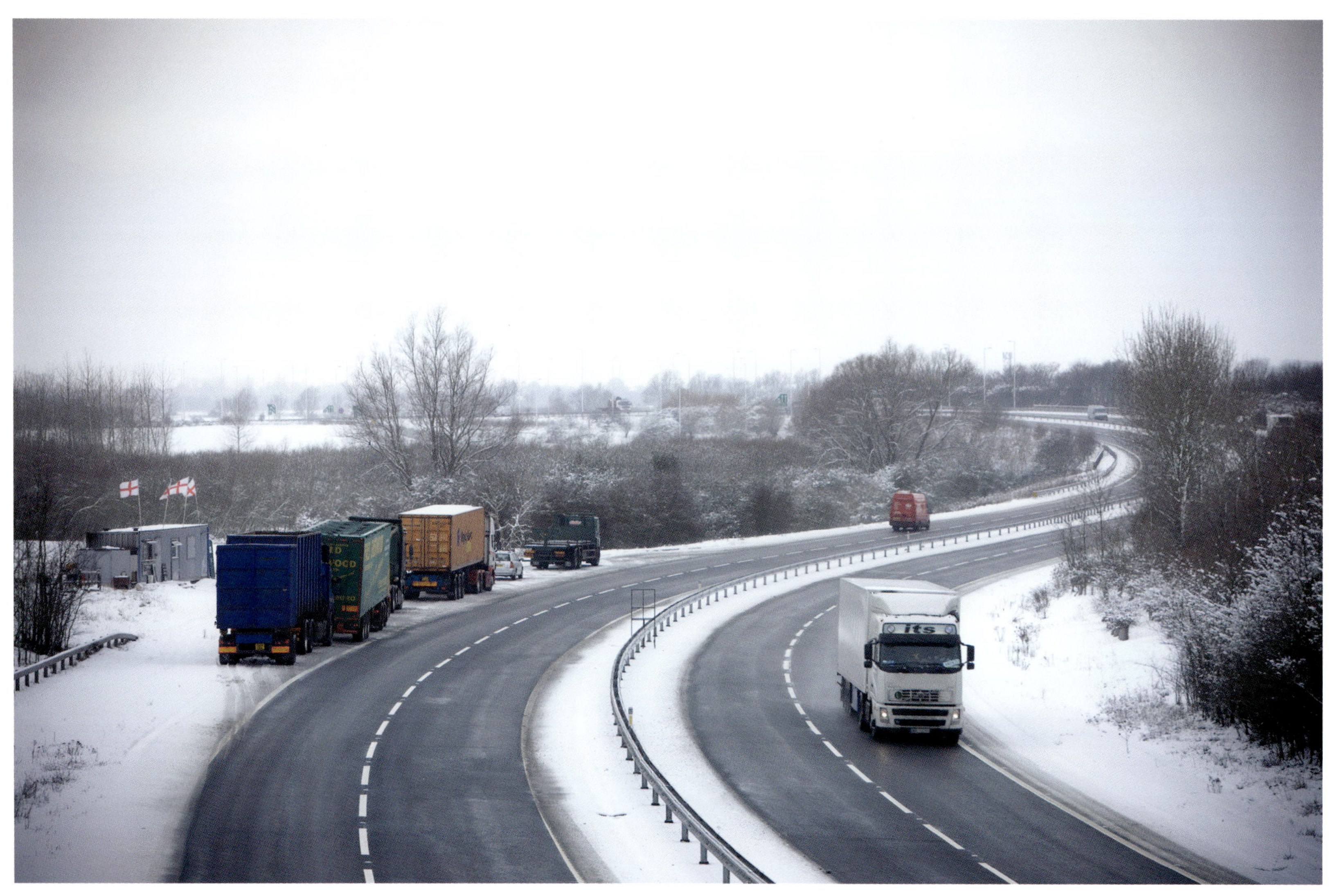

Above: Vinnies Diner – Inworth – Essex – A12
Right: Shane Walker's 'Shabbily Shack' Cafe – Kelvedon – Essex – A12

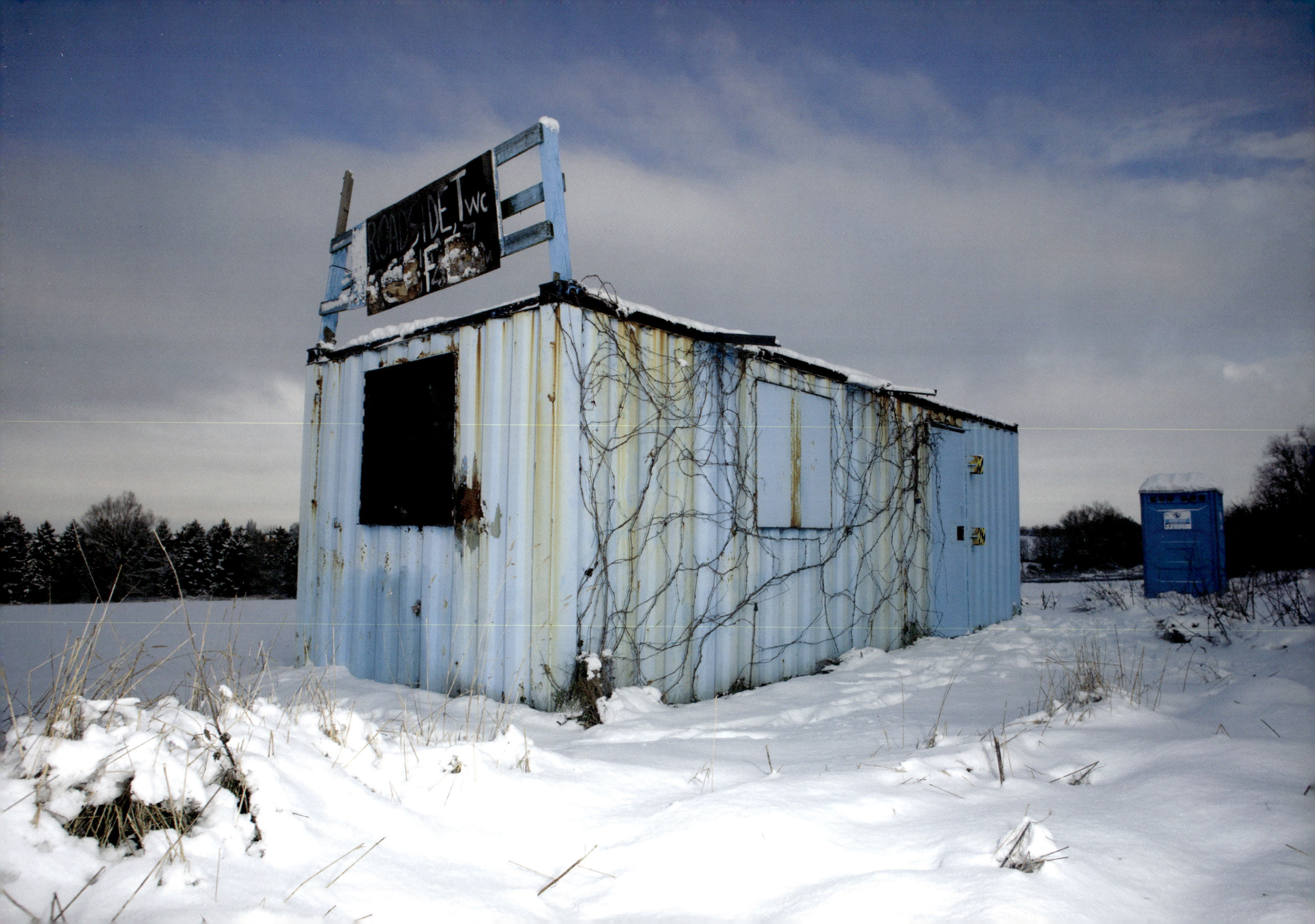
ROADSIDE T WC

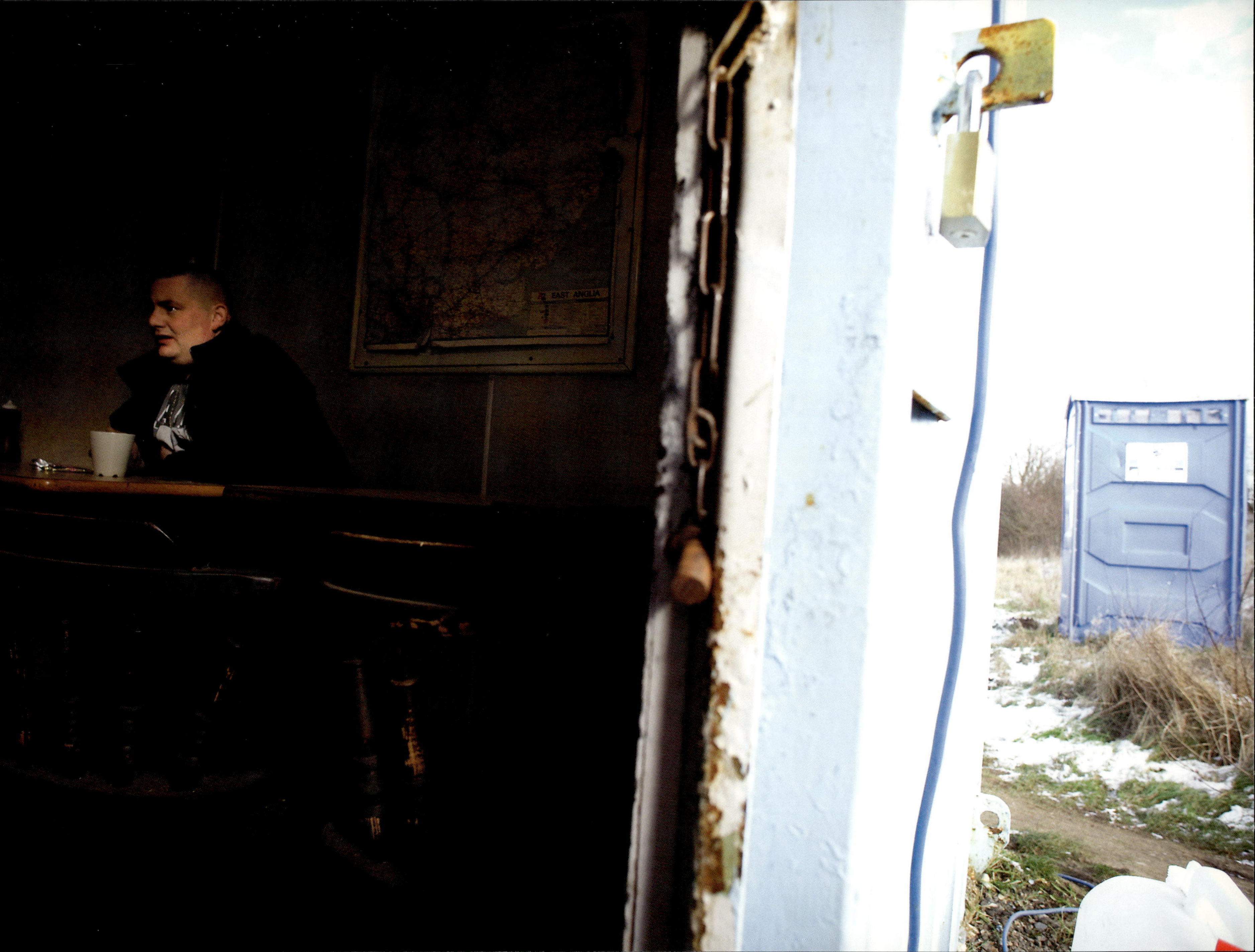

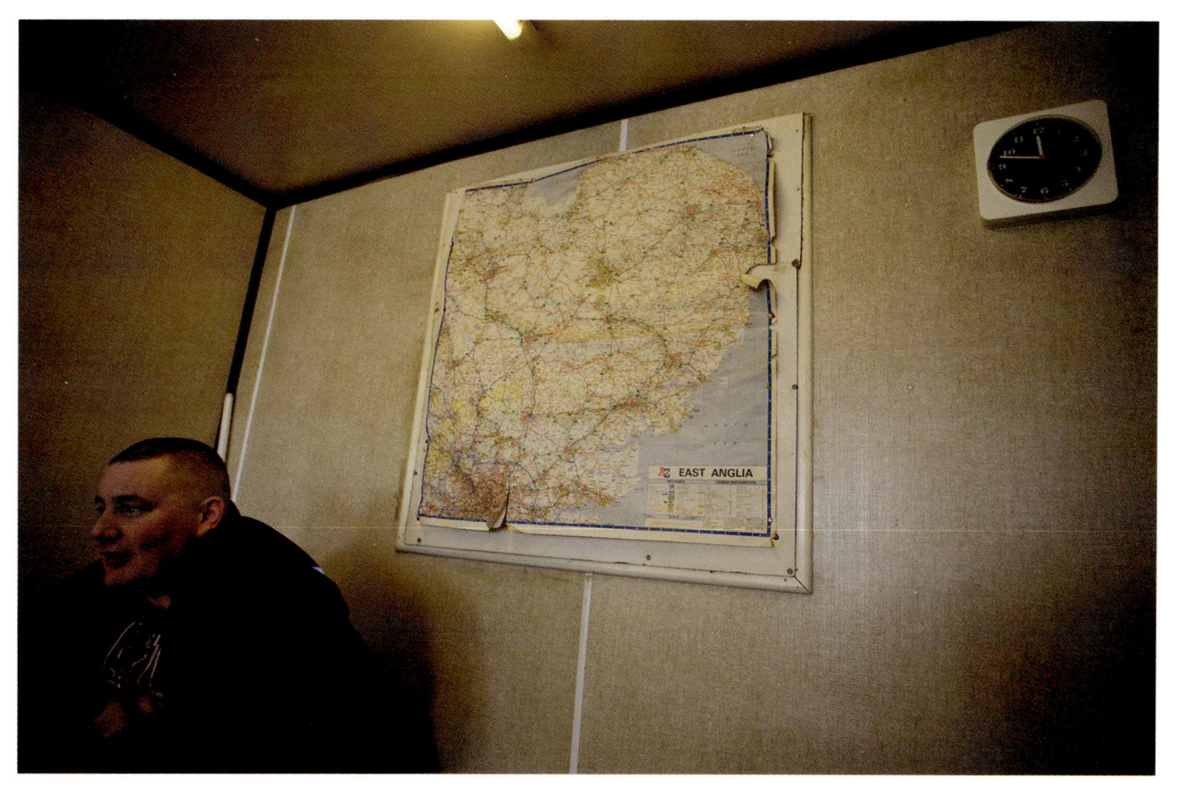



Above & left: Shane Walker's 'Shabbily Shack' Cafe – Kelvedon – Essex – A12

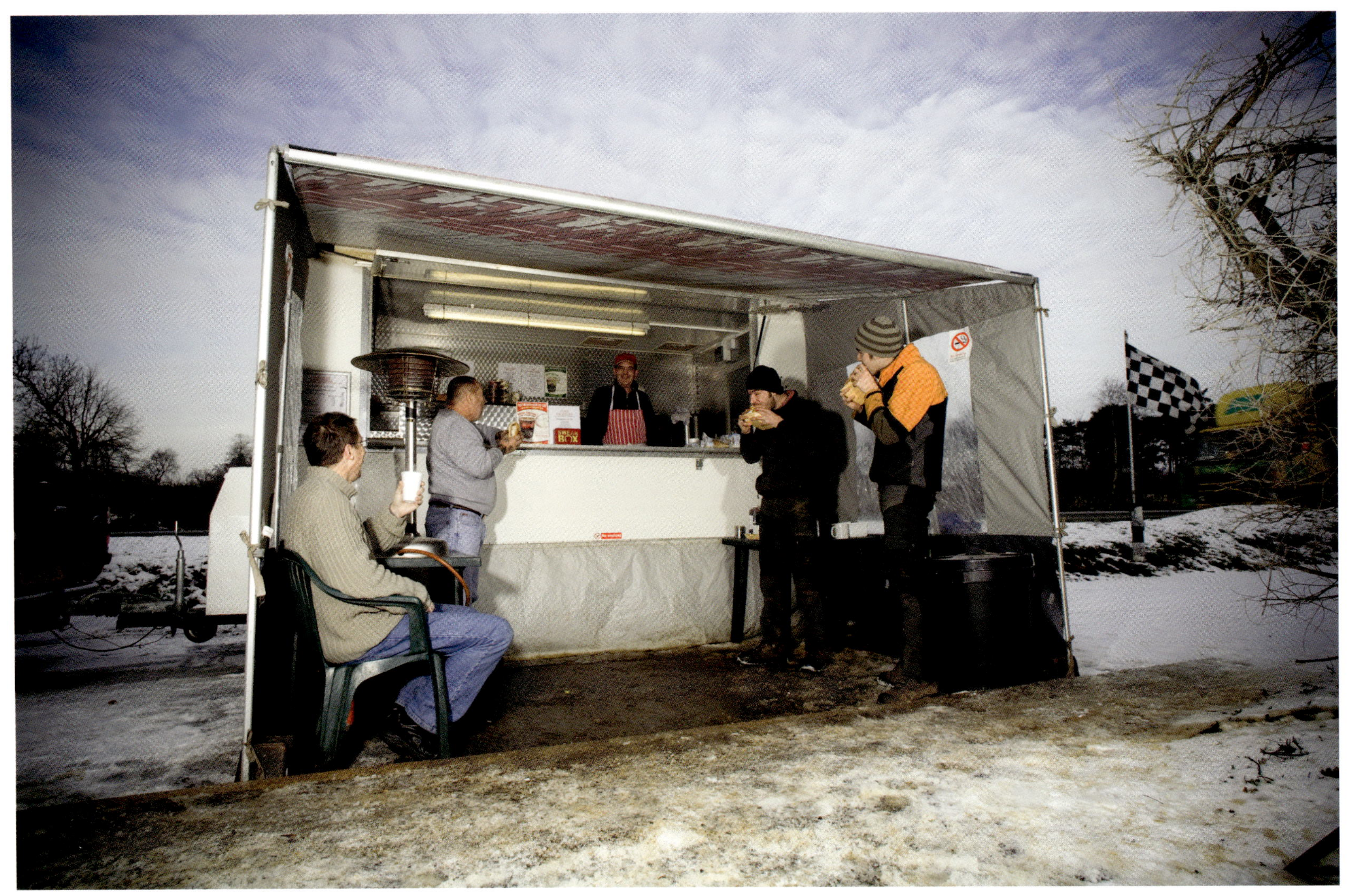

 The Pitt Stop – Benhall – Saxmundam – Suffolk – A12

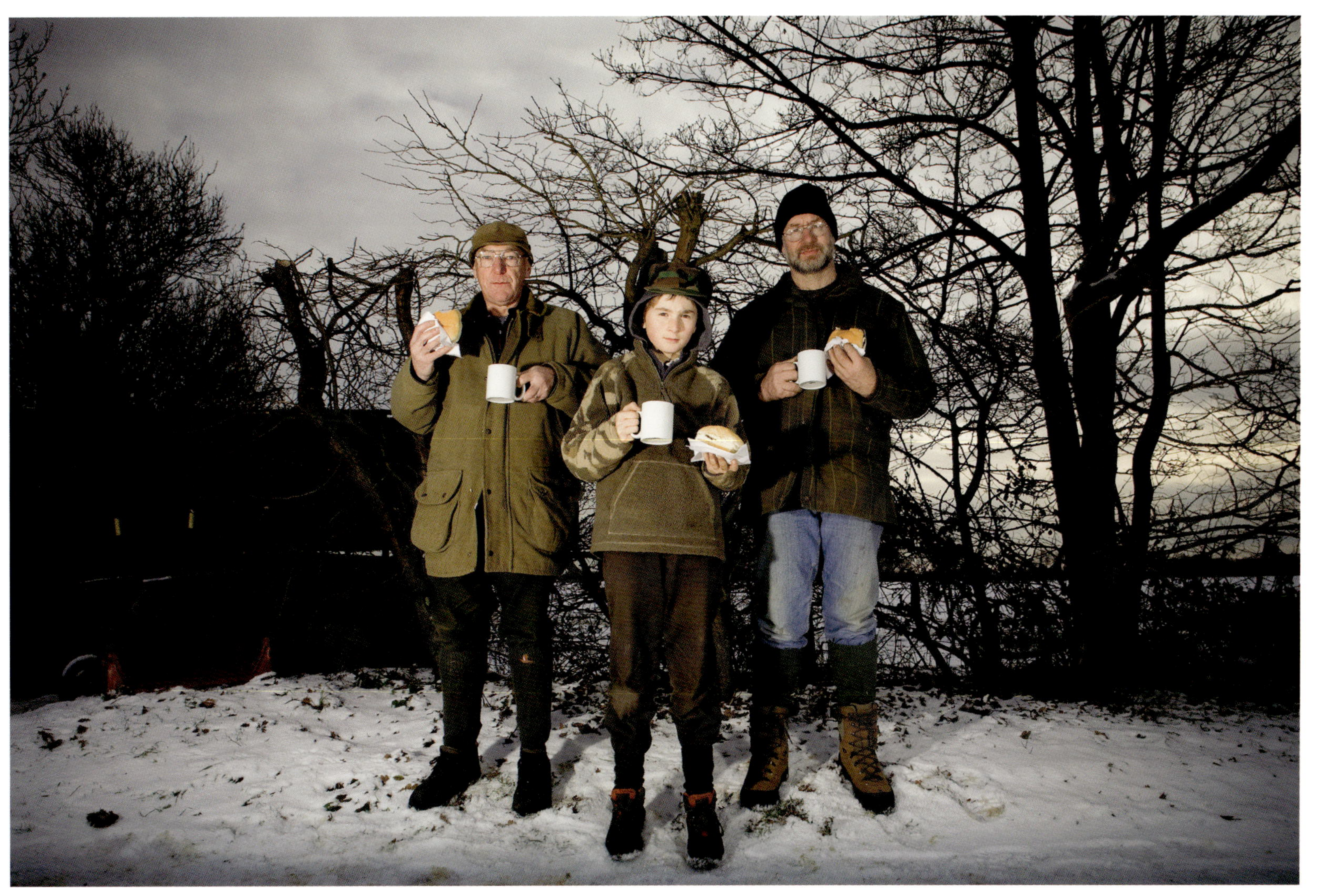

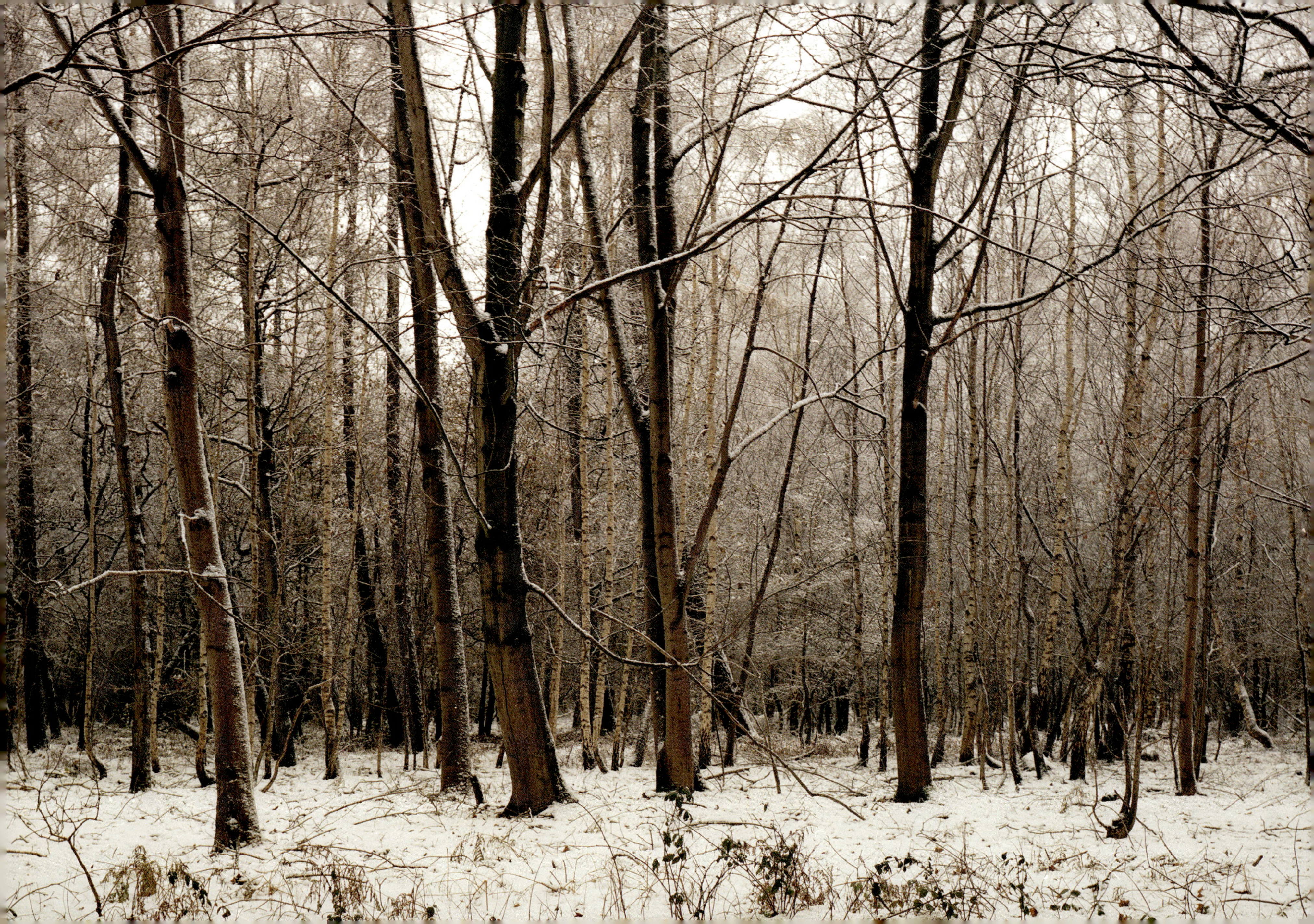

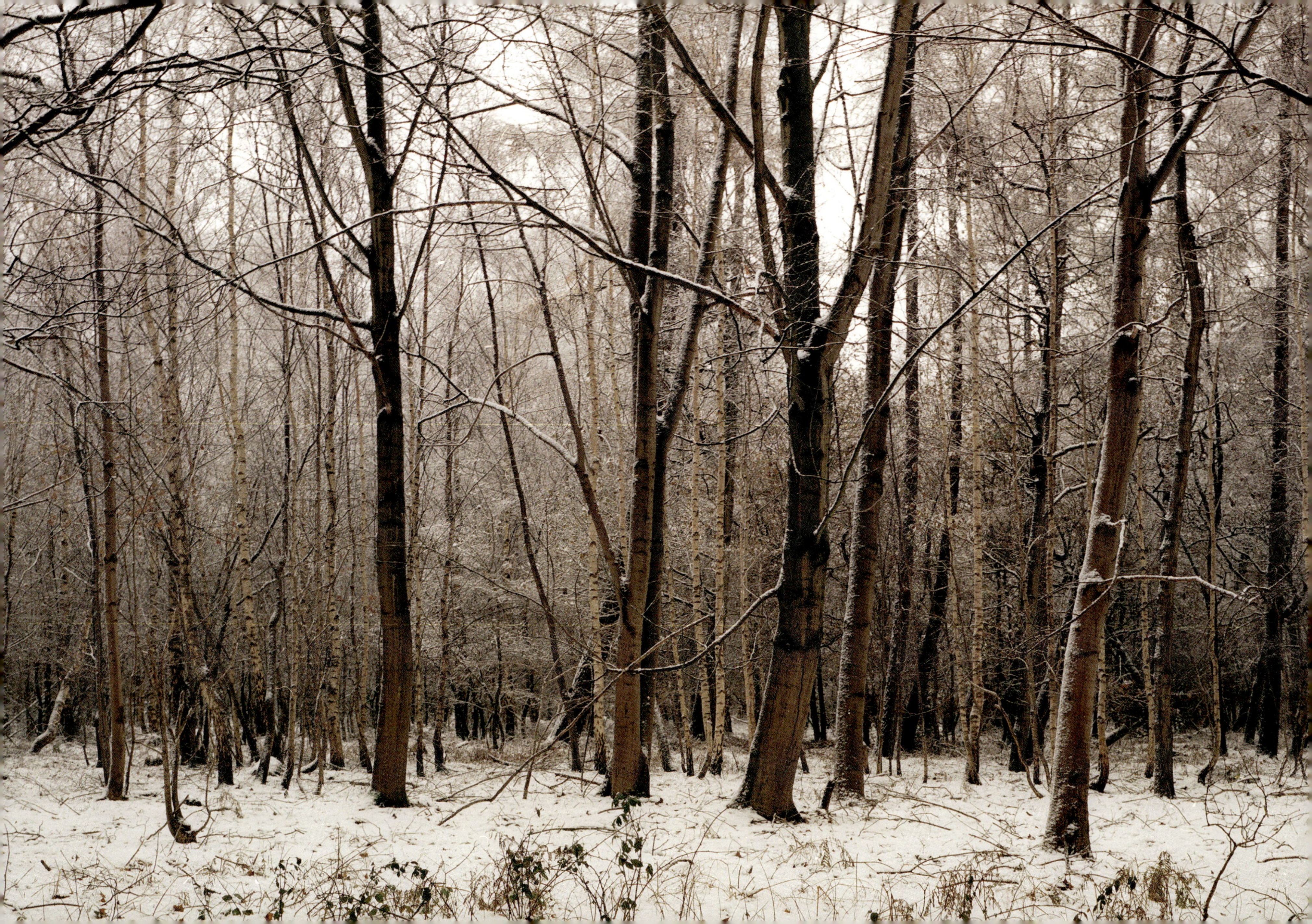

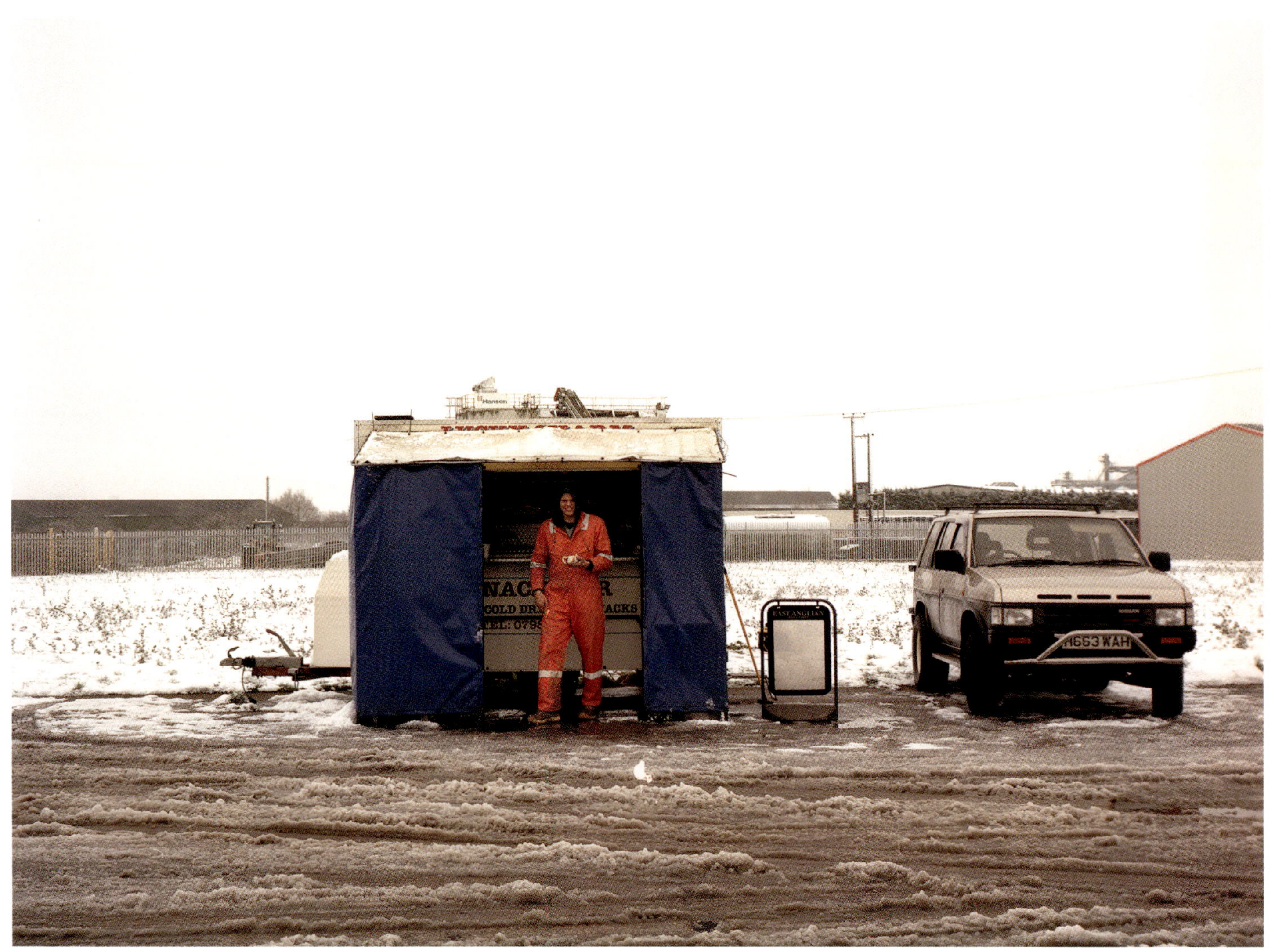

 Steel Joiner at Lucky Charms – Brome – Suffolk – A140

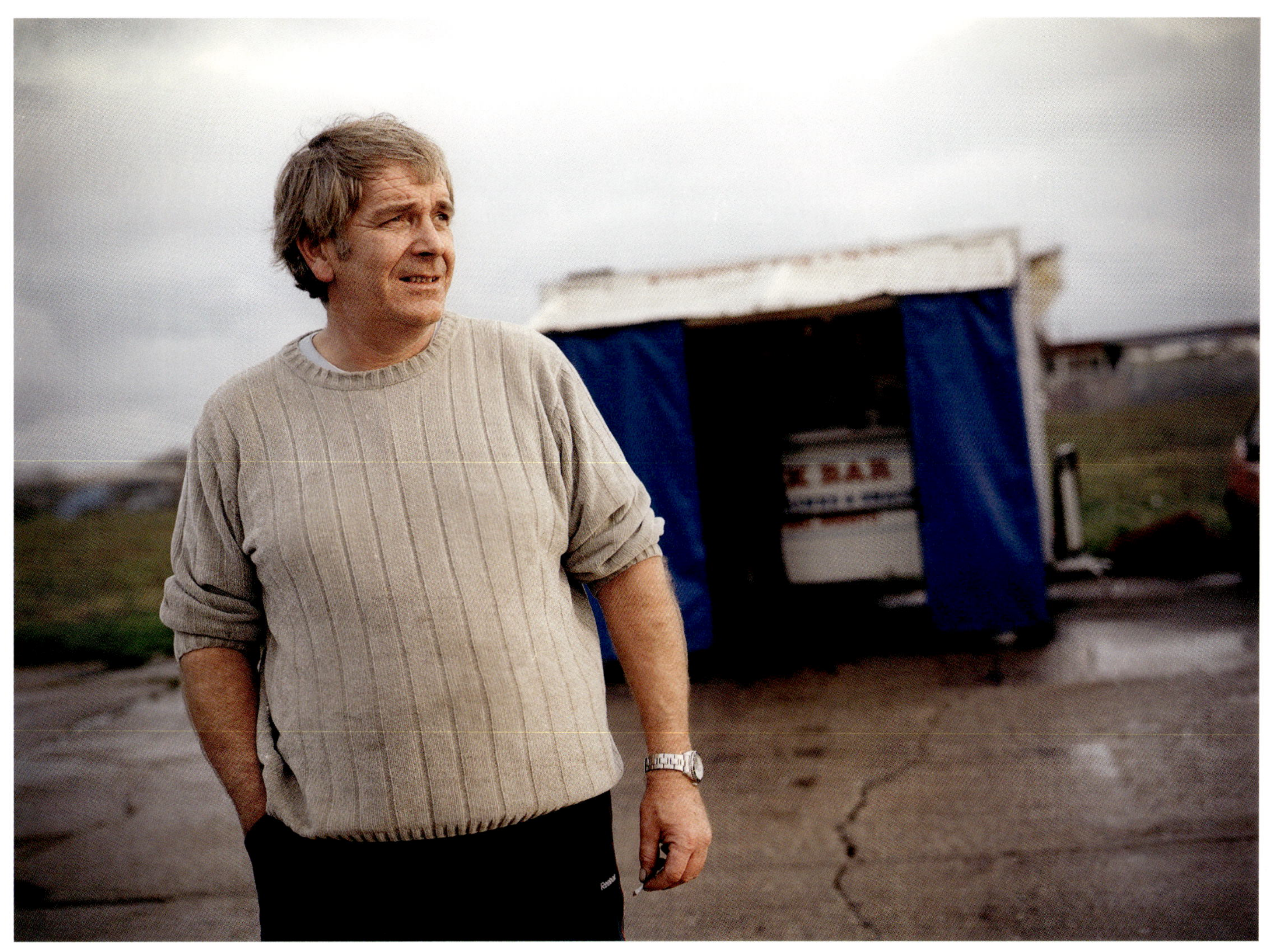

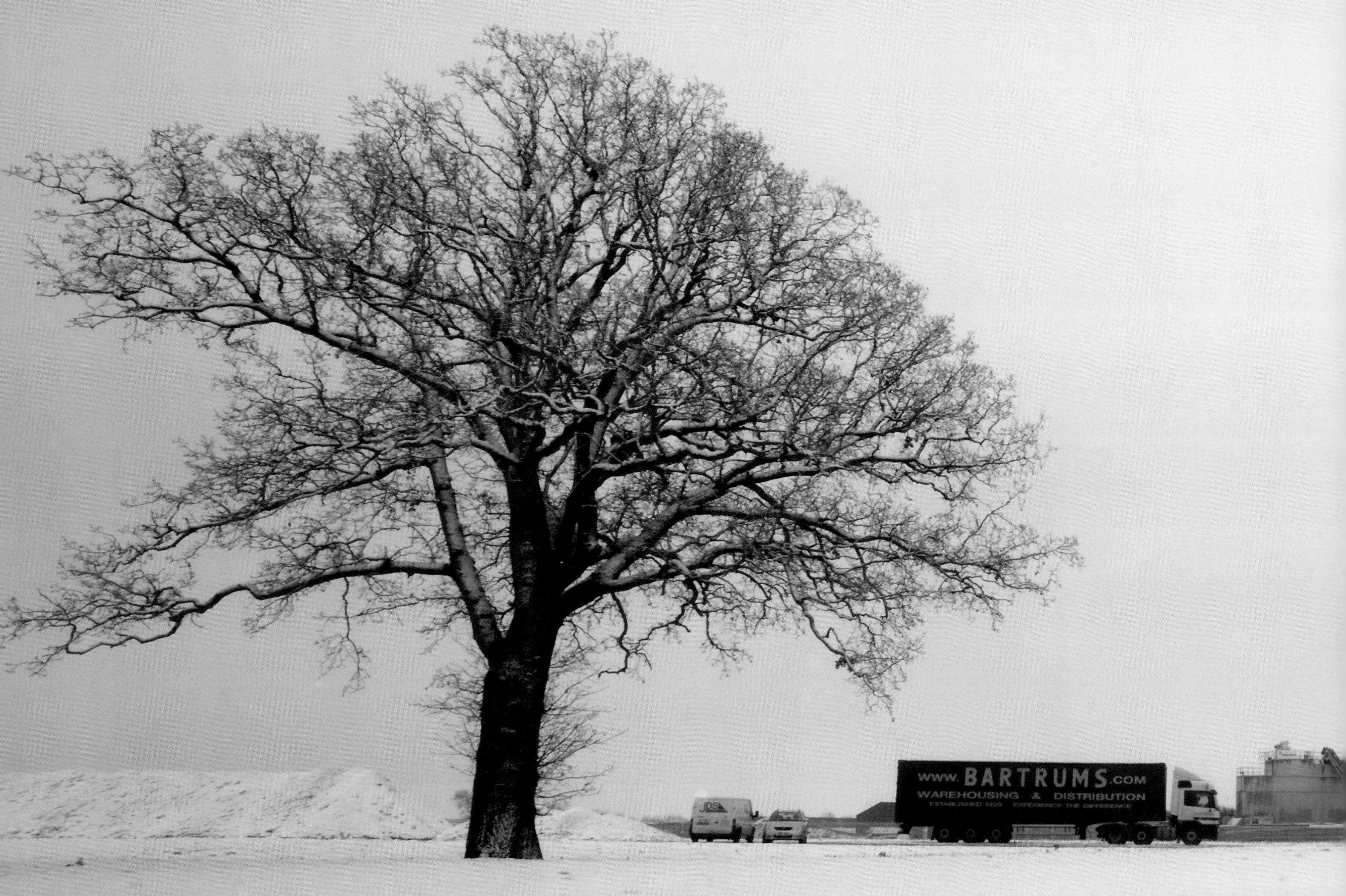

www. BARTRUMS .com
WAREHOUSING & DISTRIBUTION
JDS

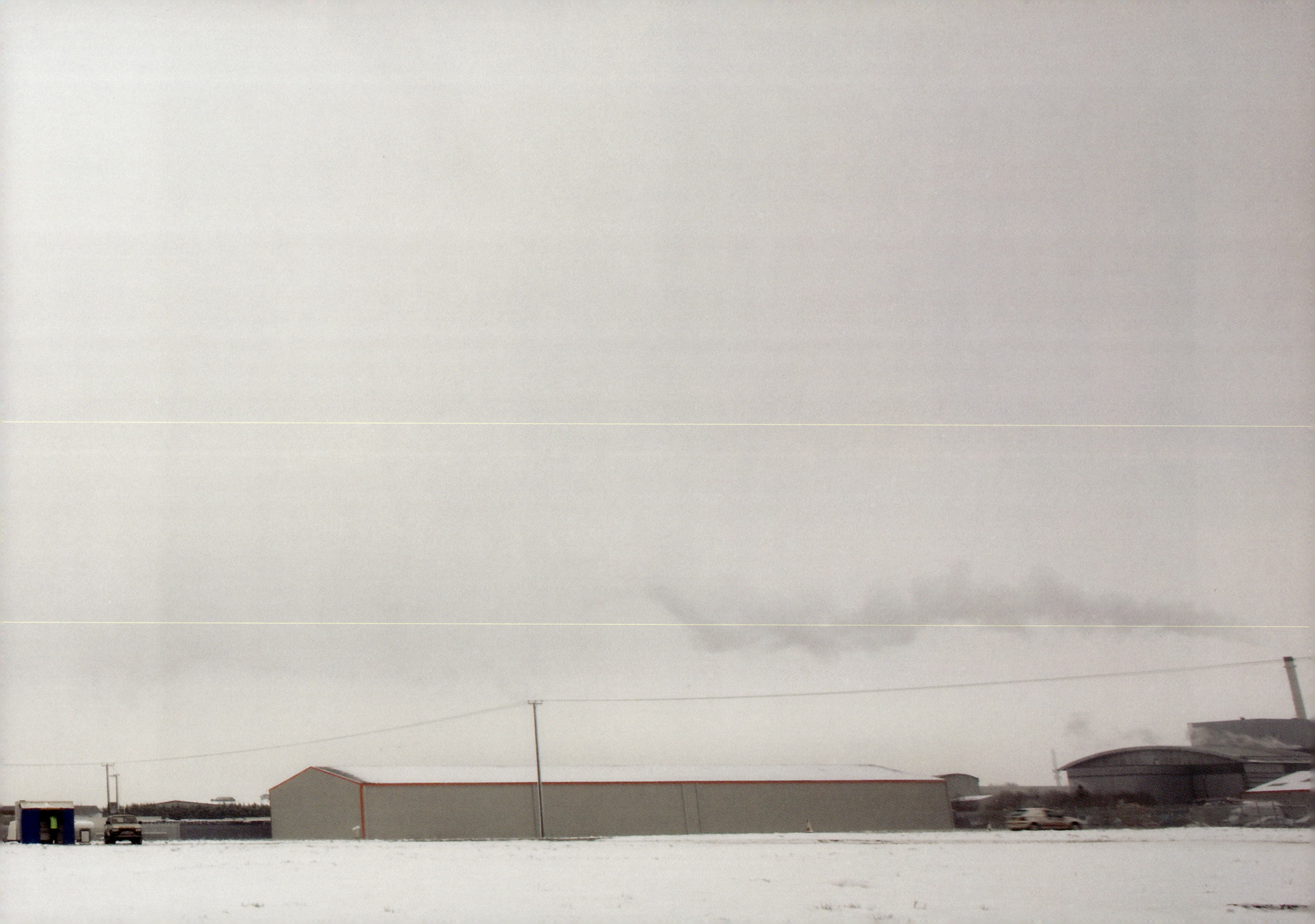

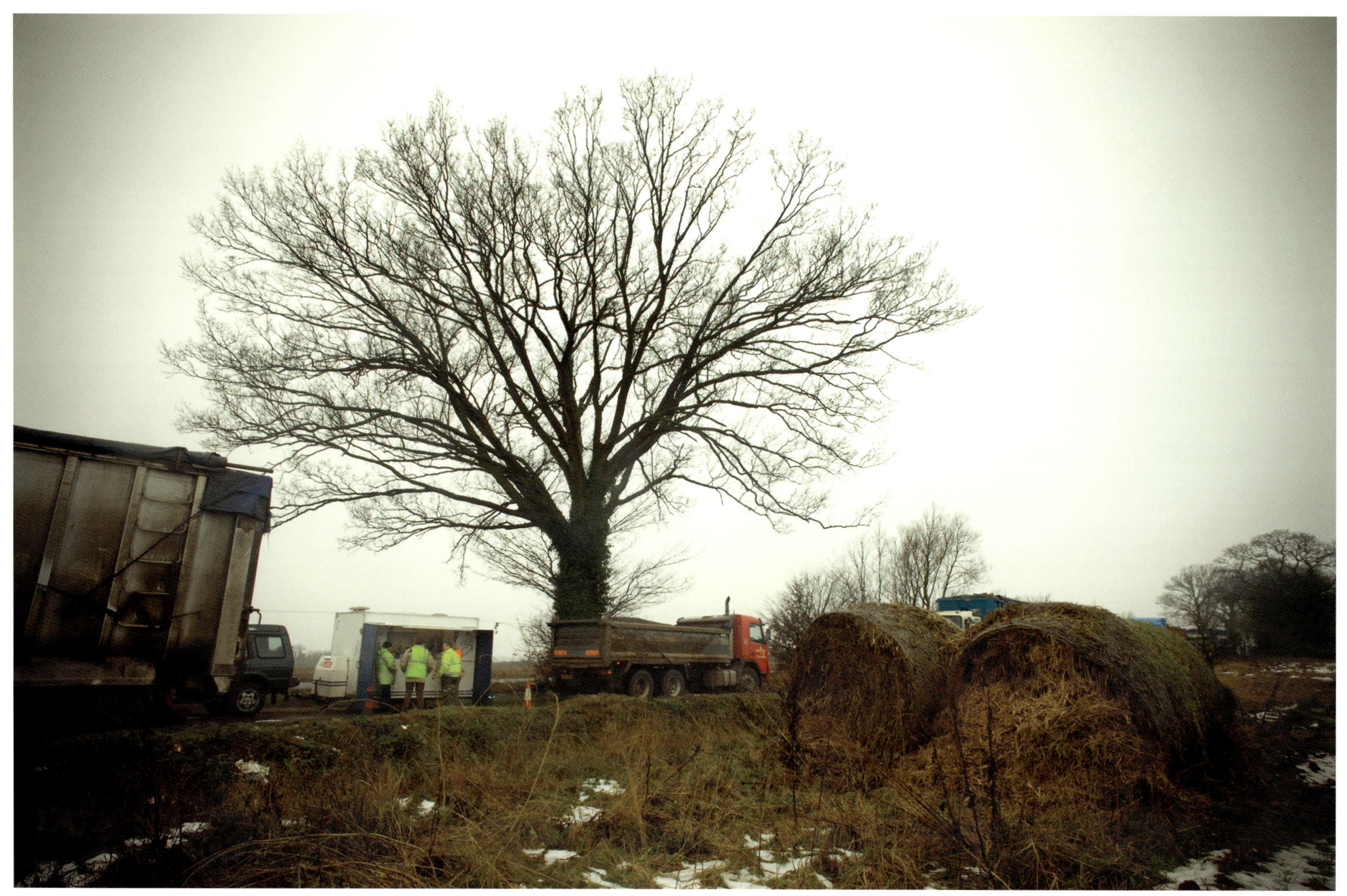

 A Wintry Morning at Kym's Catering – Crimplesham – Norfolk – A47

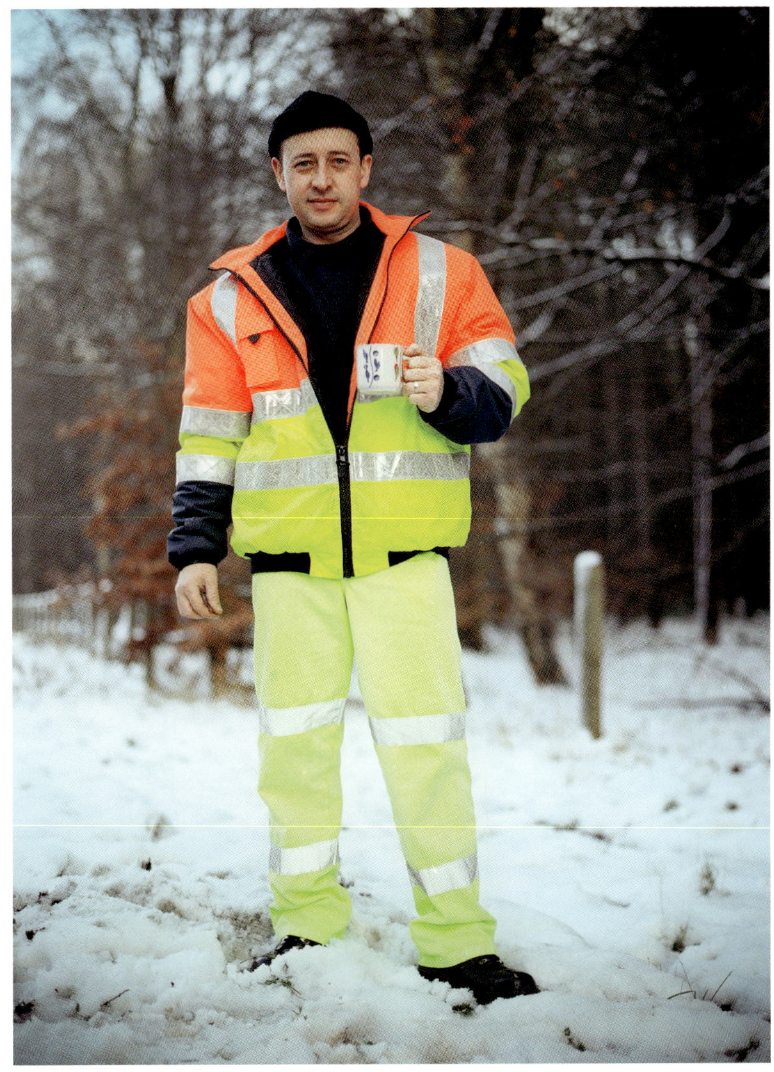

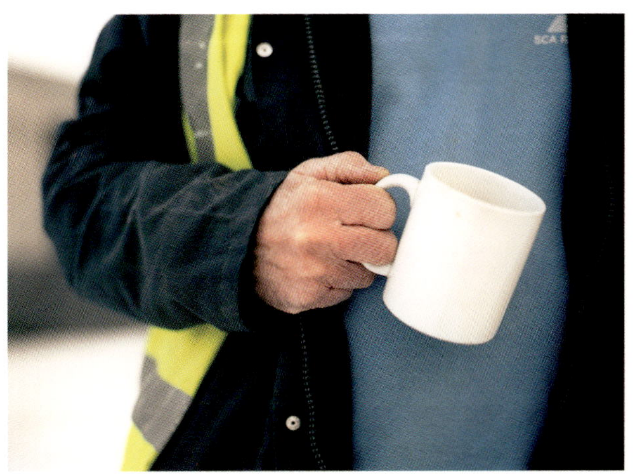

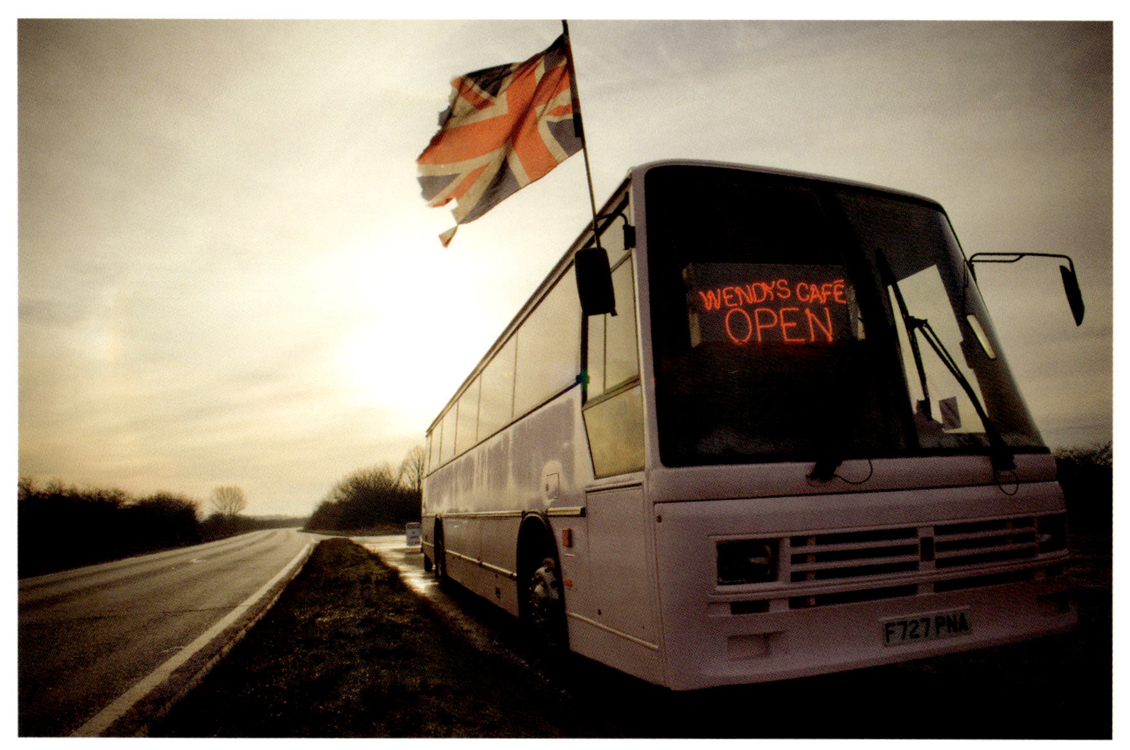


  Wendy's Bus Cafe – Kings Lynn – Norfolk – A47

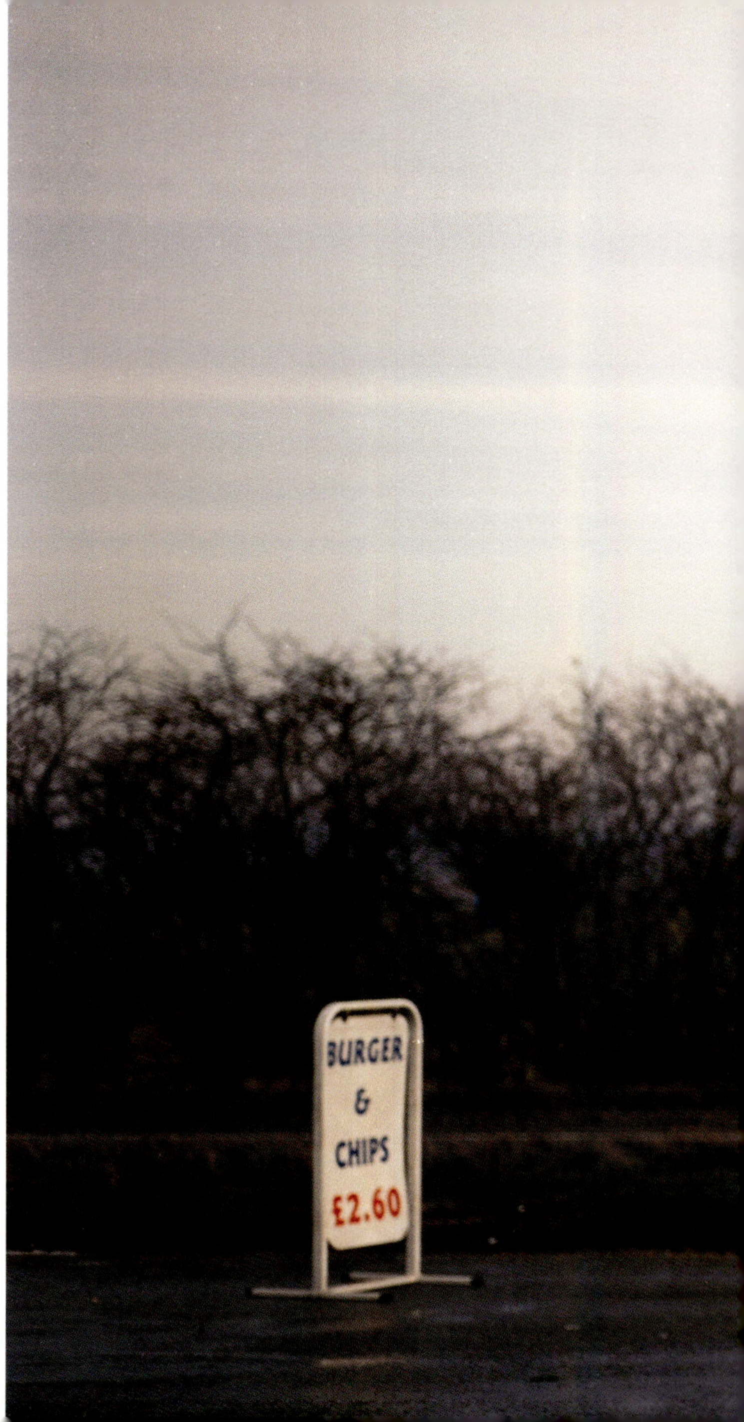

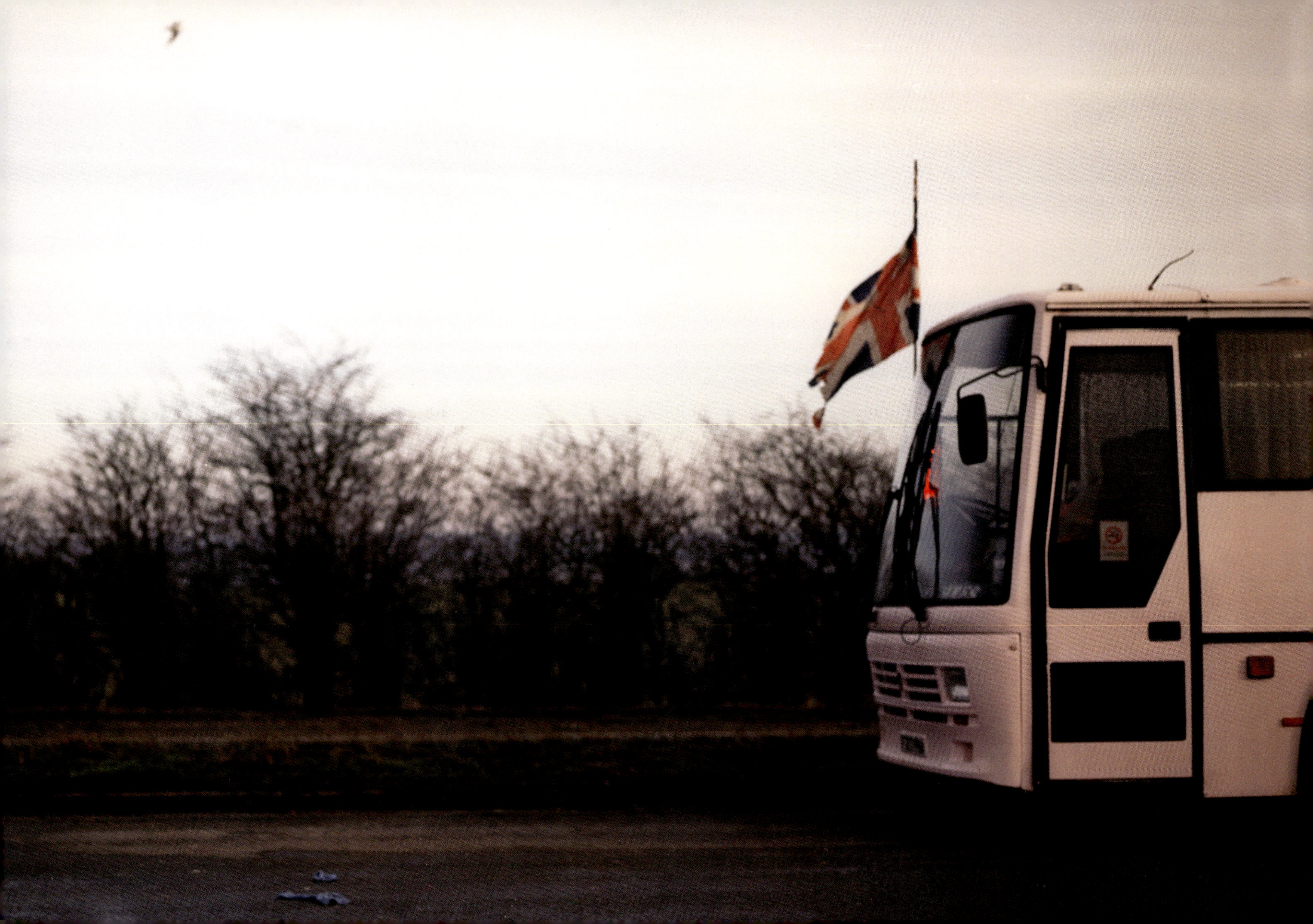

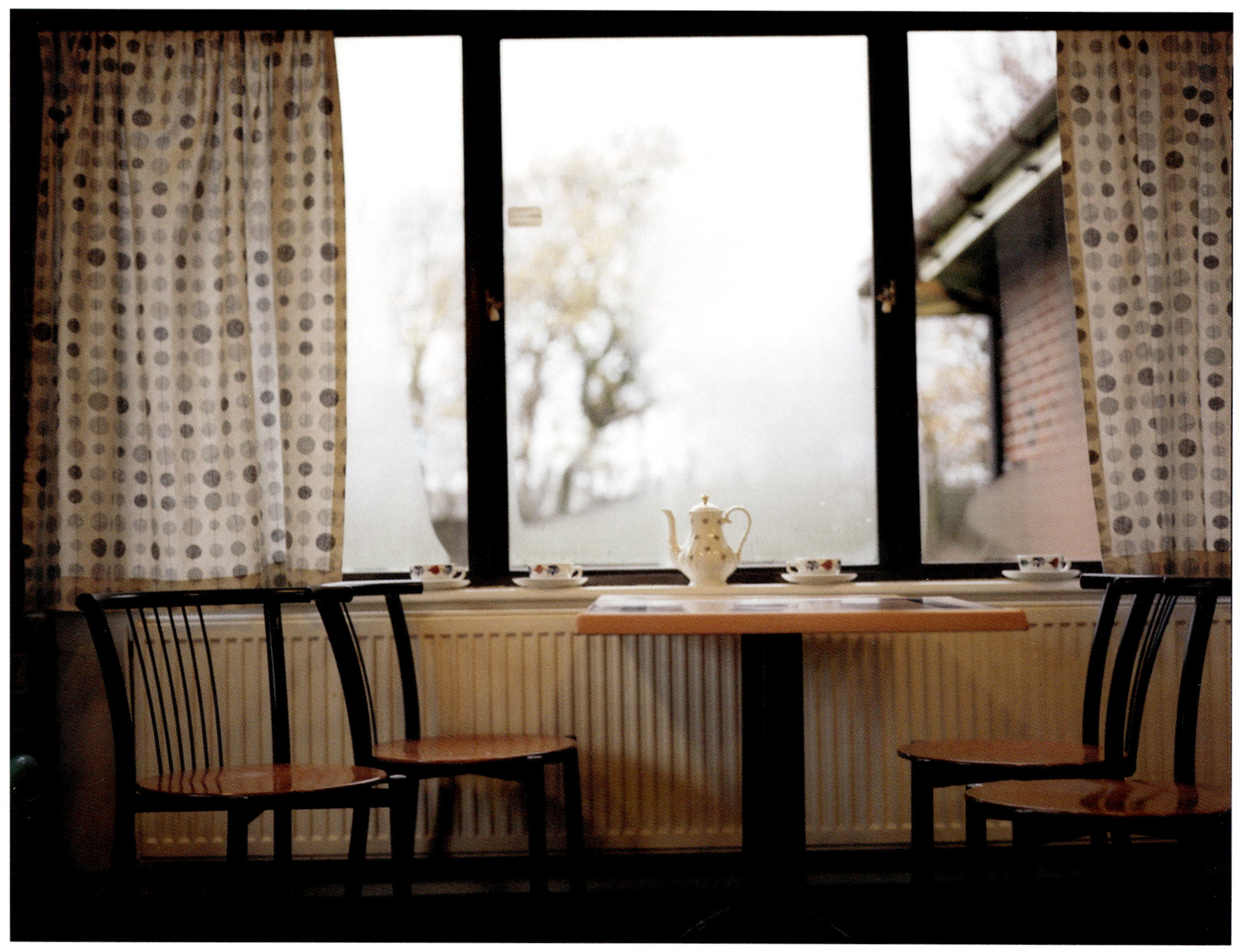

 Harvest Moon Cafe – Capel St Mary – Suffolk – A12

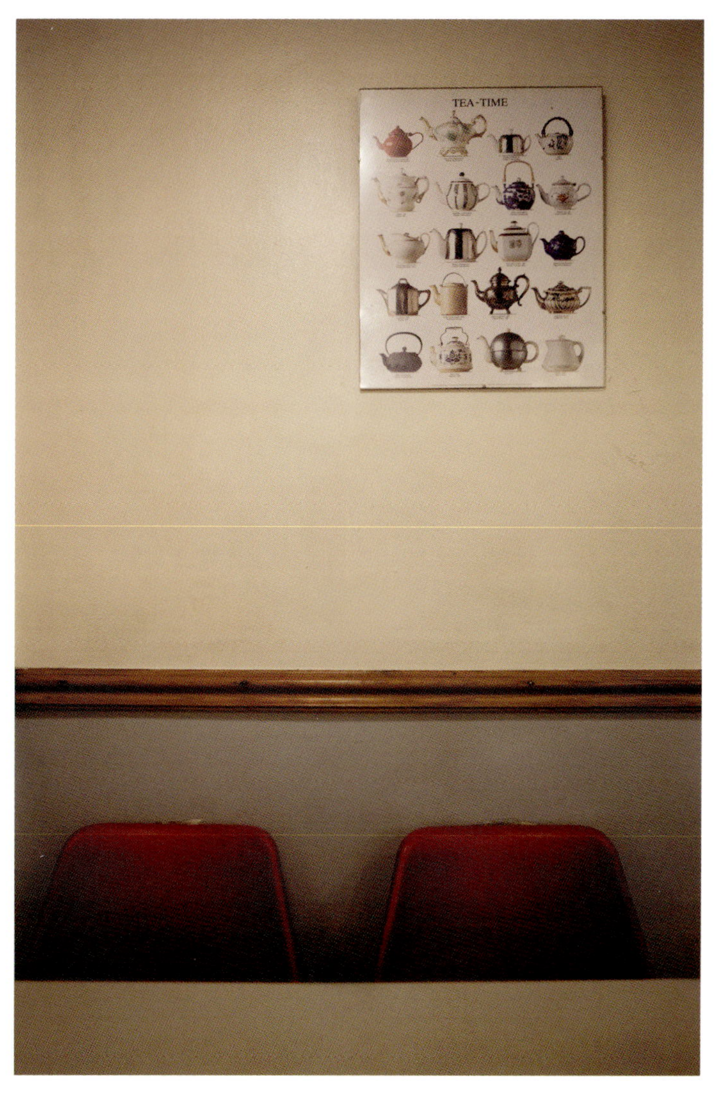



Tea Time at Stibbington Diner – Stibbington – A1     73

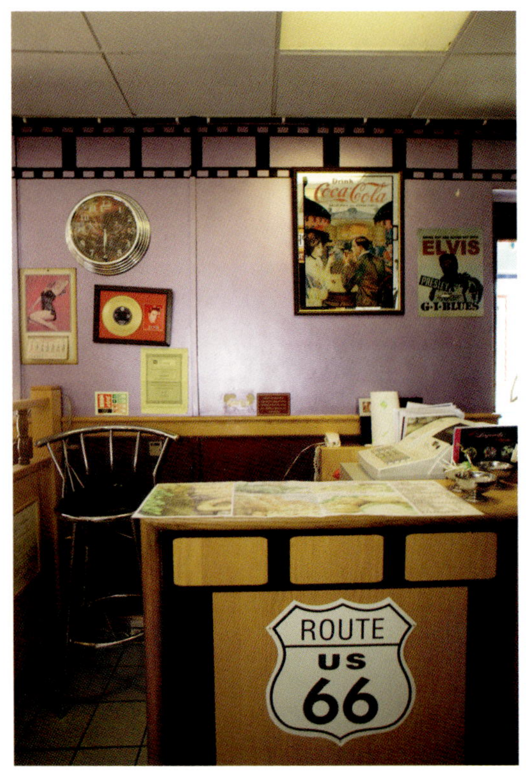
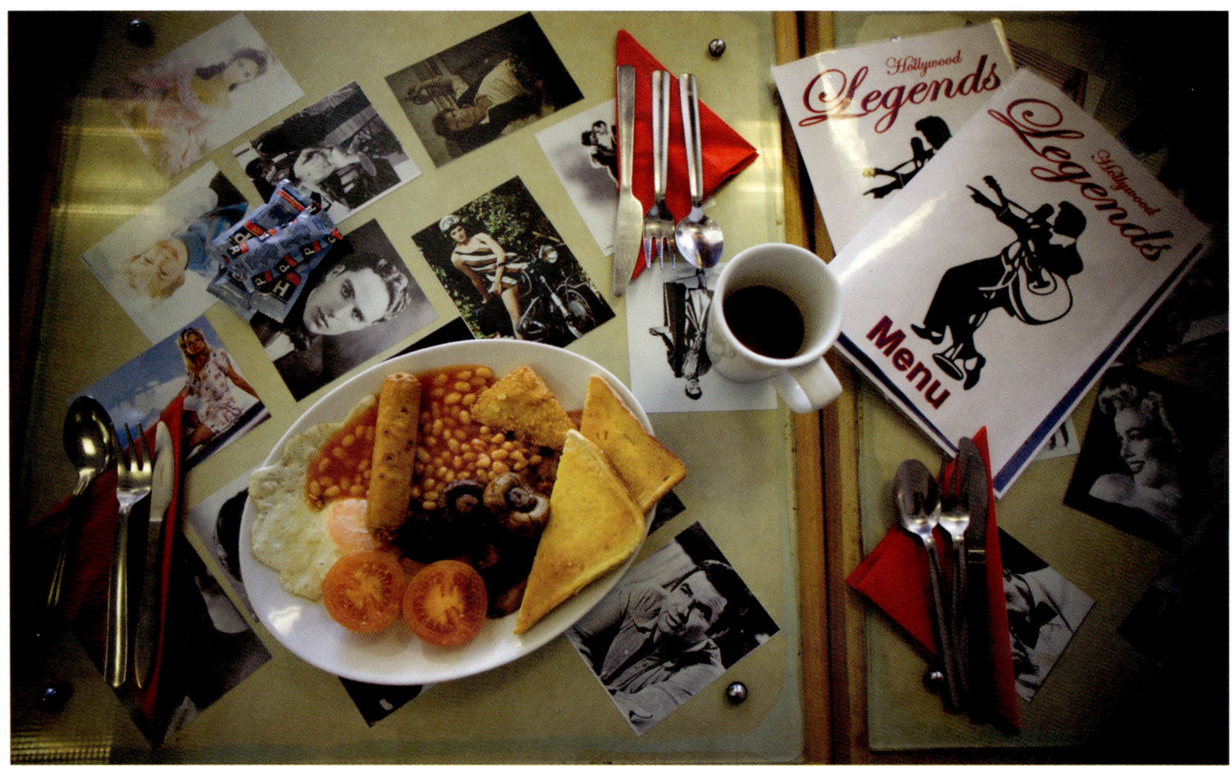

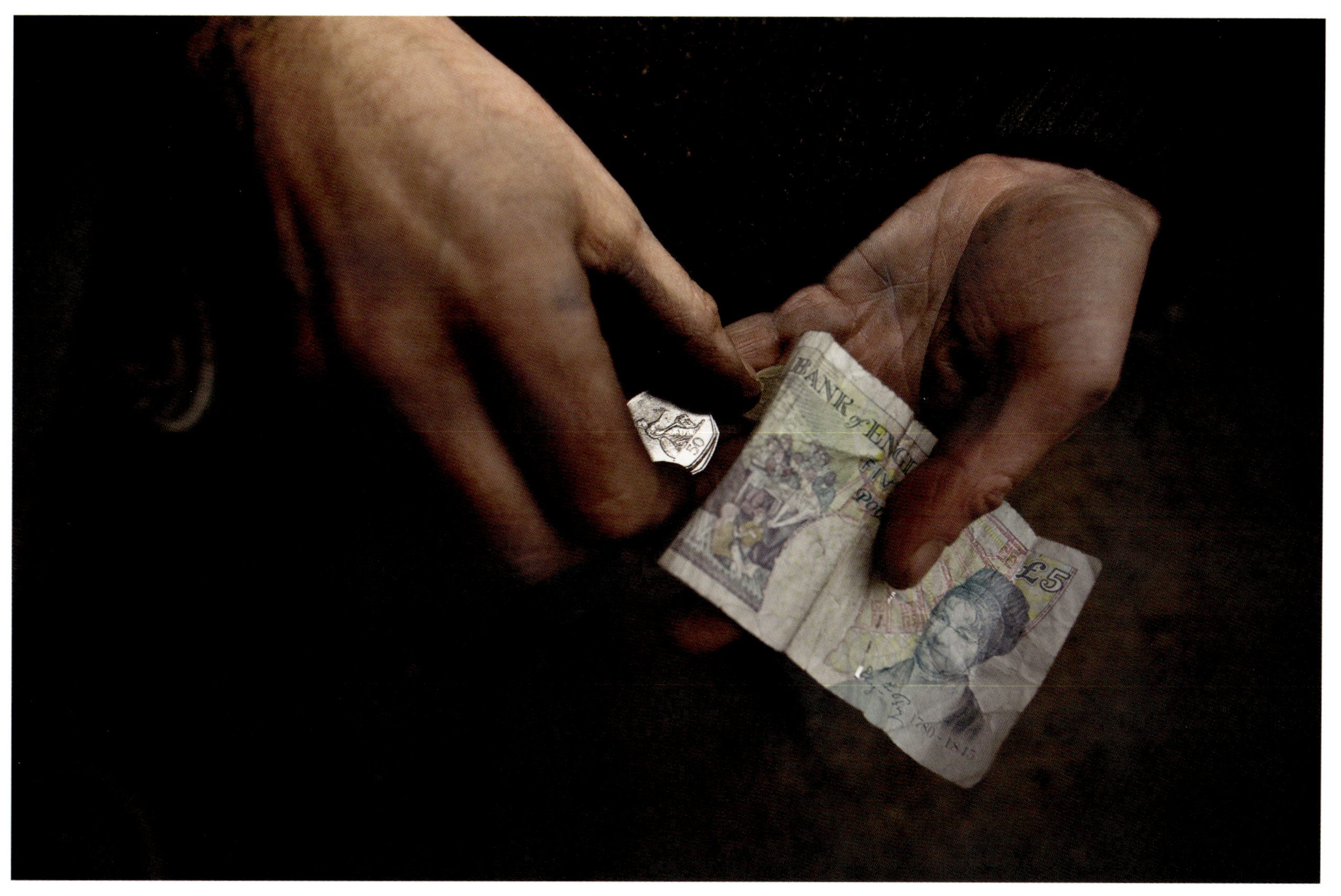

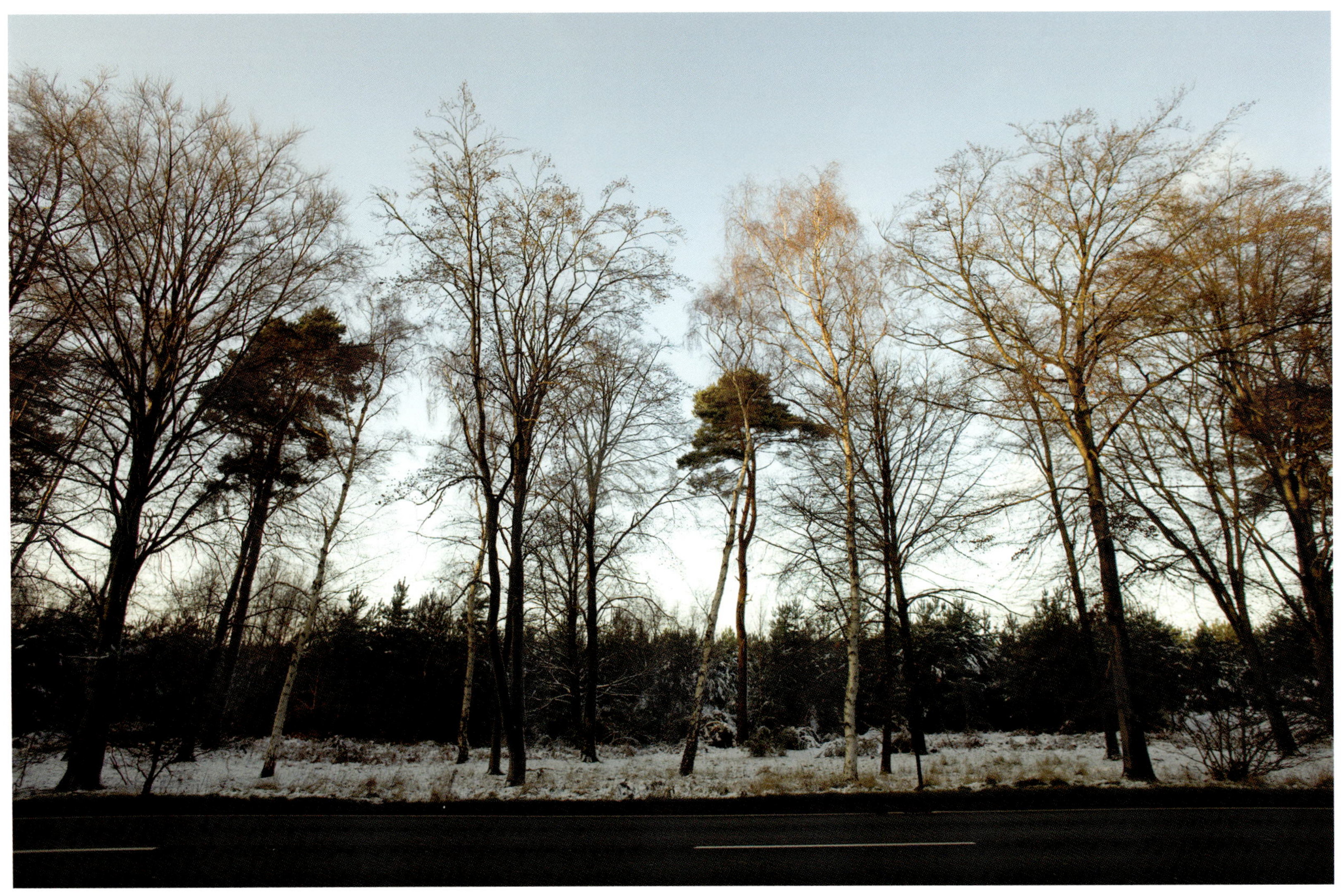

76   Norfolk-Suffolk Border – Thetford Forest – A11

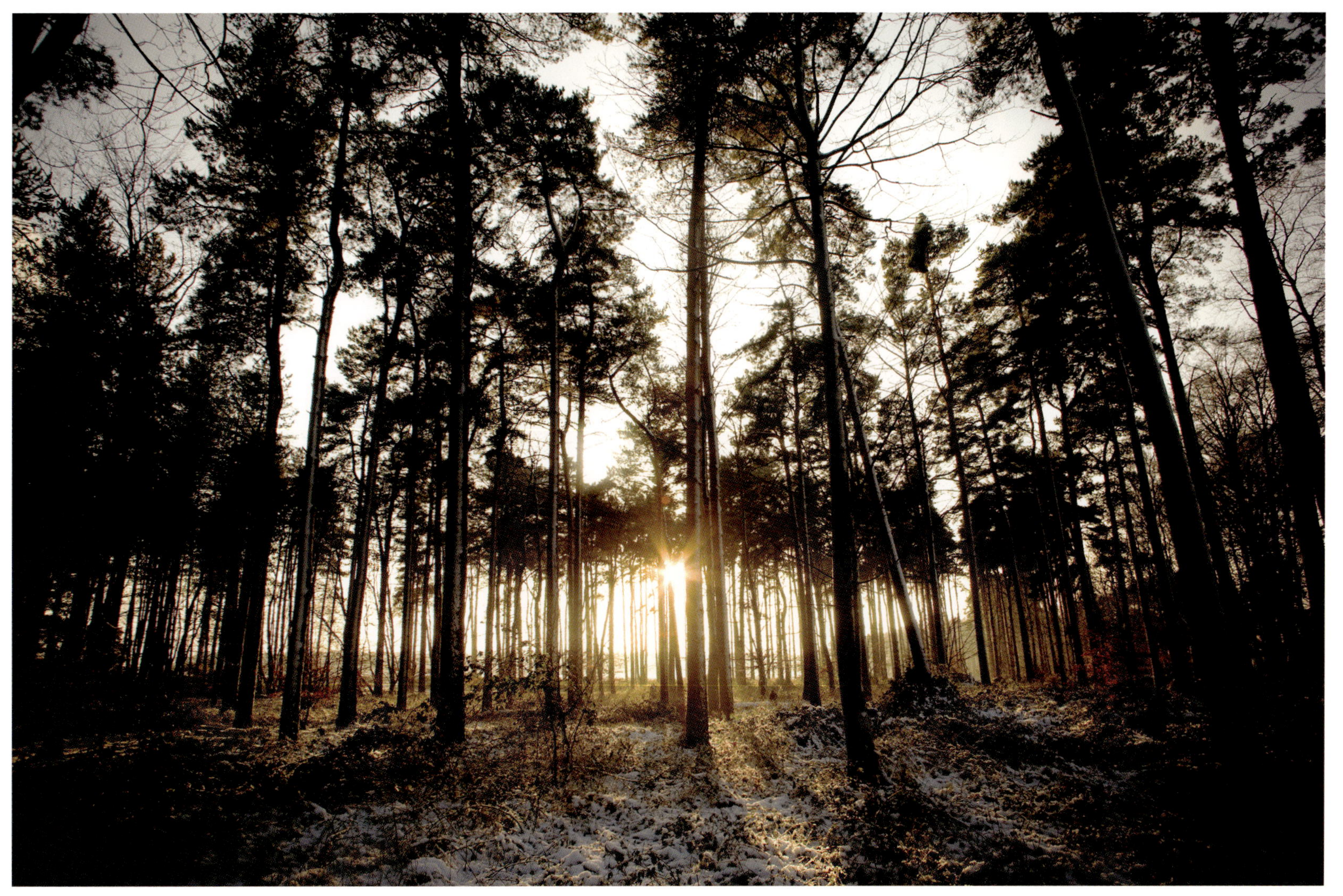

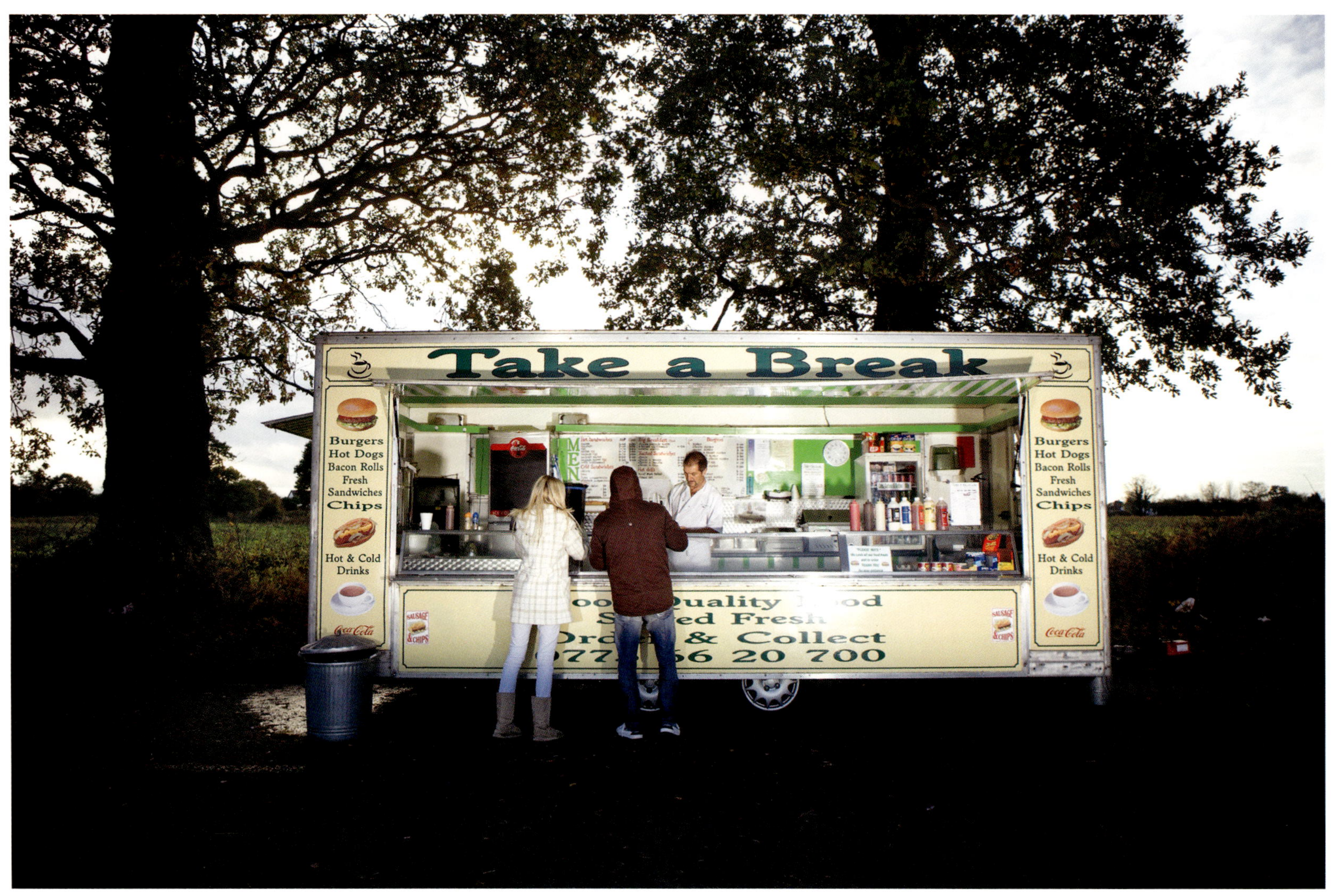


   Last Orders – Take a Break – Lowestoft – Suffolk – A12

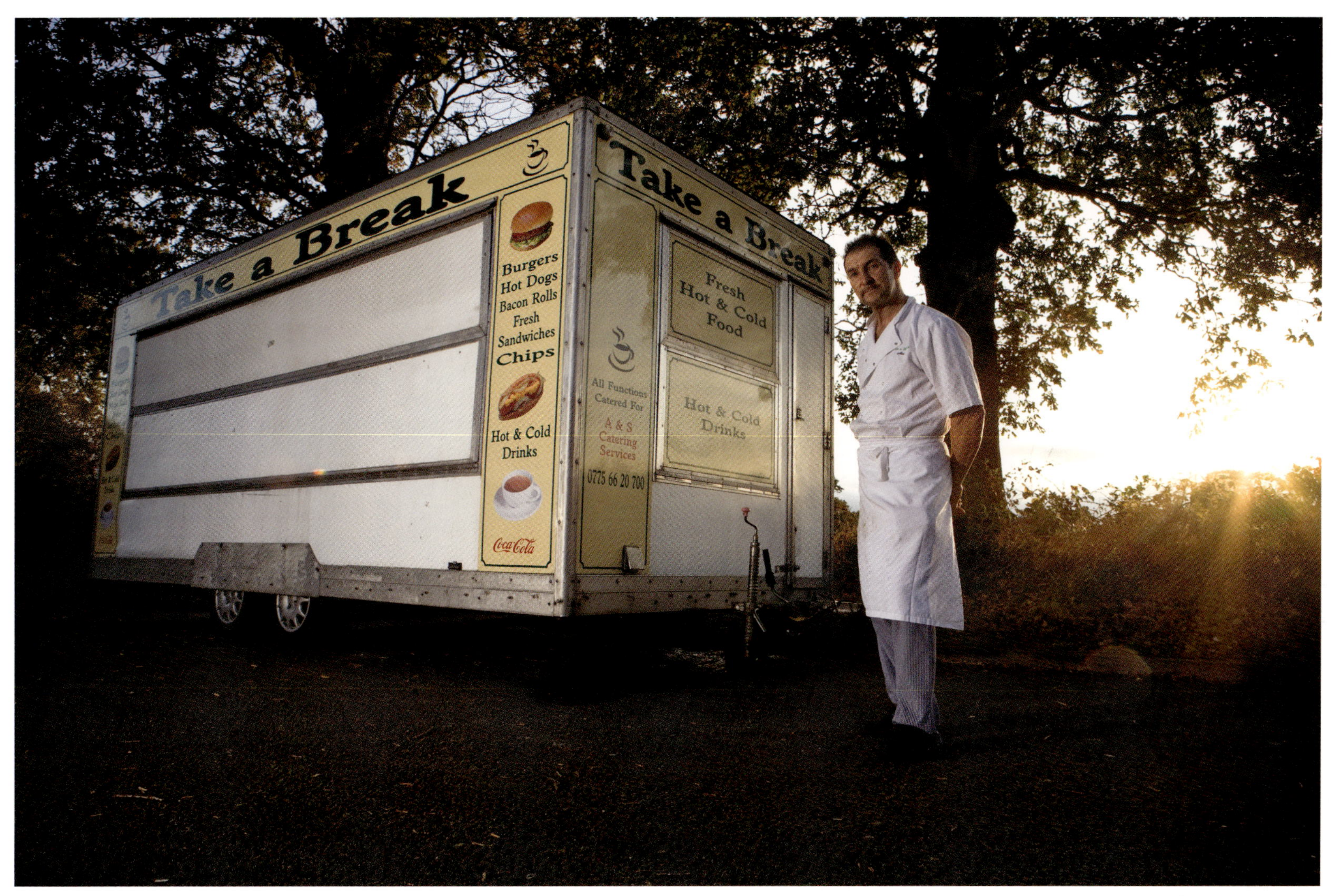


Alec – Take a Break – Lowestoft – Suffolk – A12      79

# Speedway Star

Winter of 2009/10 was unusually cold; blankets of snow covered the UK. Having spent many winters during my mid 20's living and working in the Alps, driving in the UK's snow was something I welcomed. When newsreaders warned commuters not to travel, I'd load my car and examine maps. Life on the road during these times seemed alien as only those that needed to be out and about were; farmers, the odd trucker and lone salesman were some of the folk I encountered.

In late October, before the snow laid its magnificent white mantle across the land, I ventured north along the A12, past Suffolk into Norfolk and met the A149. I'd stayed overnight somewhere and woke up to a damp, rather miserable day. The previous evening, as the sun began its descent, I'd met Alec (page 78 & 79) a retired falconer who had elected for a quieter life and opened 'Take a Break' near Lowestoft. It was here I captured some charming portraits as the sun waned its westerly course. Yet the beginnings of the next day proved different. As rain settled on the streets, I drove feeling distinctly unmotivated, yet reaching Potter Heigham, I saw the lights of a petrol station and, to my delight, parked up opposite was a bright yellow burger van with its Union Jack flowing in the wind.

Like Alec, those working or running the roadside burger vans or truck stops were full of interesting stories, often coming from intriguing backgrounds, worlds away from the rather isolated career they'd now entered. Very few were unfriendly. More often than not my chat was welcomed as the time lapse between customers could vary, especially during the harsh winters.

Robin, the owner of the van opposite, was also testament to this. I ordered a cup of tea and began chatting with him. Robin's father had been assigned to the 'D'Arcy Exploration' searching for oil throughout Persia (present day Iran), and Robin had been brought up in Australia and read clinical psychology at University in Brisbane. He owed the name of his weather-beaten burger van, 'Speedway Star', to his boat, which he was currently restoring. As he talked, notions of adventure and excitement formulated in my mind at the thought of traveling with the oil explorers. I'd also visited Brisbane in my late teens and recalled the joy I'd experienced wandering in the city. I felt admiration tinged with sadness, that on this miserable morning, an exotic character like Robin was confined to his Speedway Van in a layby on the A149.

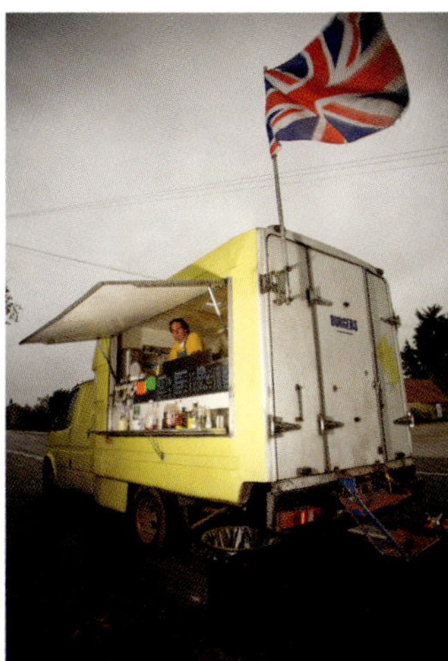
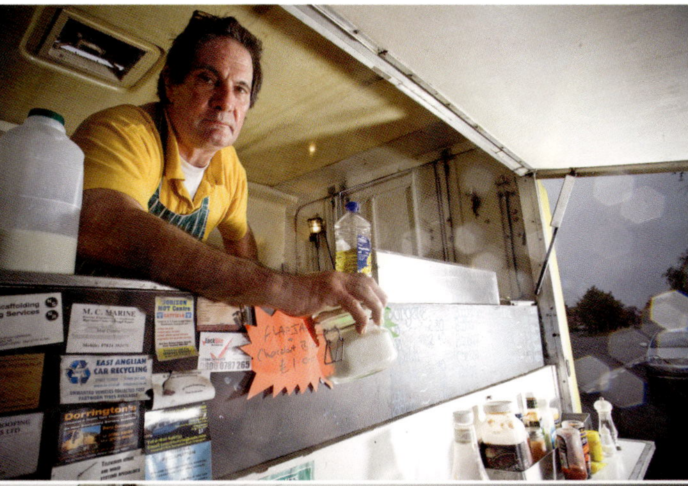
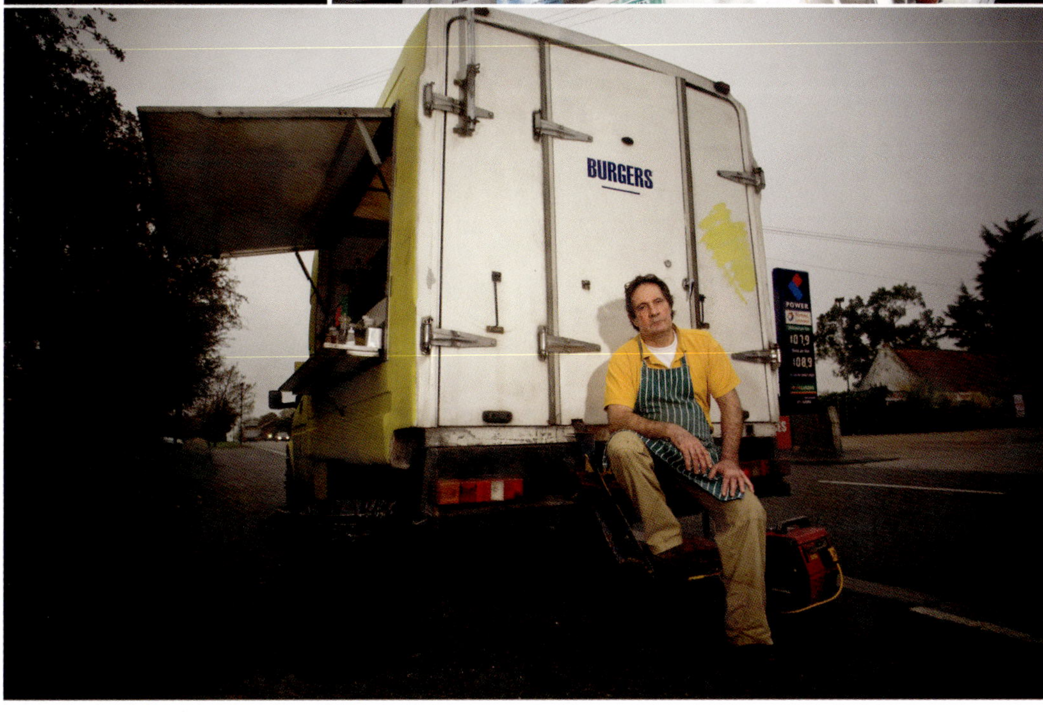

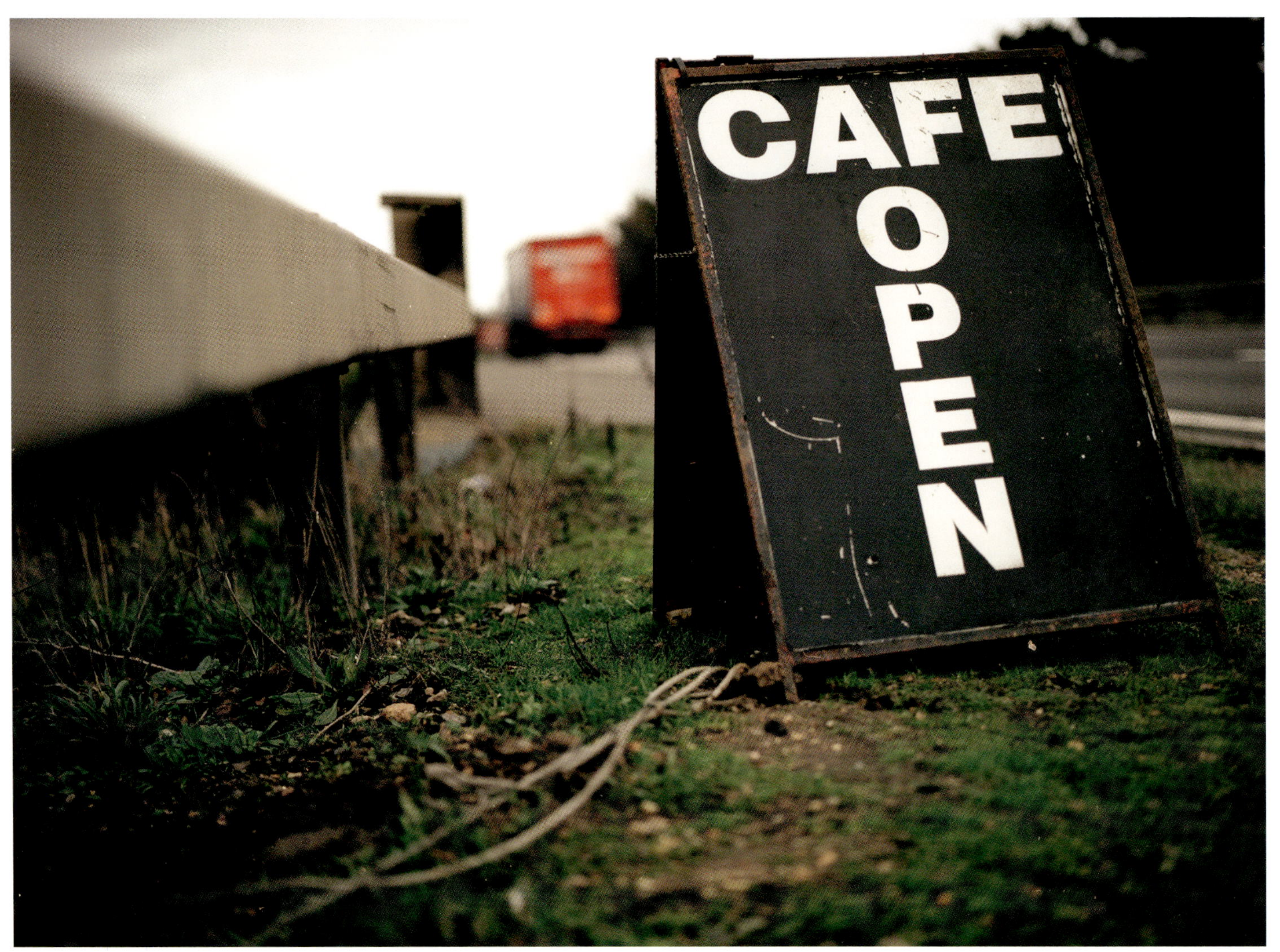


 Roadside Signs – Stratford St Mary – Suffolk – A12

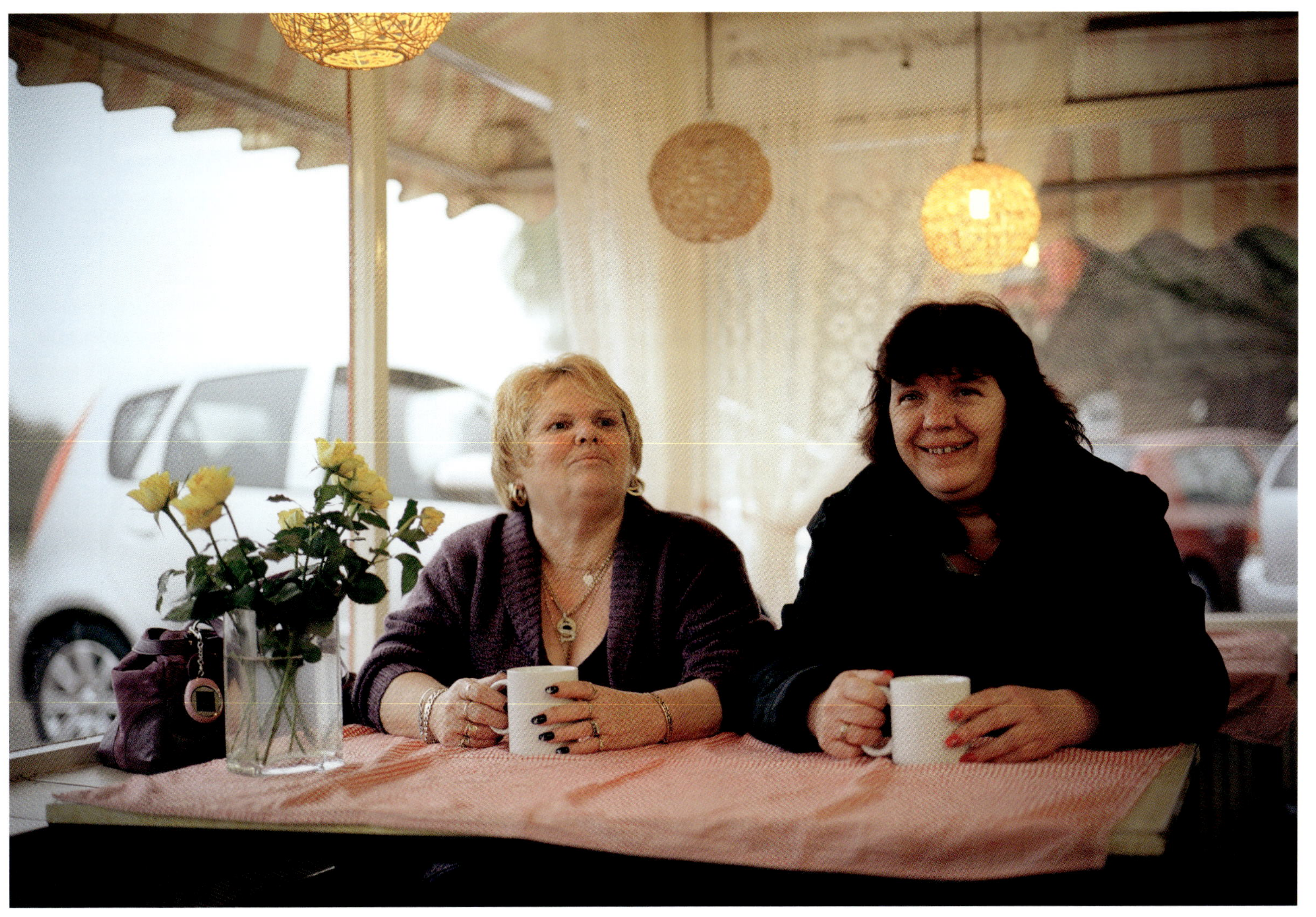

Sandra & Lorraine – Red Lodge 24hr Cafe – Red Lodge – Suffolk – B1085

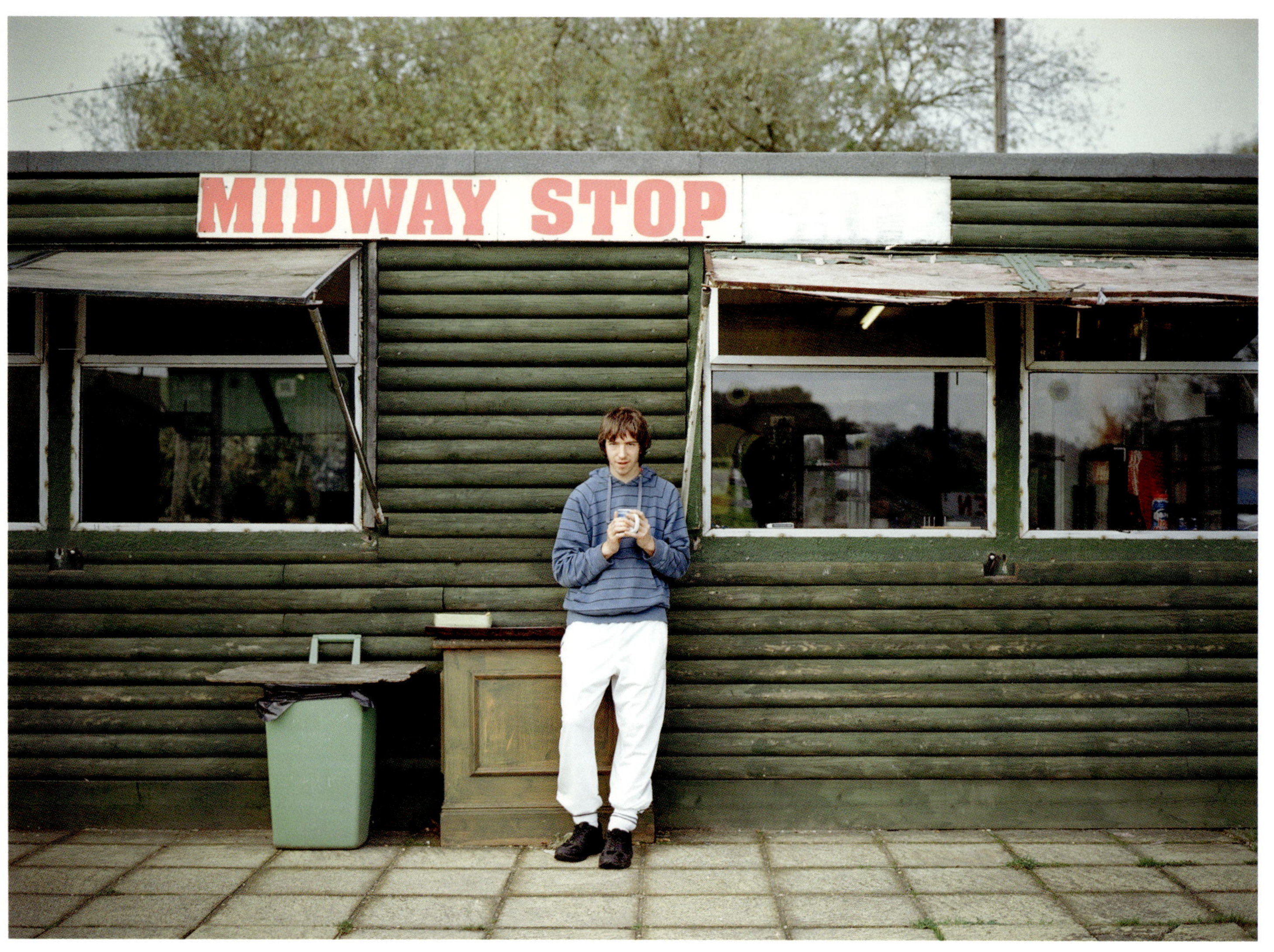



84      Shane Anderson – Midway Stop Cafe – Haughly New Road – Suffolk – A14

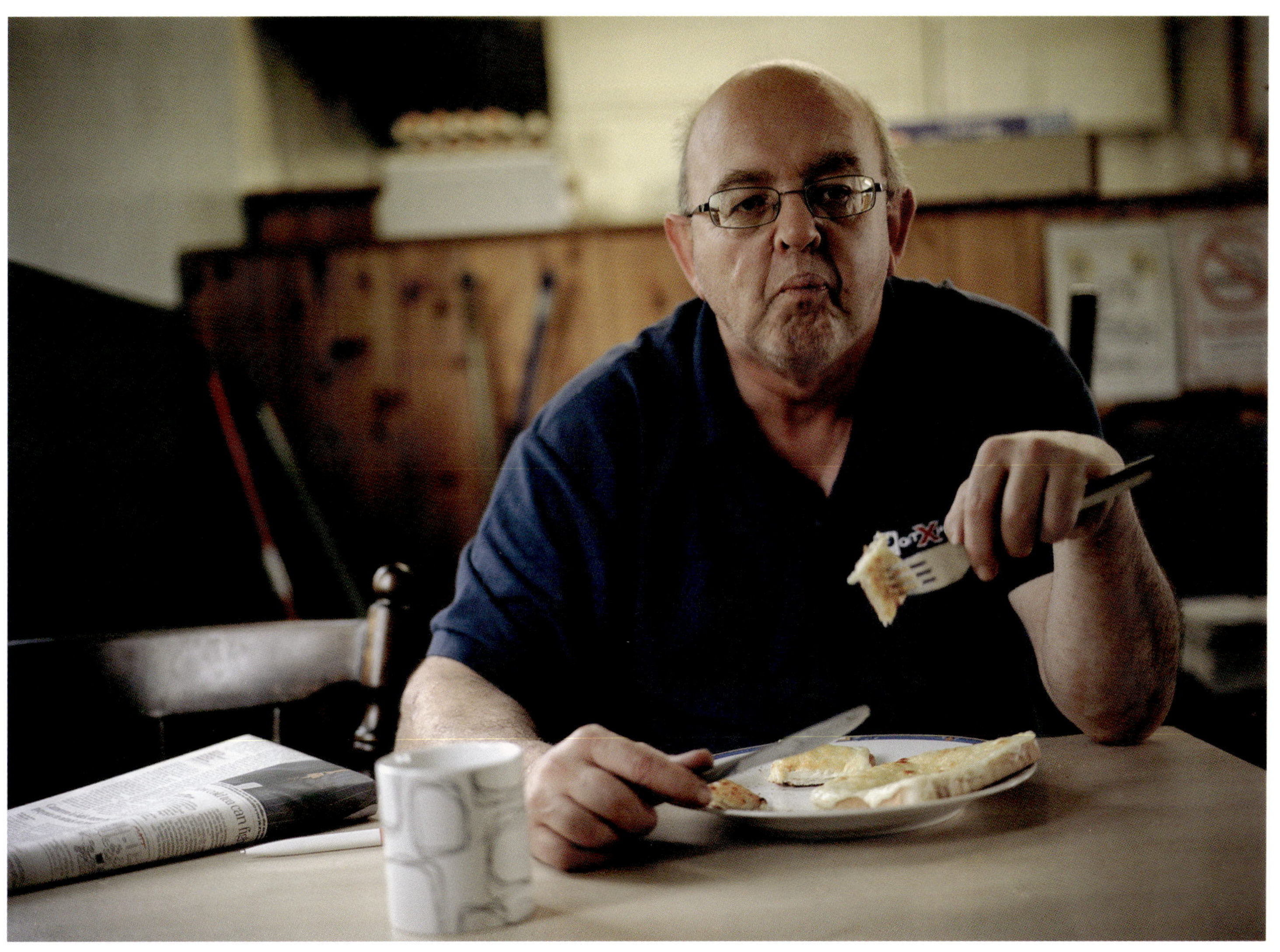

Steve 'Jess the Trucker' James – Midway Stop Cafe – Haughly New Road – Suffolk – A14     

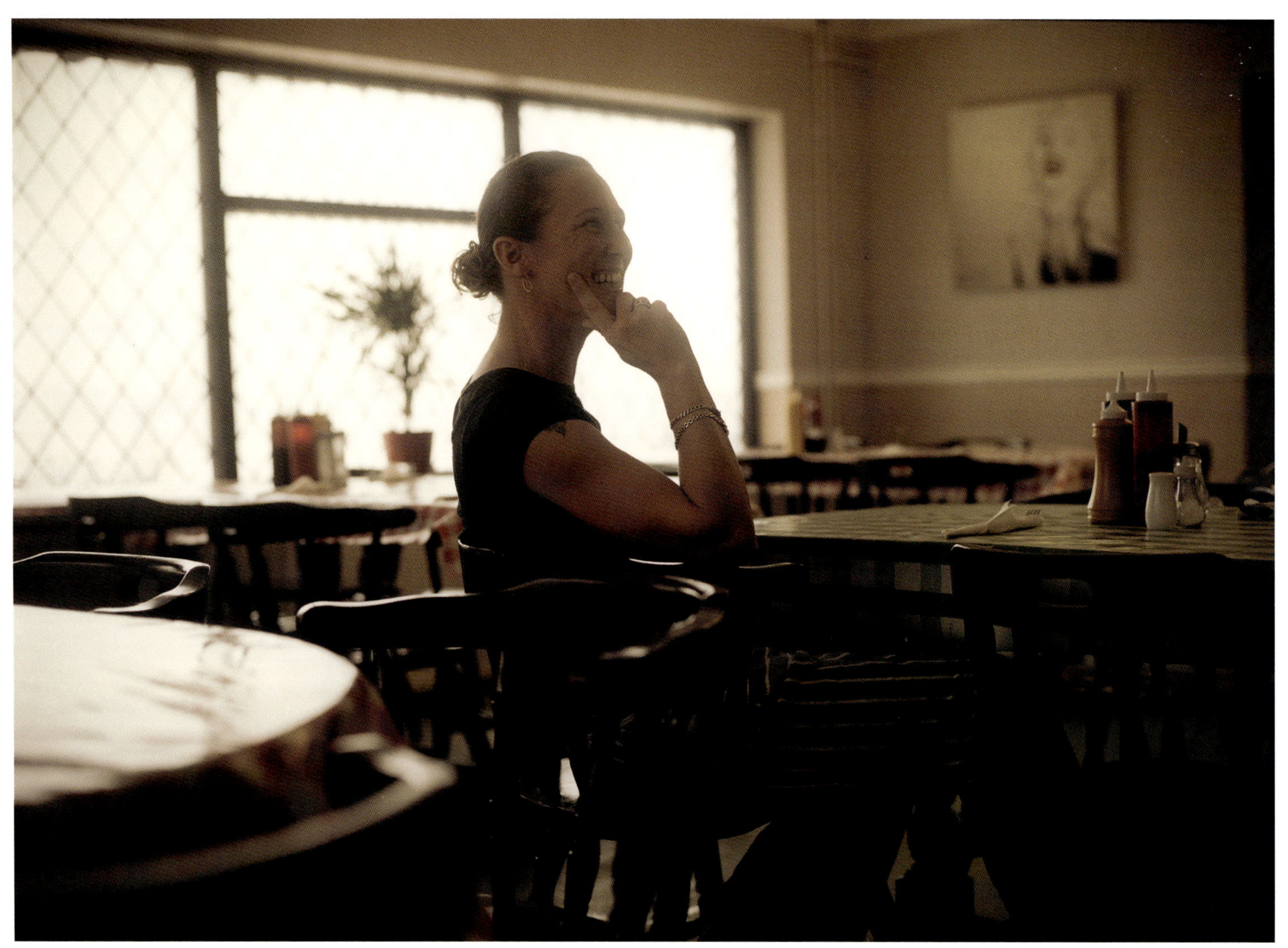

  Emma Stevens – D's Cafe – Hatfield Peverel – Essex – A12

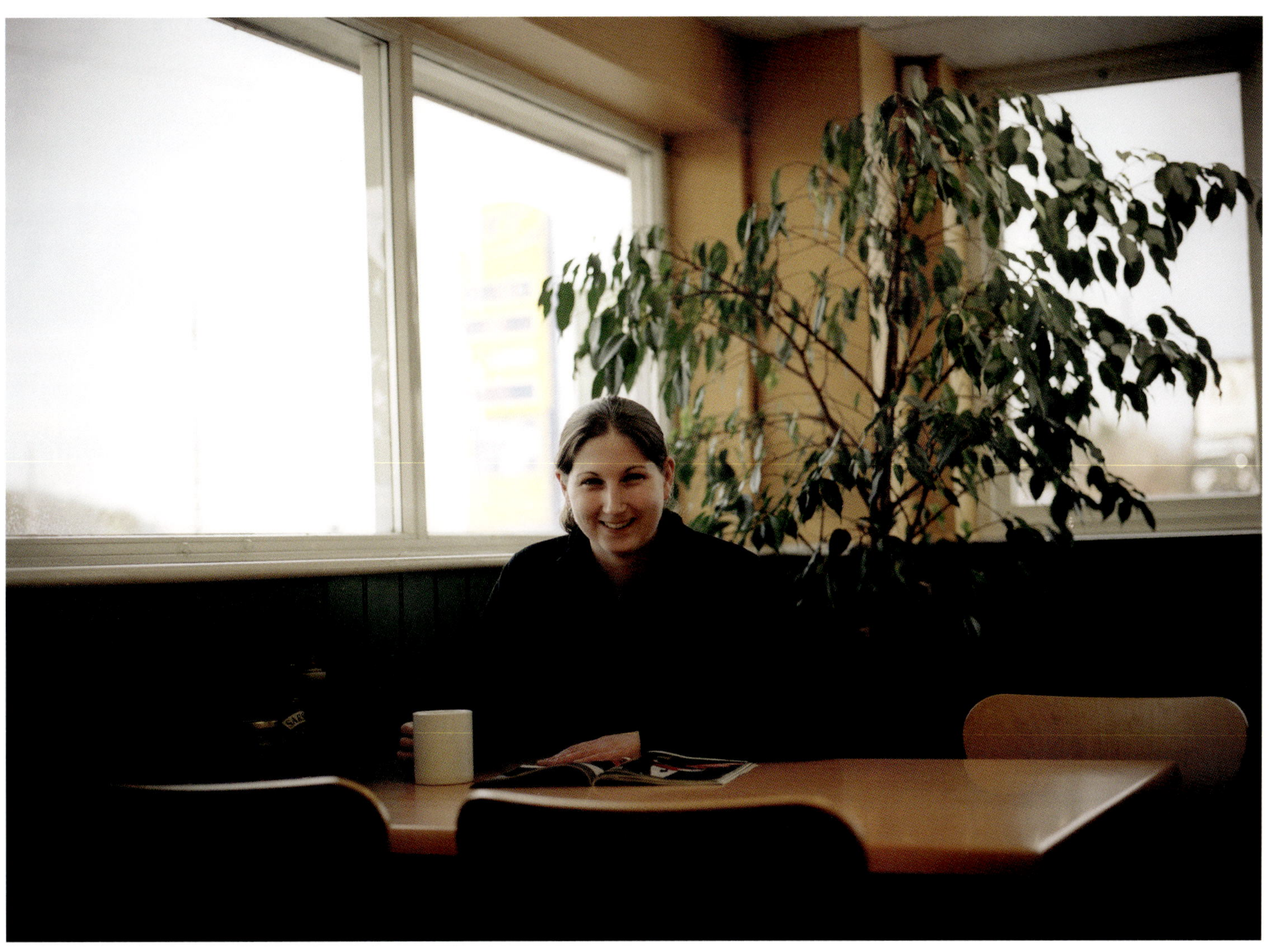

Claire Foreman taking a break at Lilly's Pantry – Darsham – Suffolk – A12

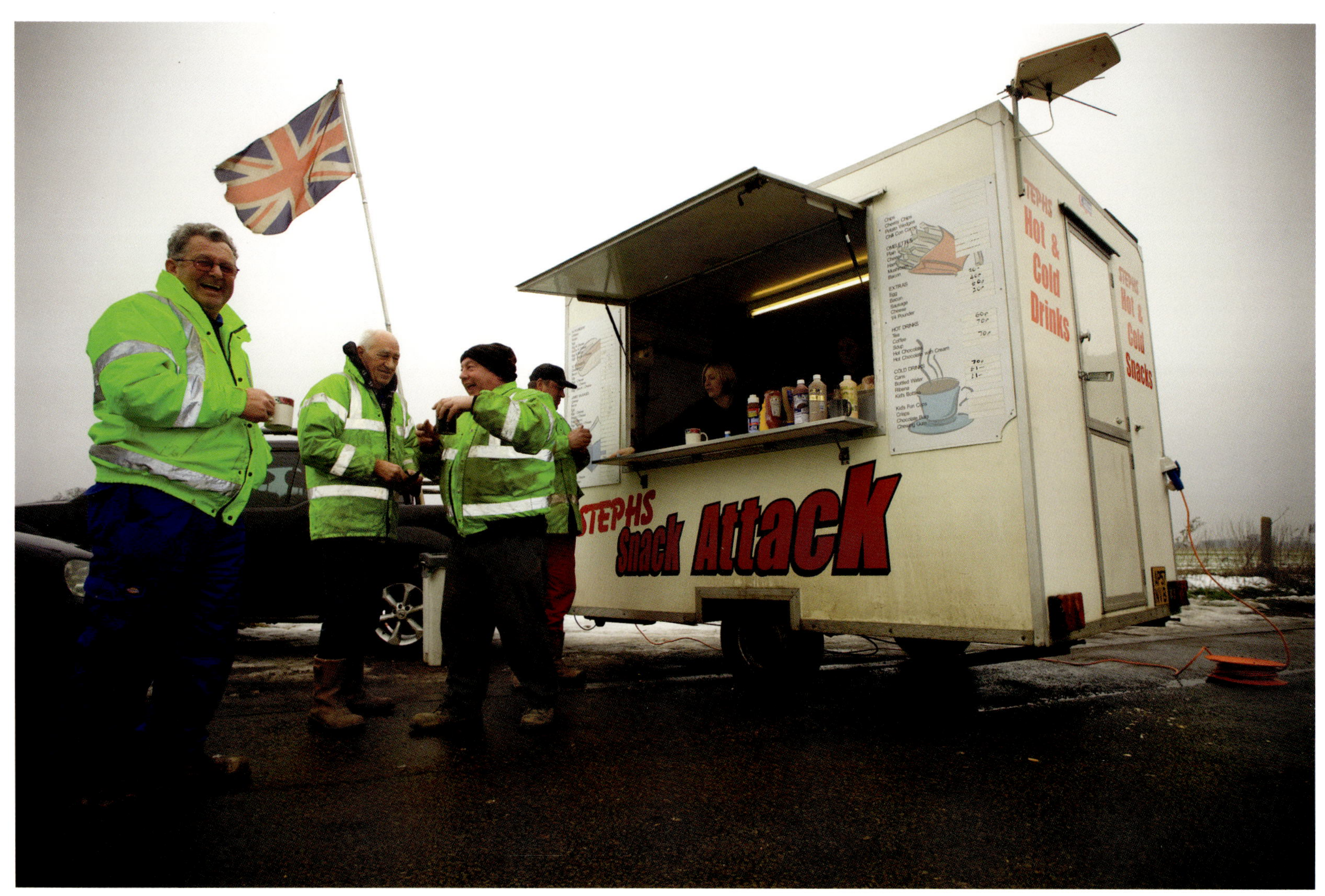




Sugar Beet Drivers – Steph's Snack Attack – Acle – Norfolk – A17

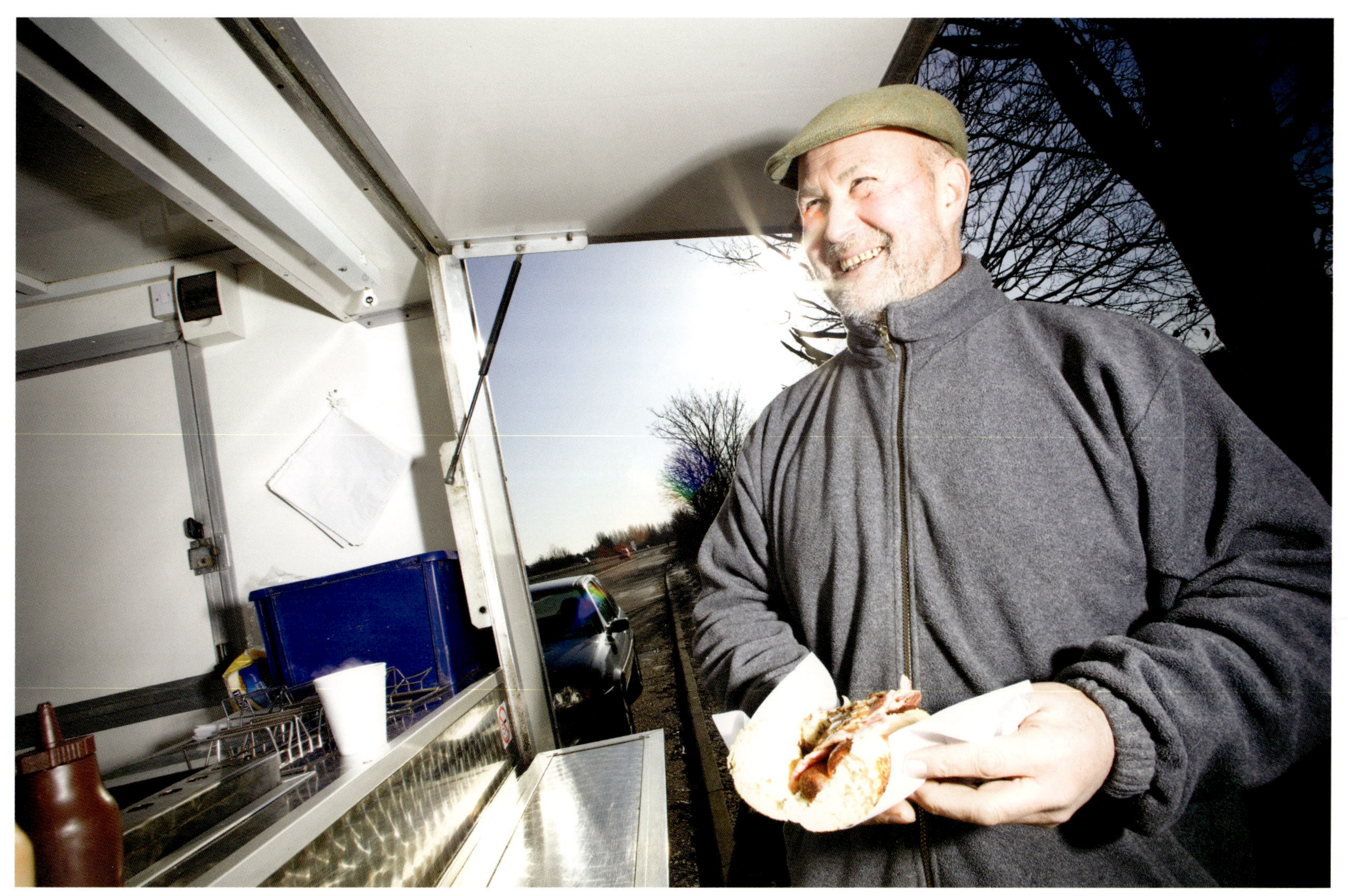

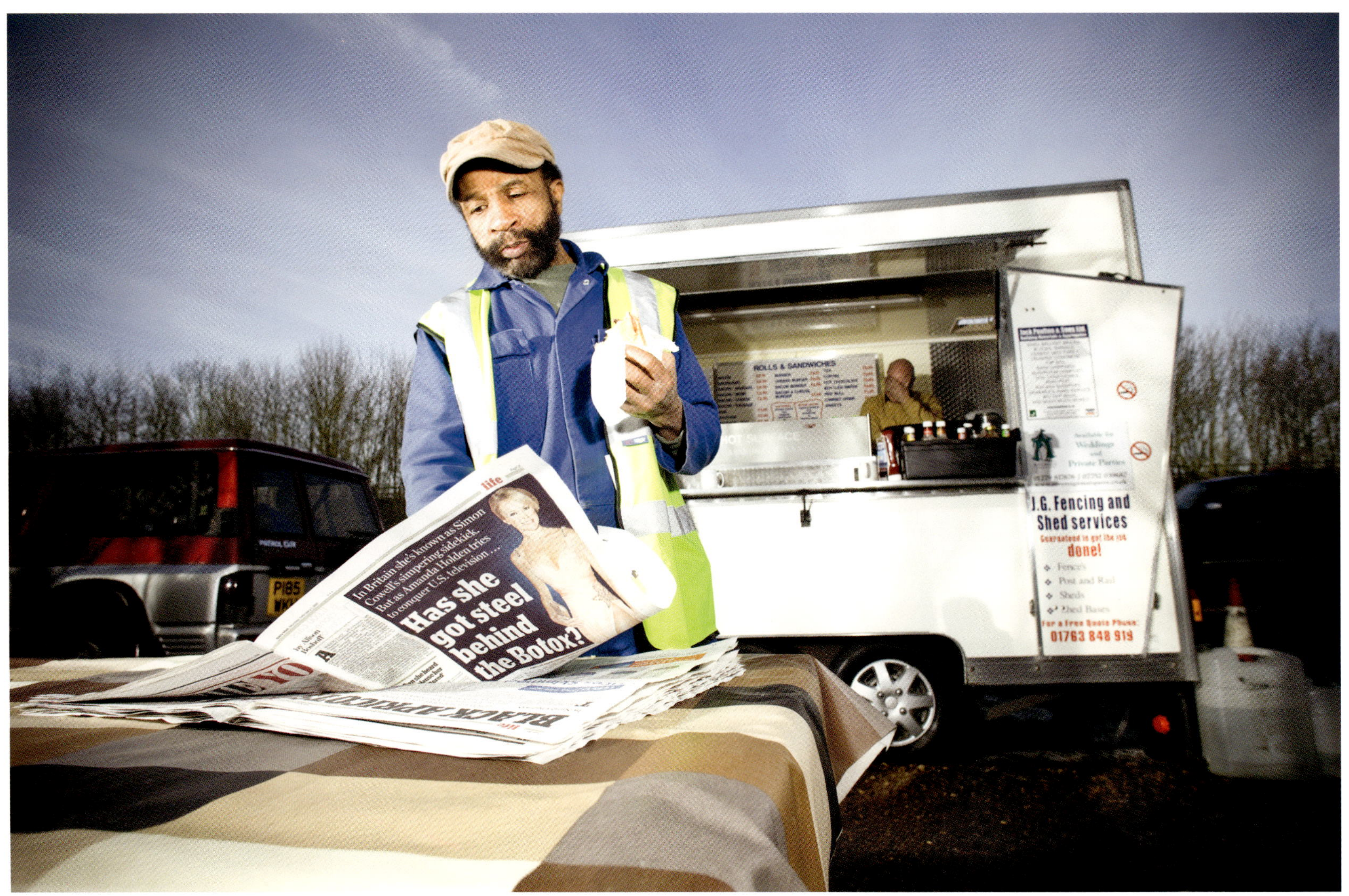



90  Lee Swanson's Snack Bar – Bishop Stortford – Hertfordshire – A120

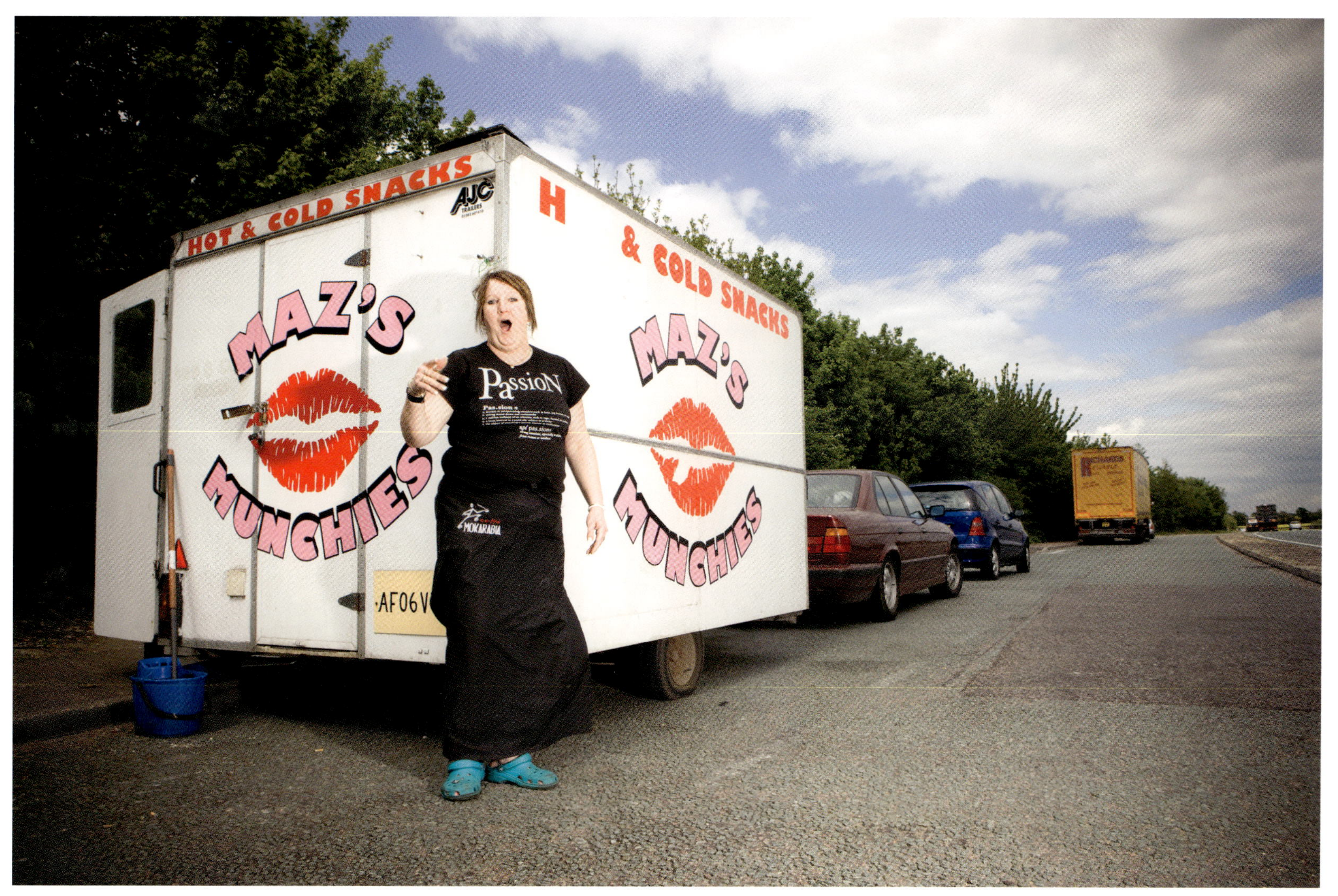


Maz's Munchies – Cambridgeshire – A11          91

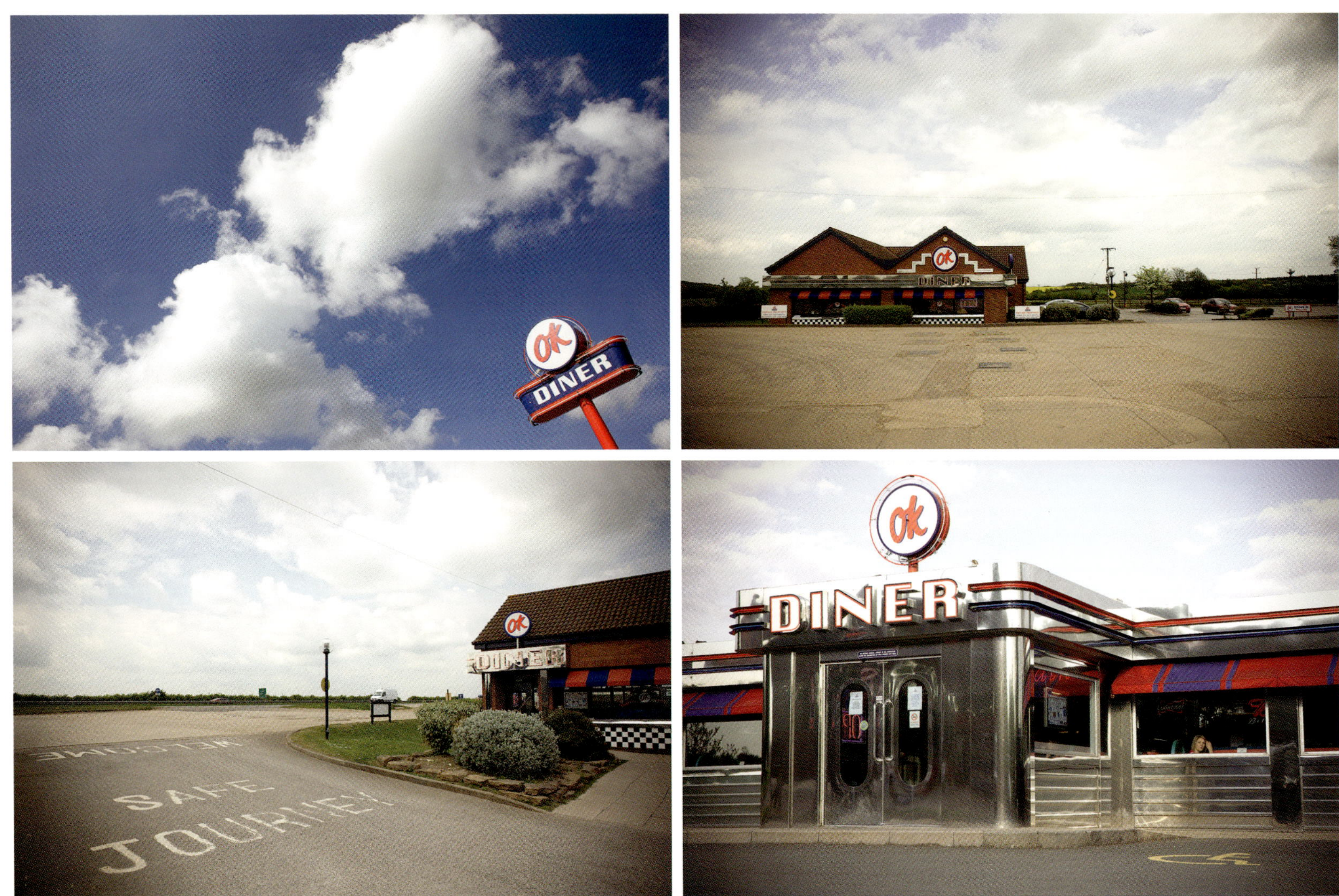


  OK Diners on the A1 – East Anglia

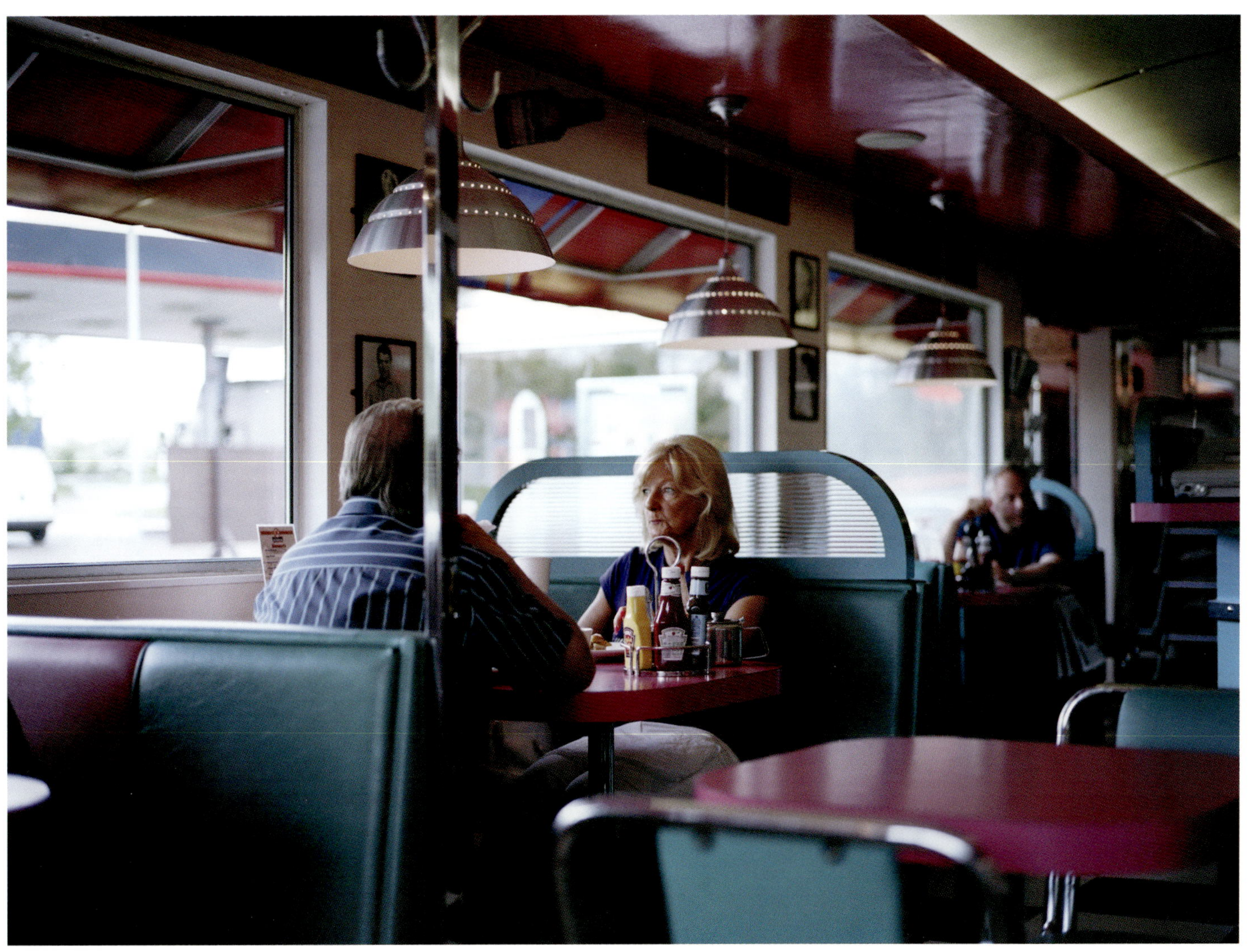

Out for Lunch at OK Diner – Tickencote – Rutland – A1　　93

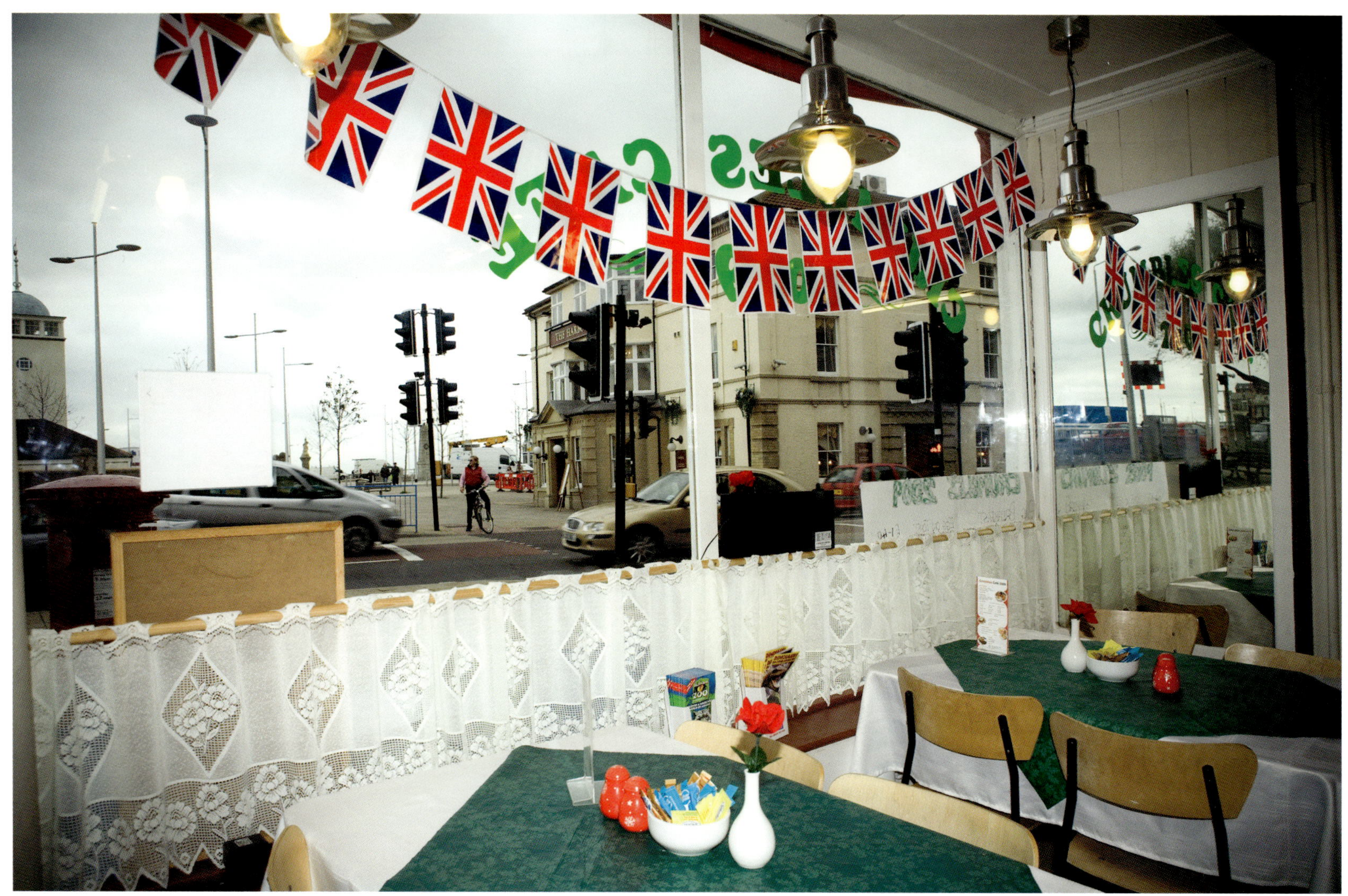

94  Crumbles Cafe – Lowestoft – Suffolk – A12

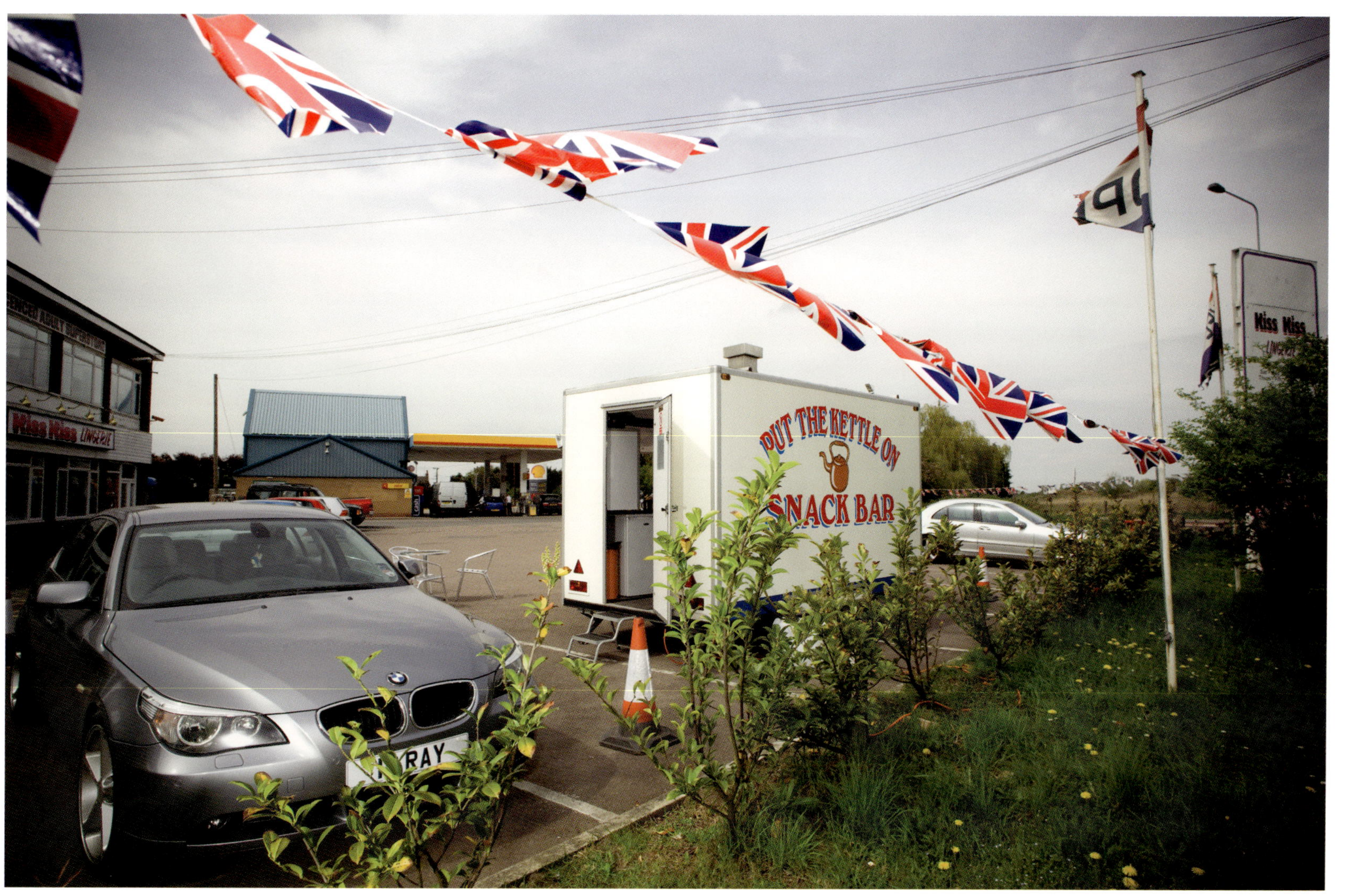



Put the Kettle On – Guyhirn – Cambridgeshire – A47

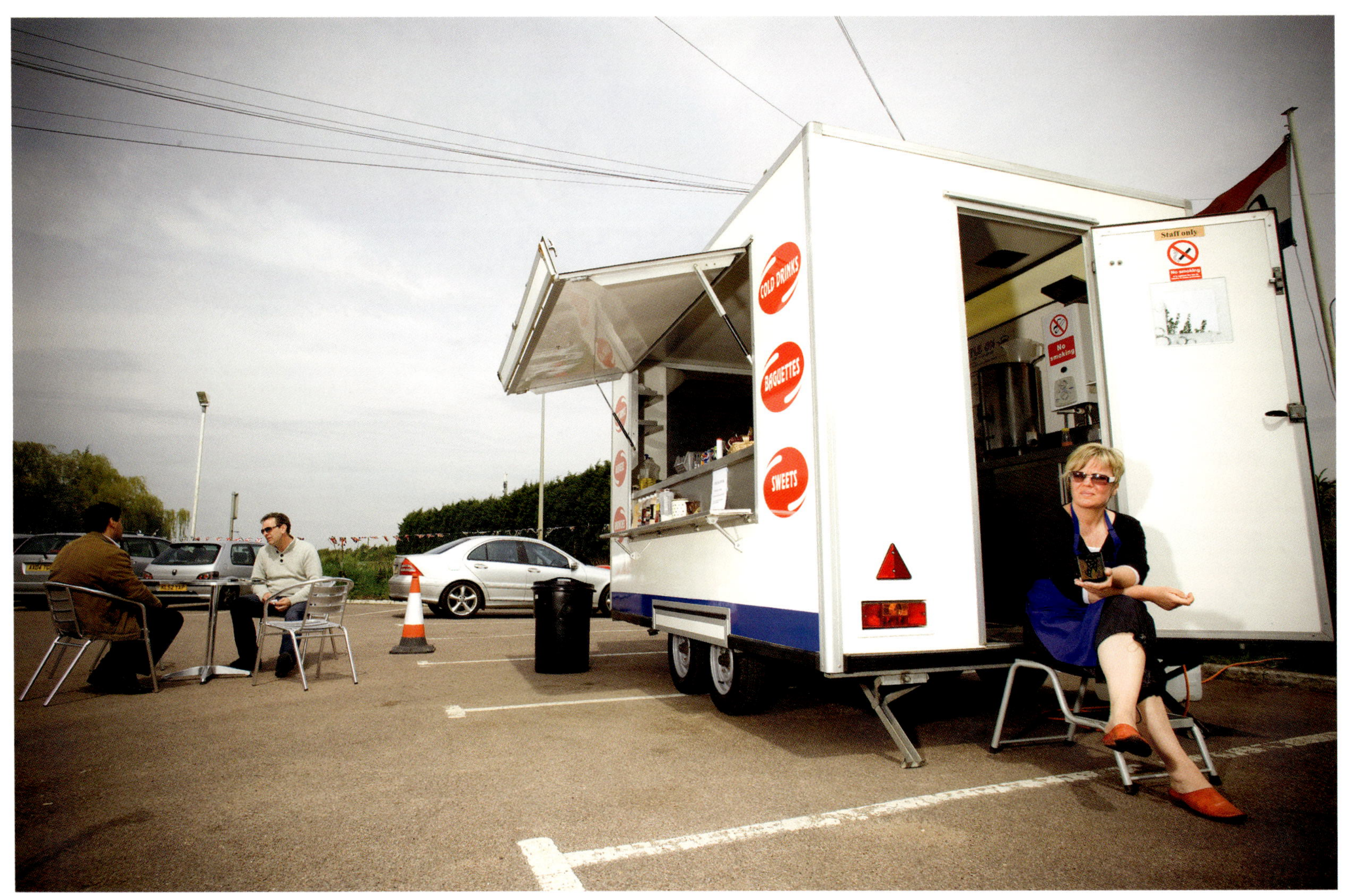


COLD DRINKS
BAGUETTES
SWEETS
Staff only
No smoking

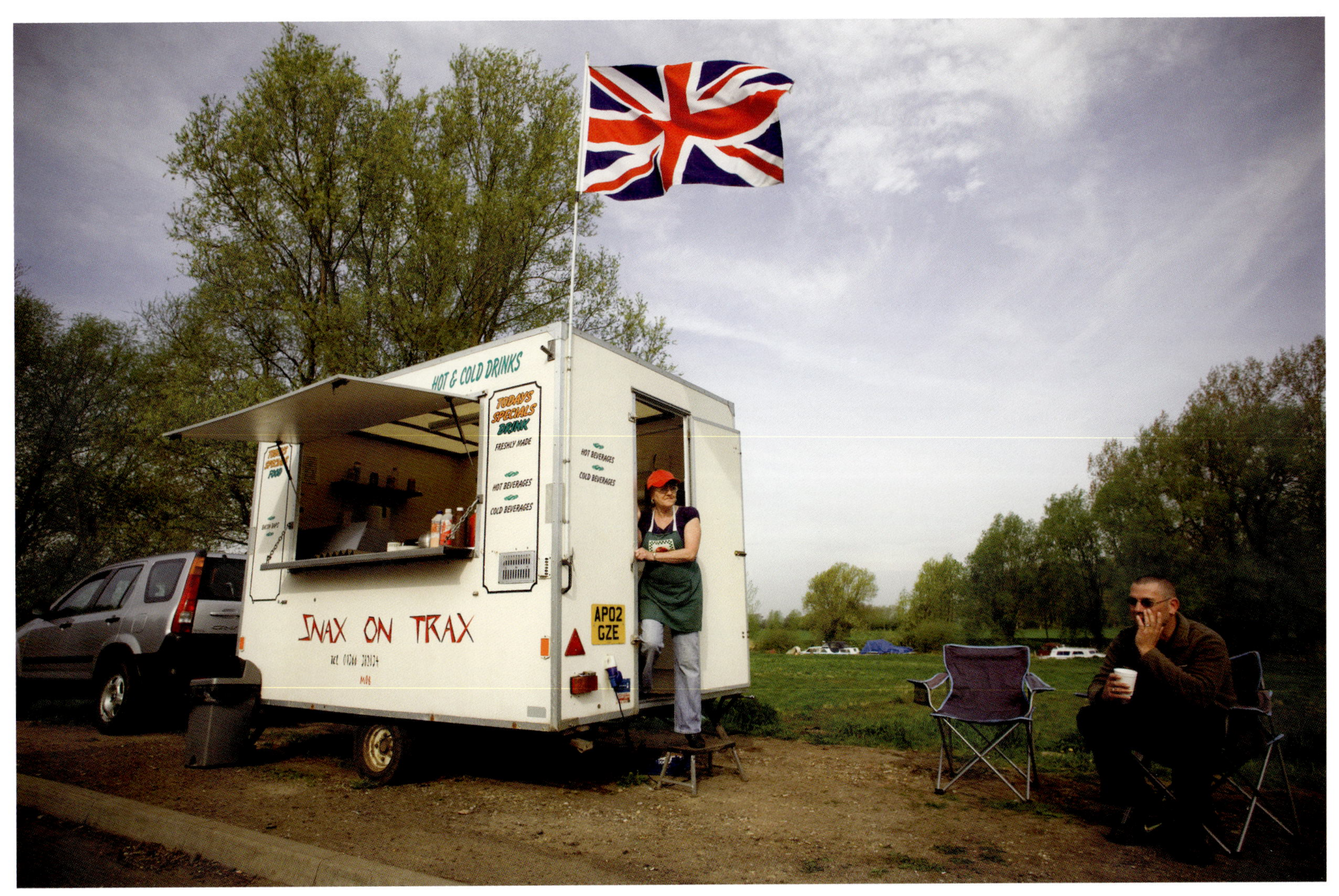


Lunch by the River Wissey – Hilgay – Norfolk – A10

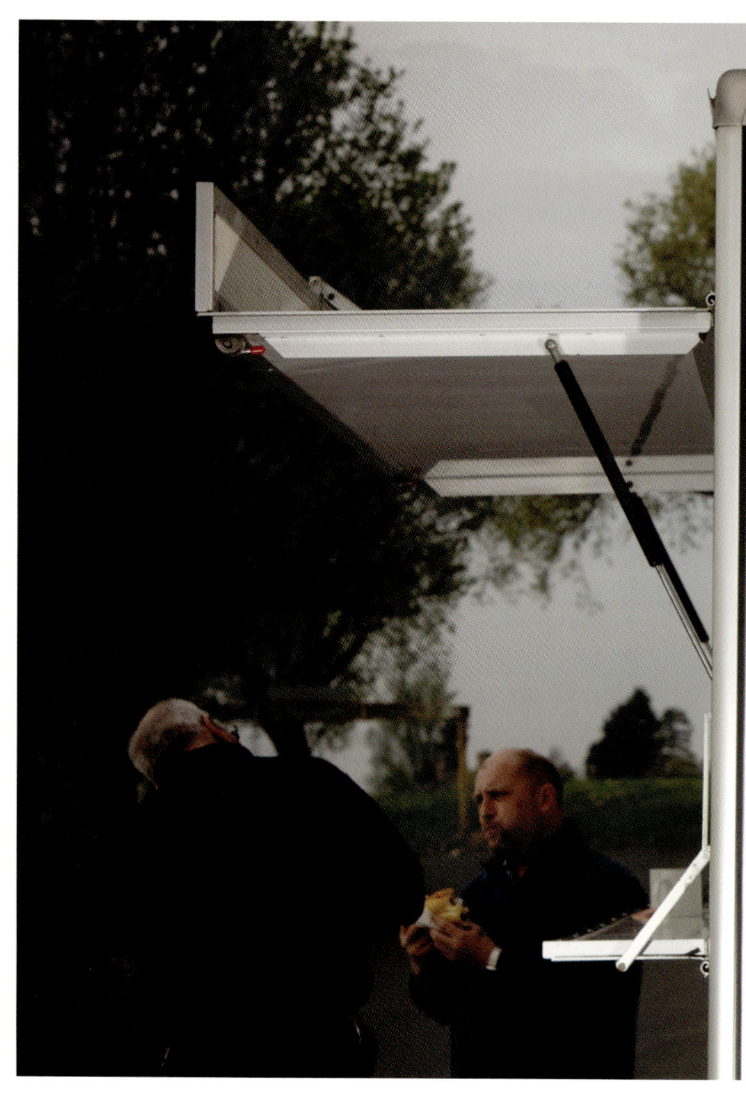
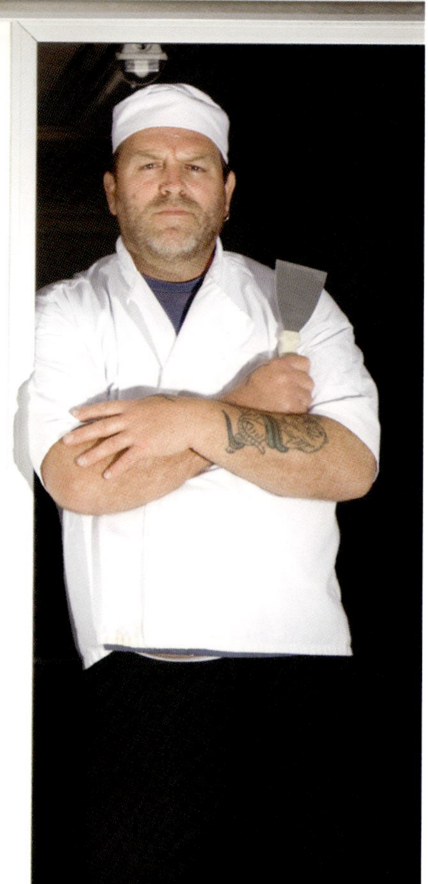




Steve – Steve's Burger Van – Littleport – Cambridgeshire – A10

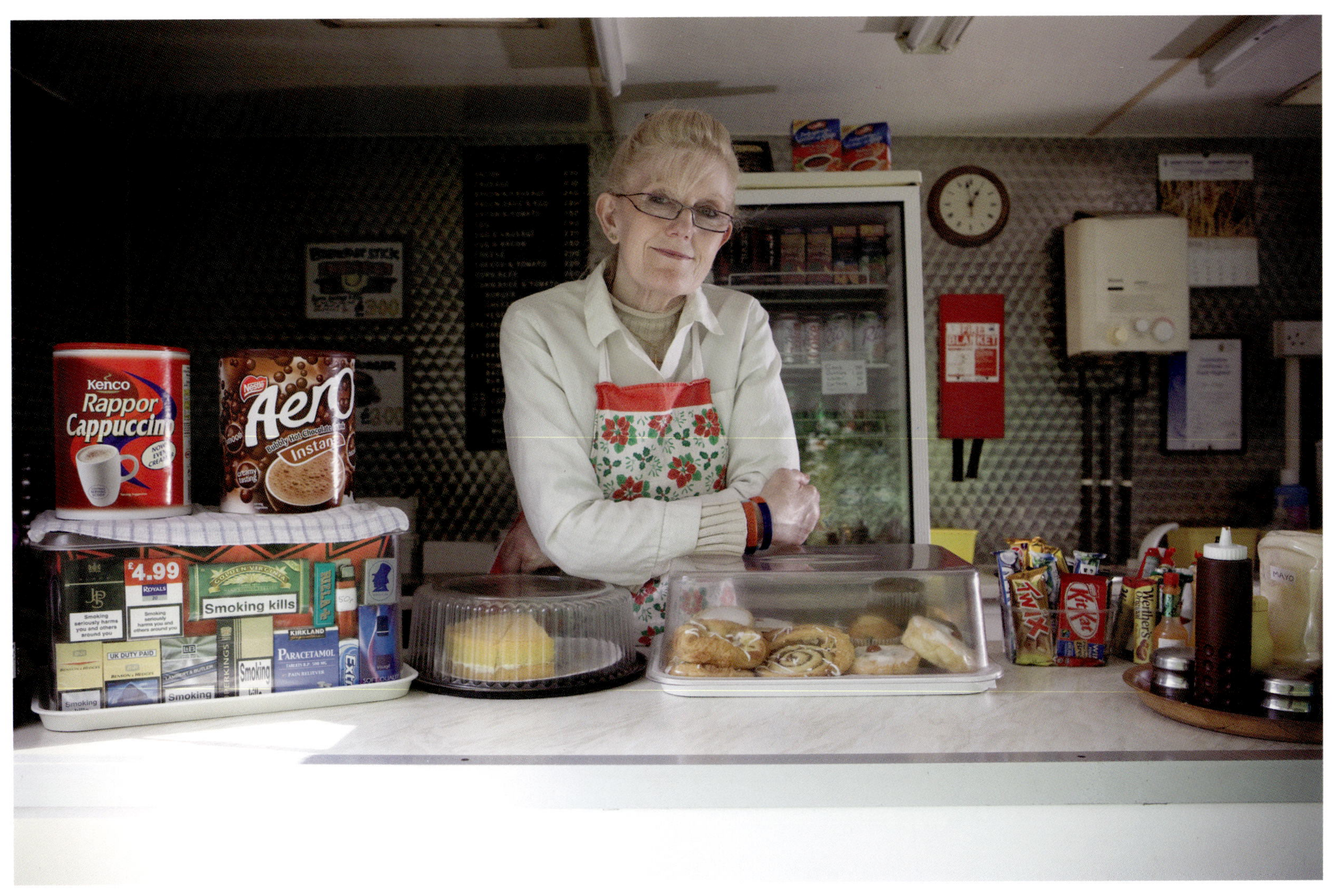



Daisy – Daisy's Catering – Fourwentways – Cambridgeshire – A11

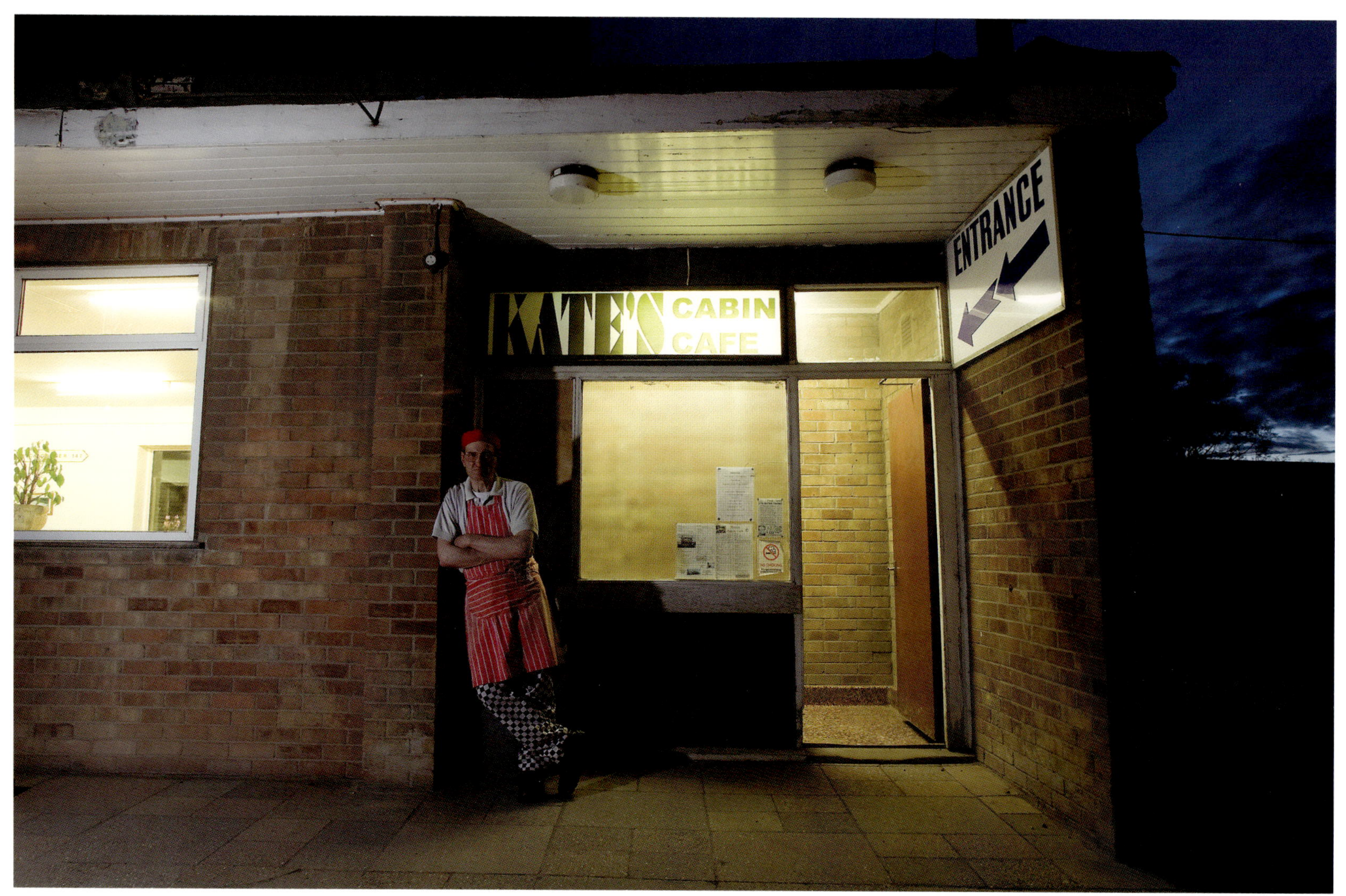



100    Dave Williams – Kate's Cabin – Stilton – Cambridgeshire – A1

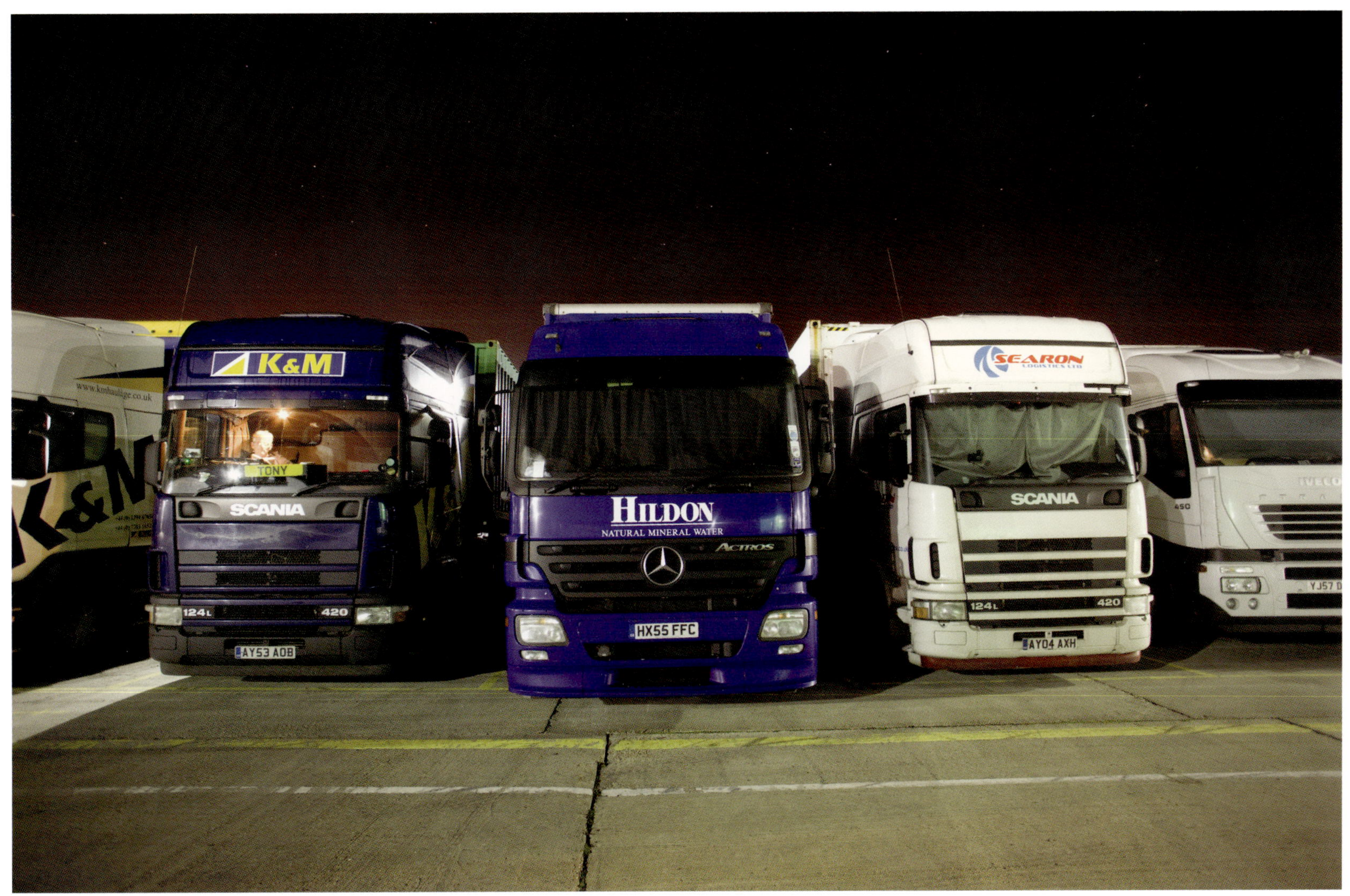

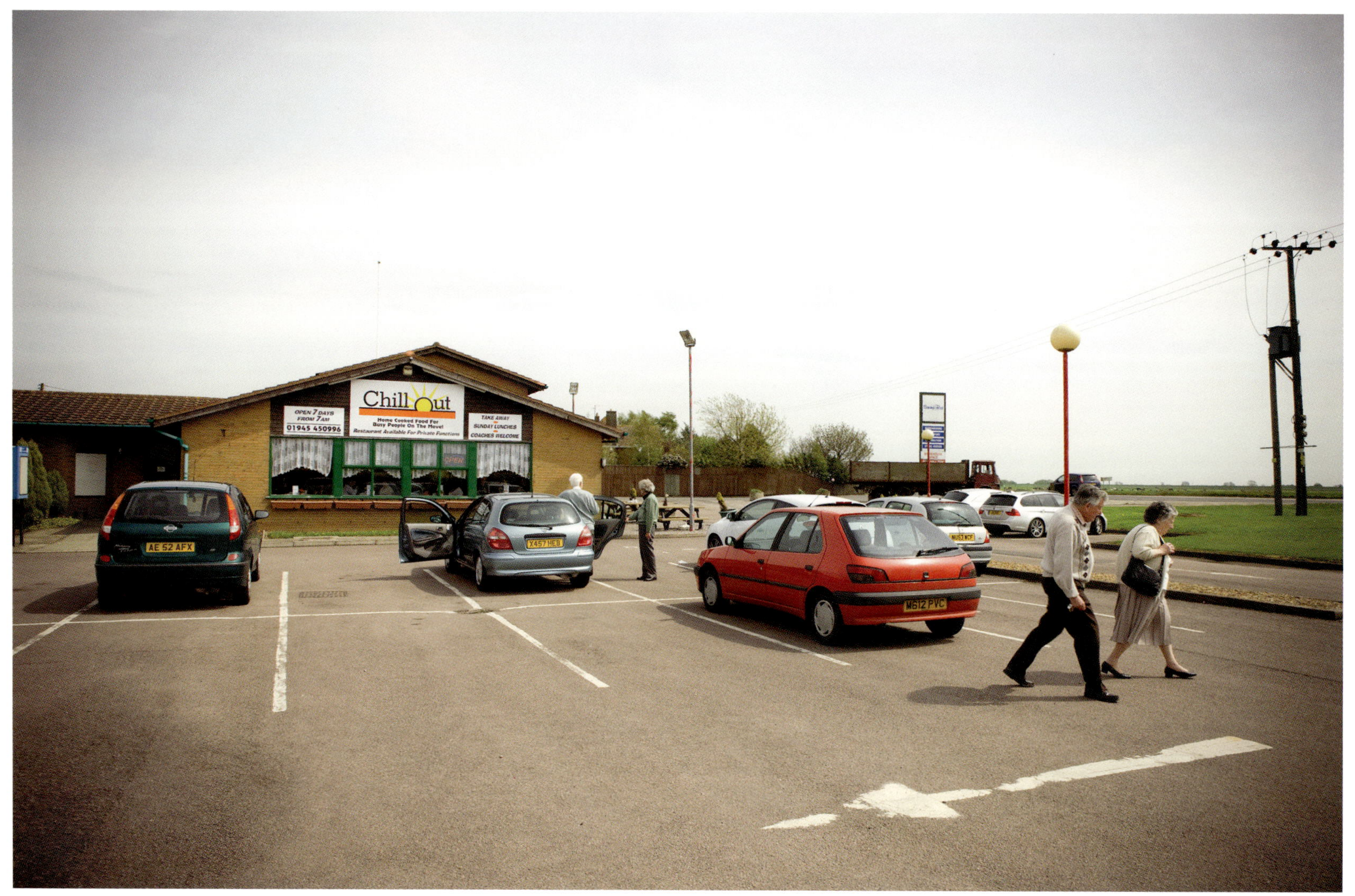

Chill Out
OPEN 7 DAYS
FROM 7AM
01945 450996
Home Cooked Food For
Busy People On The Move!
Restaurant Available For Private Functions
TAKE AWAY
SUNDAY LUNCHES
COACHES WELCOME
AE 52 AFX
M612 PVC

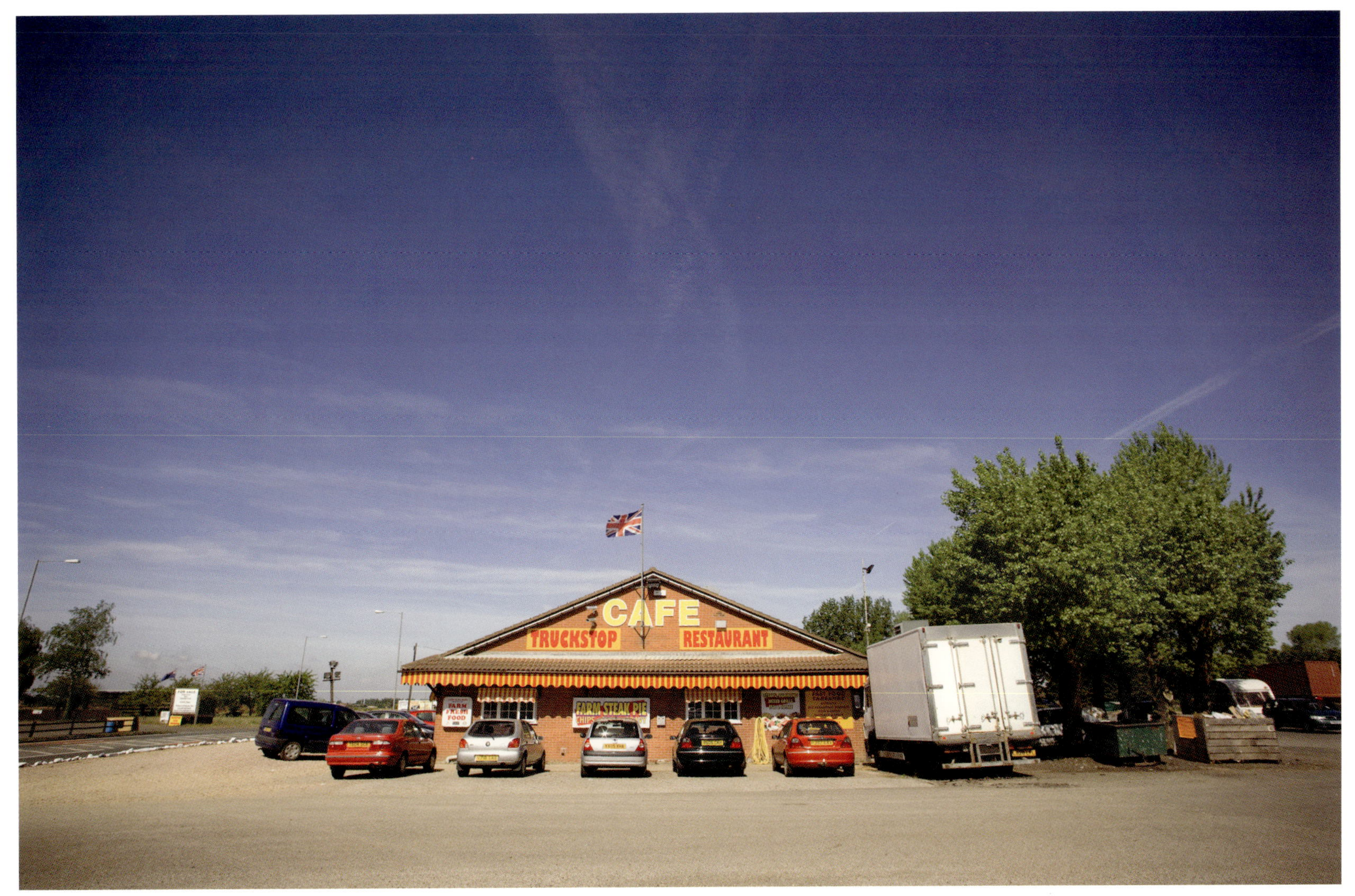

CAFE
TRUCKSTOP     RESTAURANT
FARM STEAK PIE
CHIPS

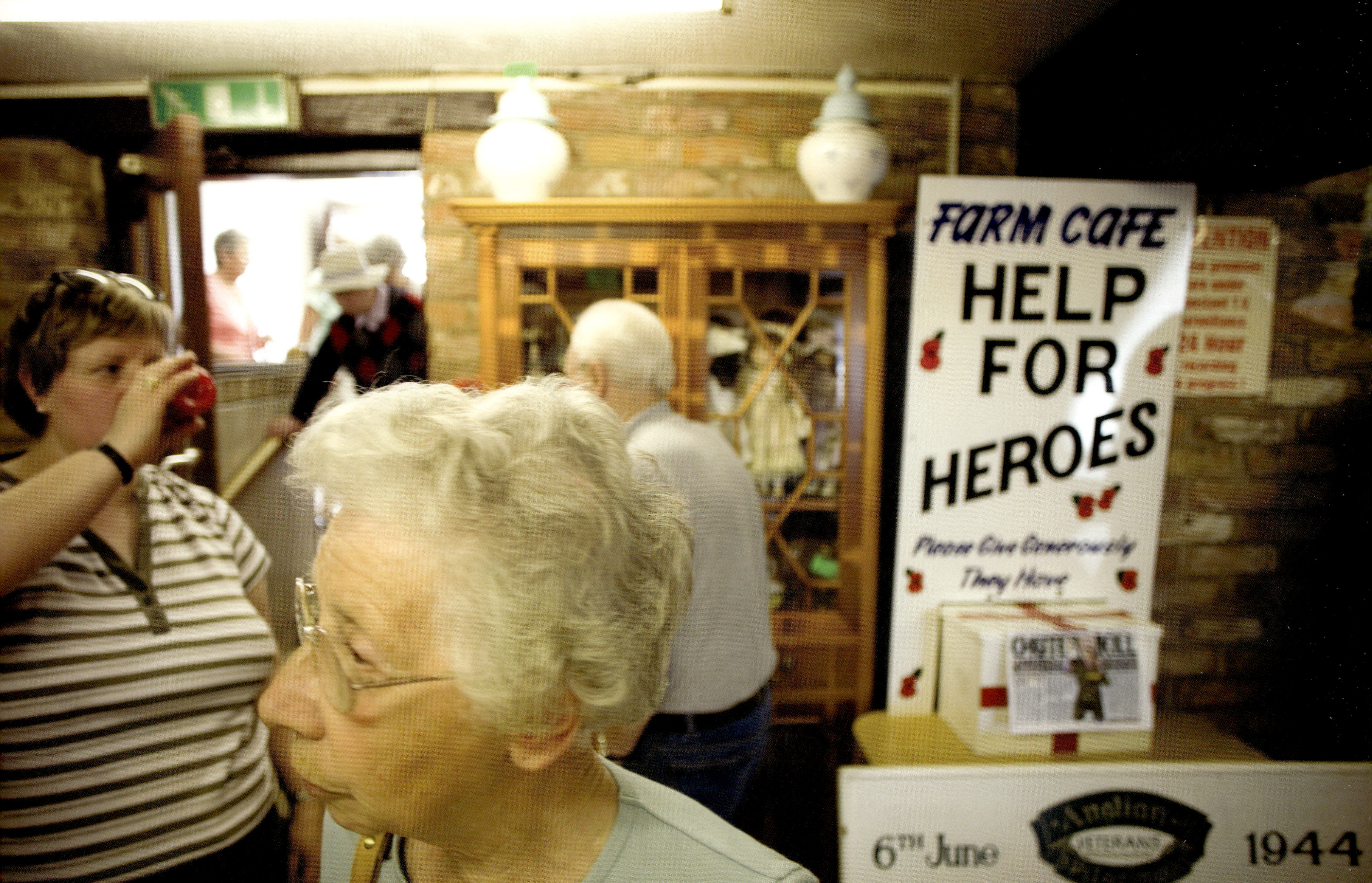
FARM CAFE
HELP
FOR
HEROES
Please Give Generously
They Have
6TH June
1944

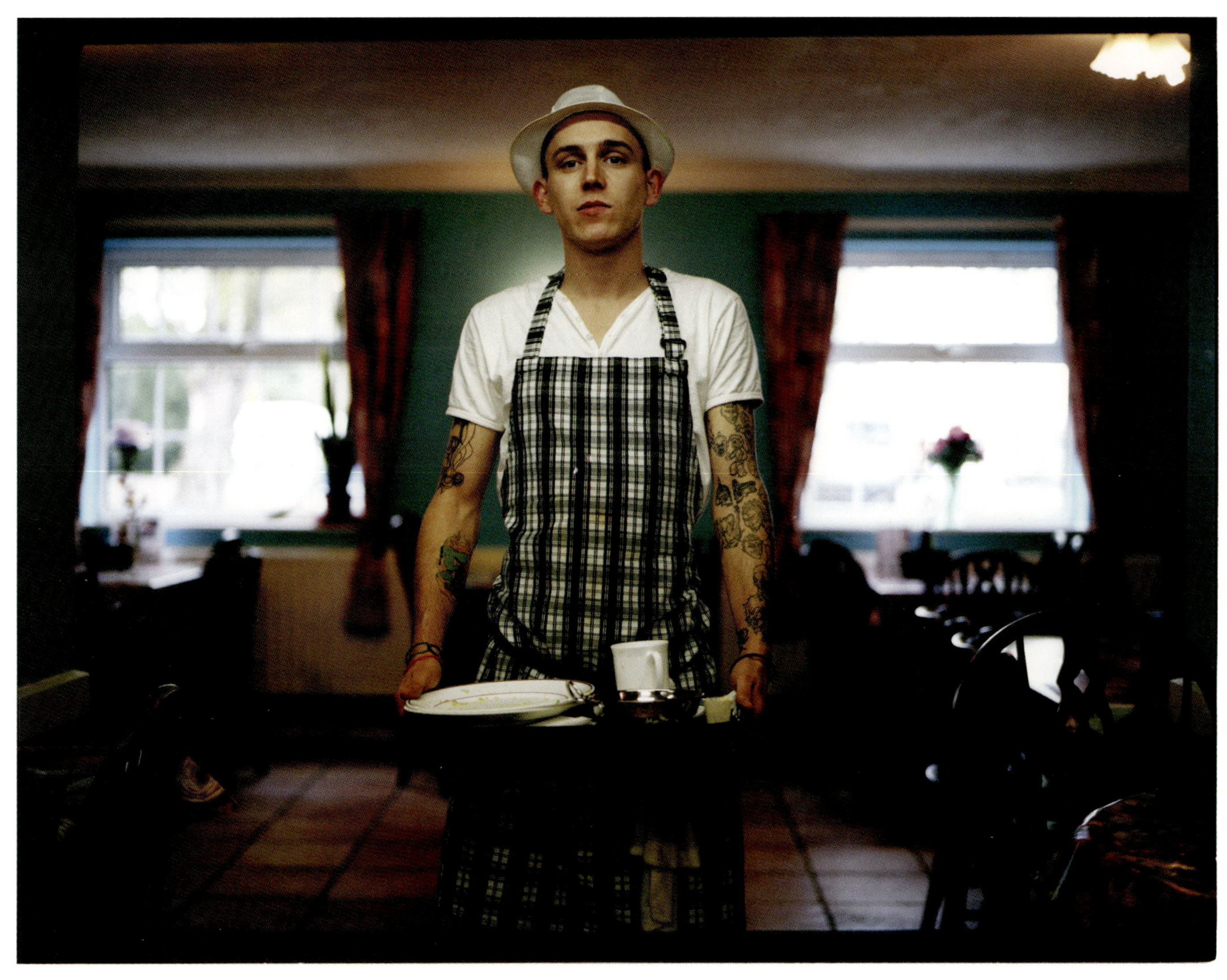

Above: Jon – The Farm Cafe – Holbeach – Norfolk – A17
Left: Coach Arrival – The Farm Cafe – Holbeach – Norfolk – A17

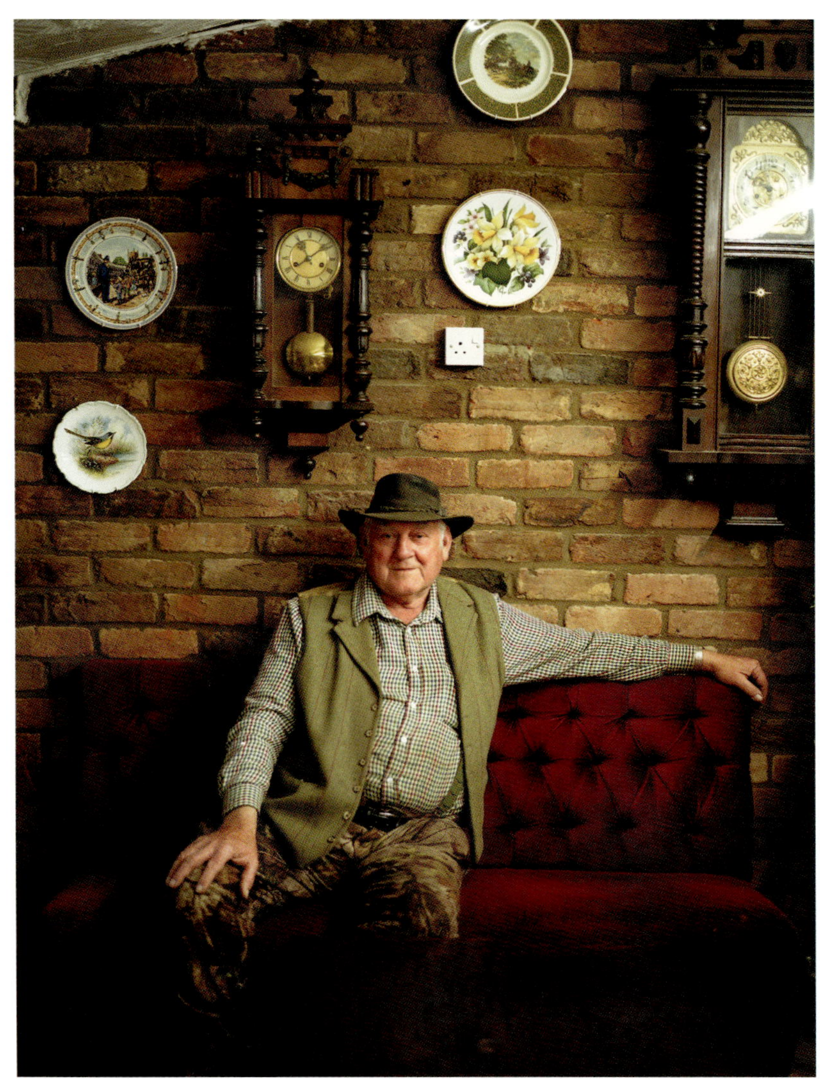

     Bill – The Farm Cafe – Holbeach – Norfolk – A17

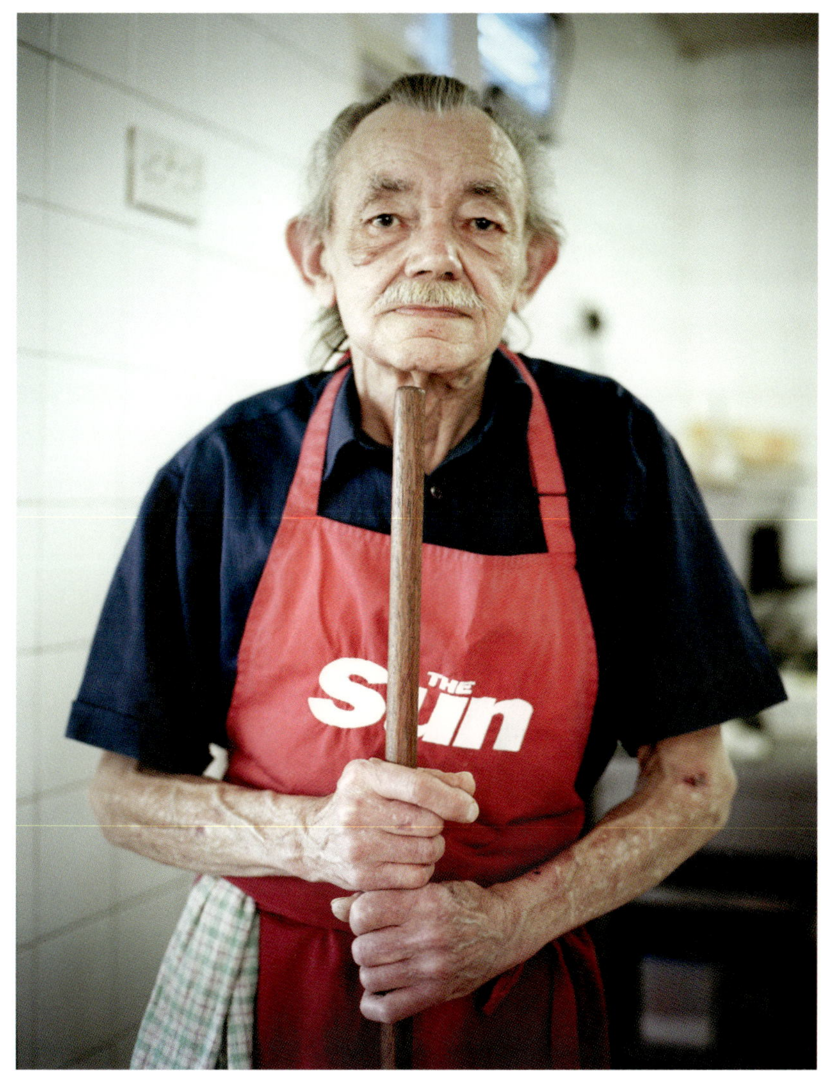

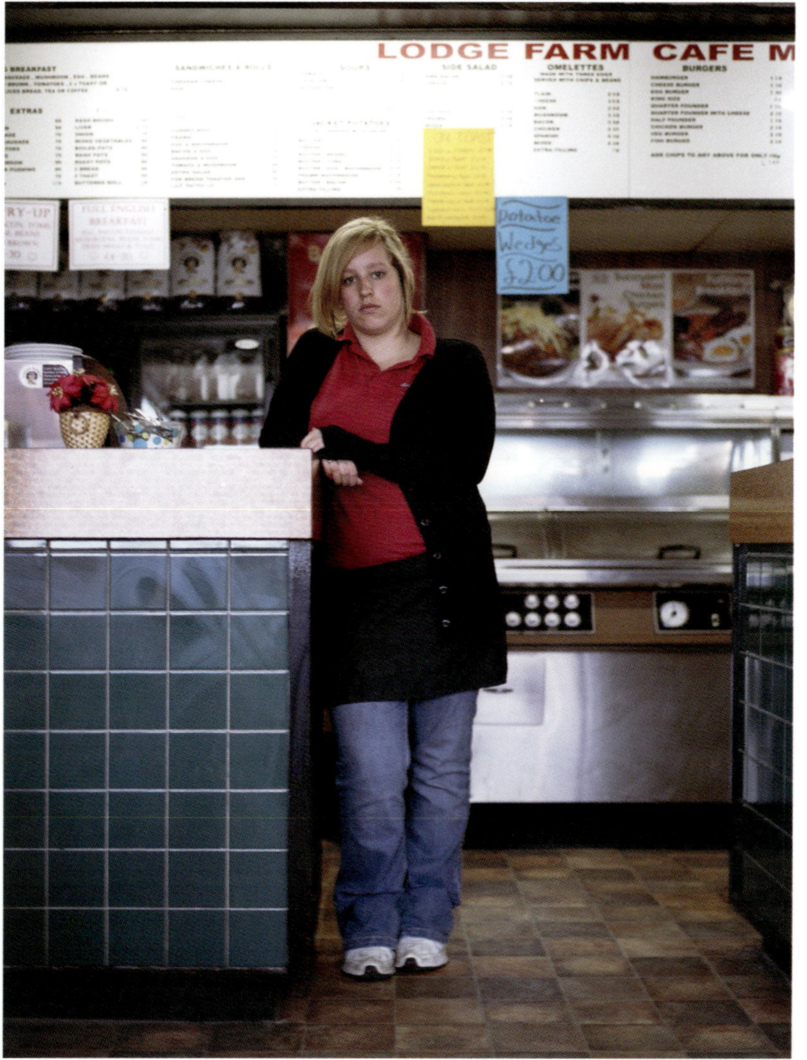

Above: Shana – Lodge Farm Cafe – Holbeach – Norfolk – A17
Above left: Jon – The Green Welly – Chatteris – Cambridgeshire – A141

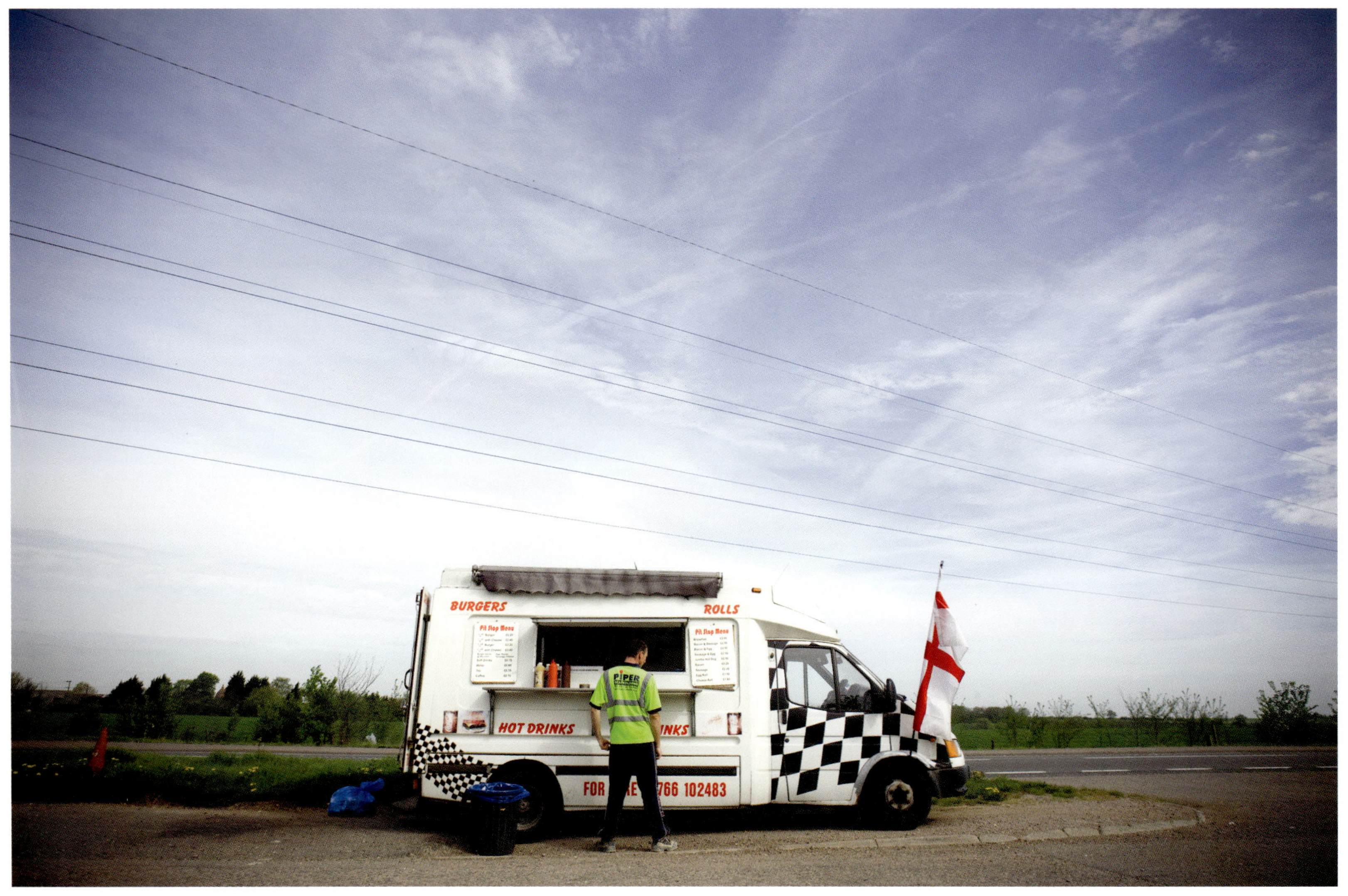



   Dominic's Burger Van – St Neots – Cambridgeshire – A428

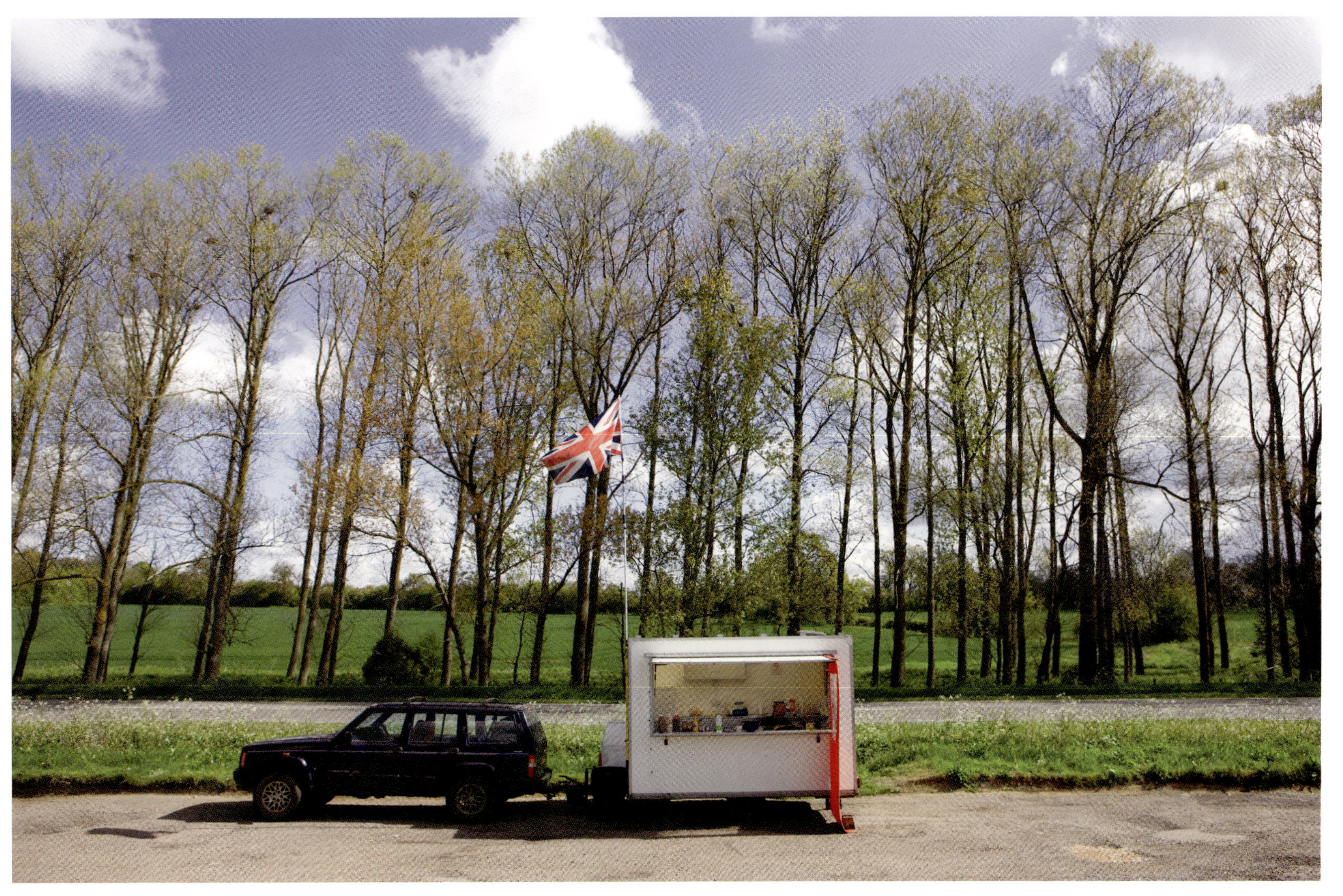

B&S Snacks – Haverhill – Suffolk – A1307    109

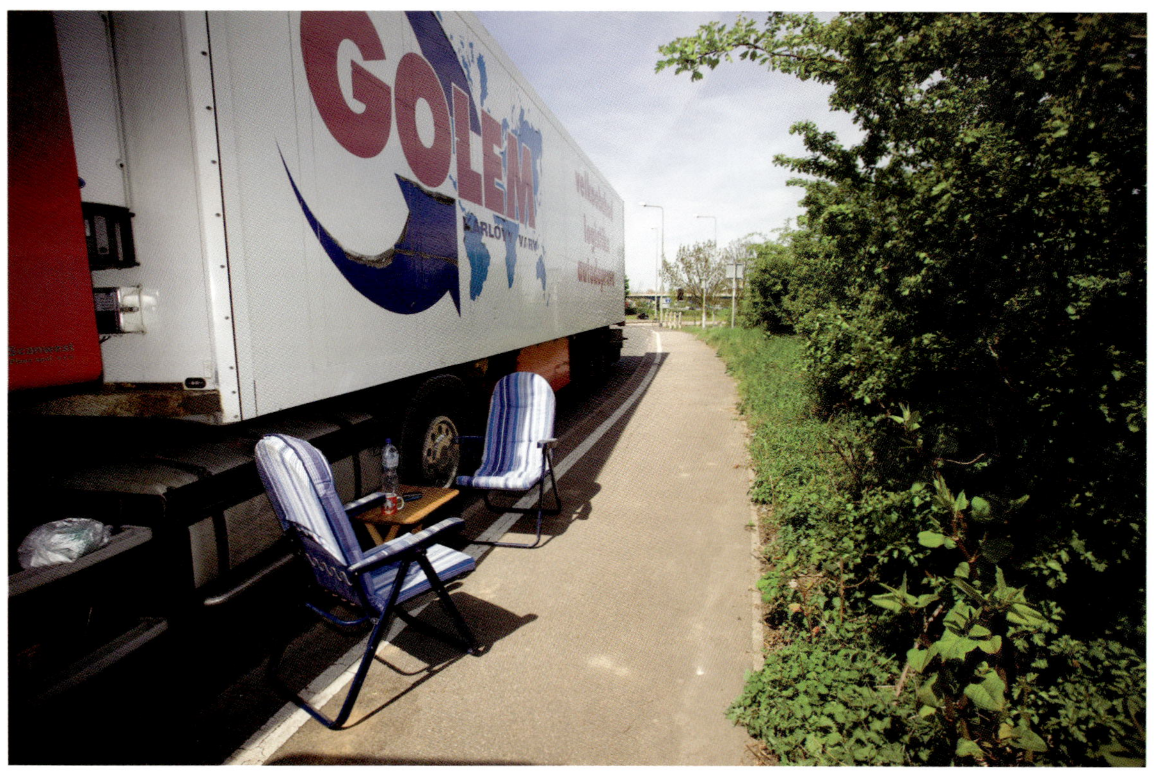


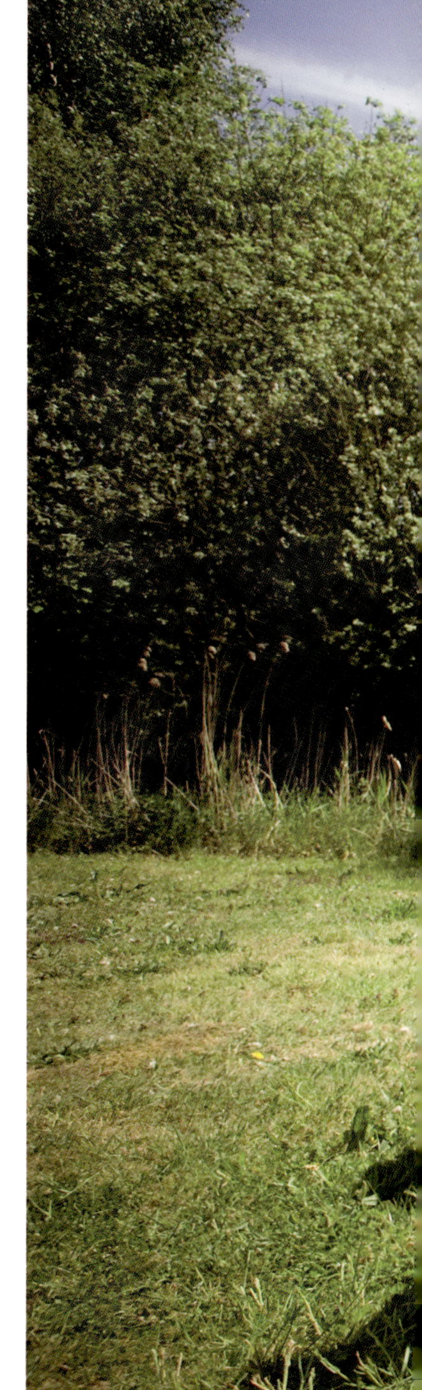

Above: Jack's Burger Van – Kings Lynn – Norfolk – A10
Right: John, Jacqui & Friends – Jack's Burger Van – Kings Lynn – Norfolk – A10

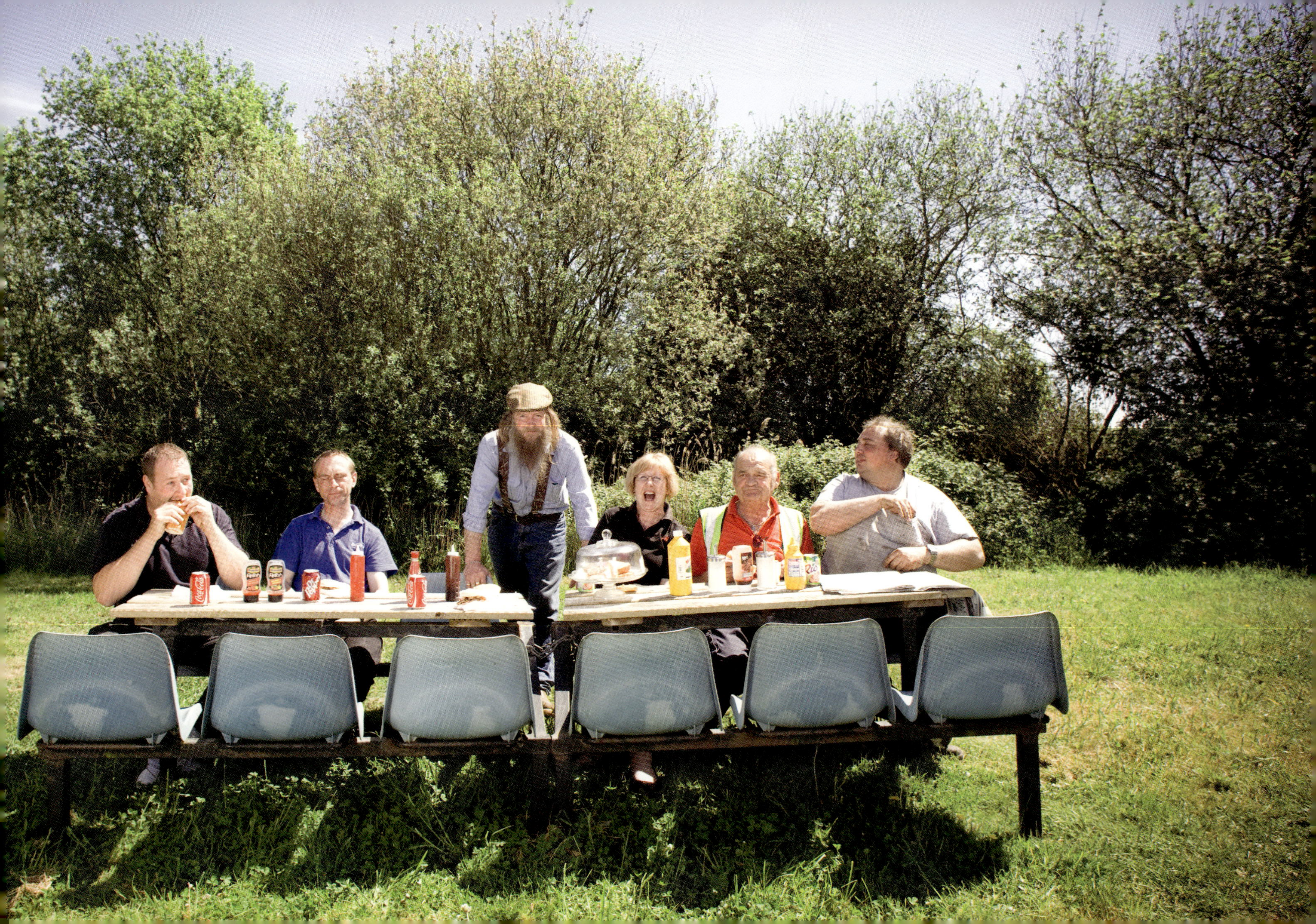

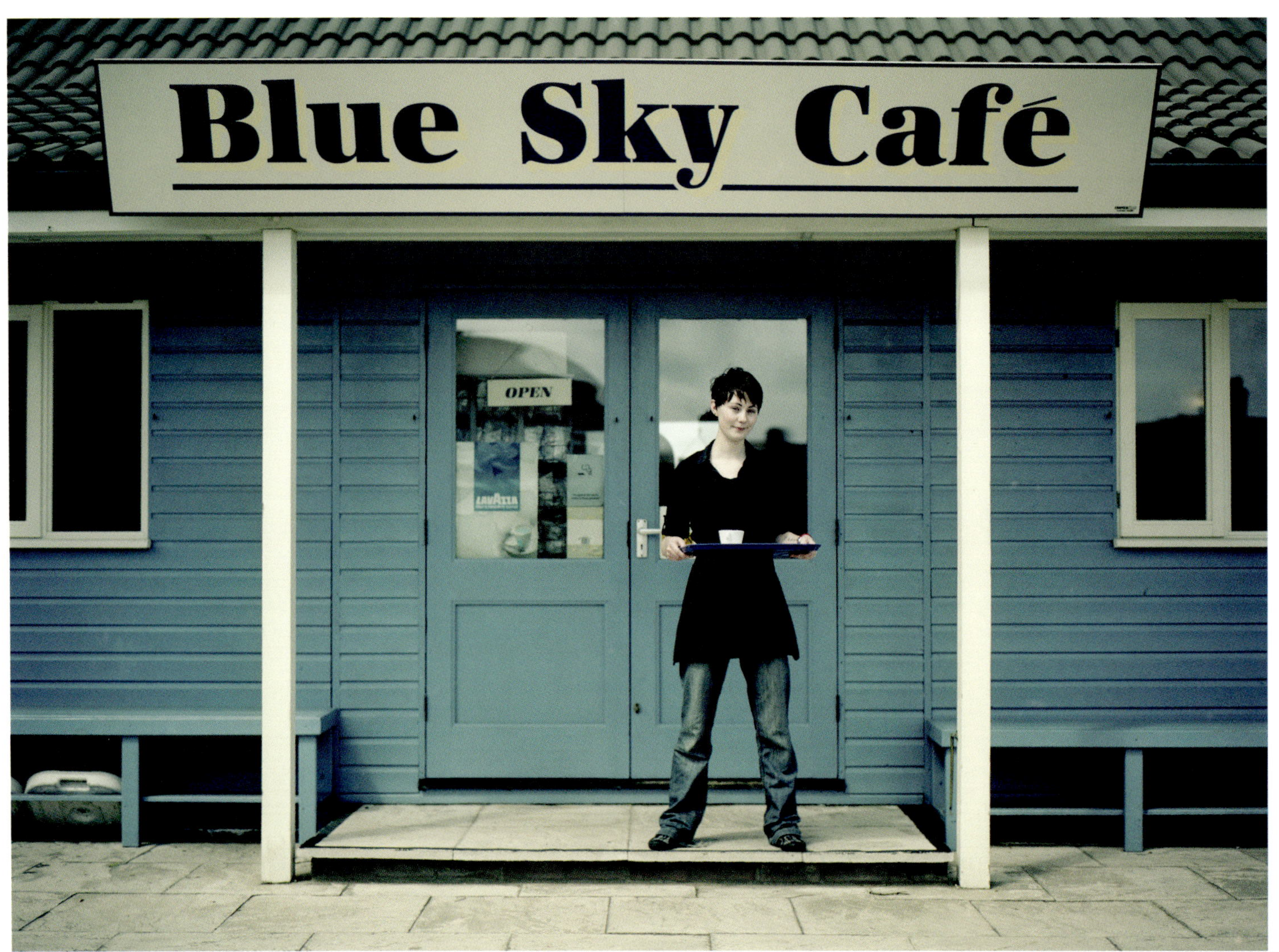

Blue Sky Café
OPEN
LAVAZZA

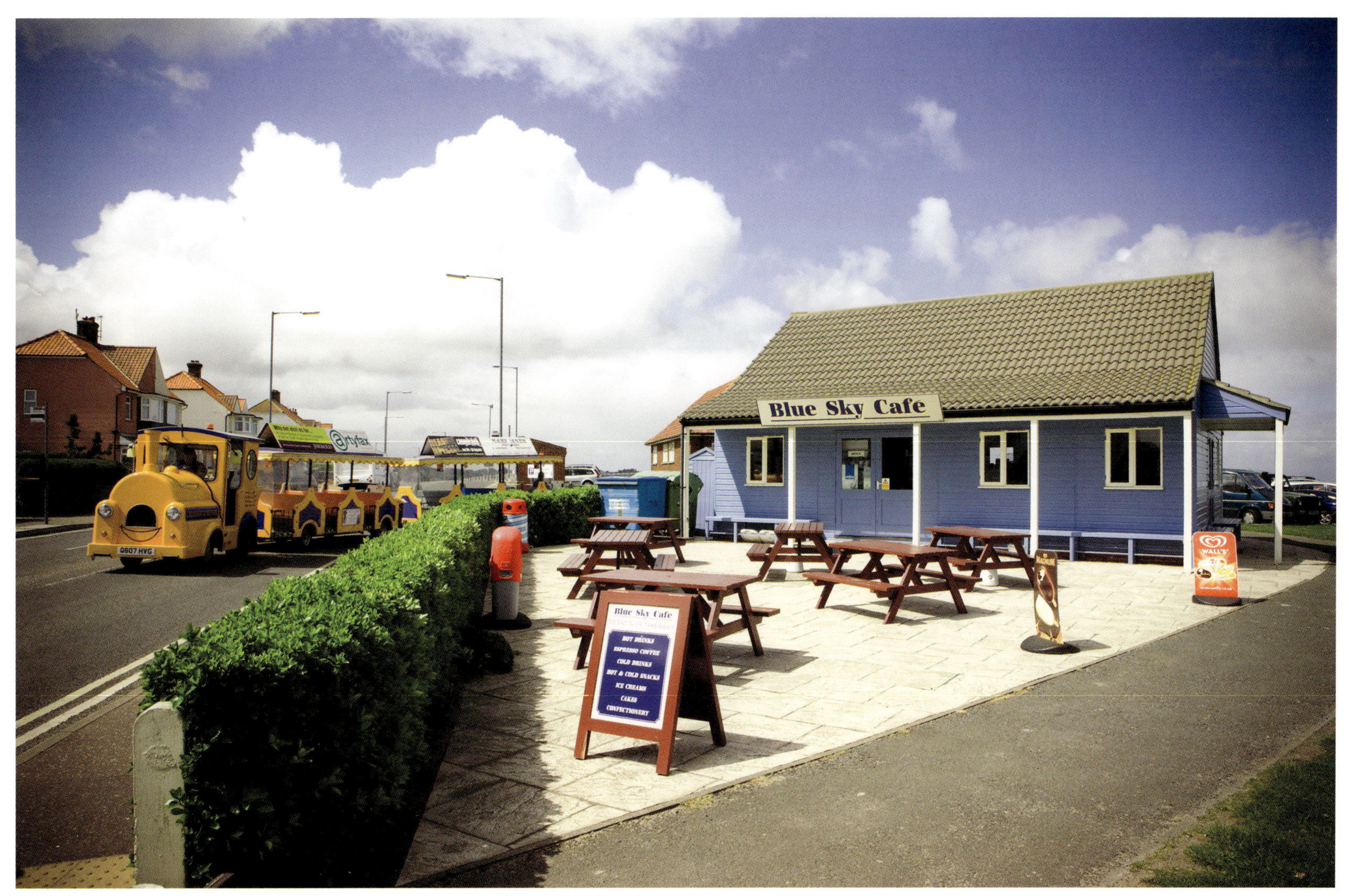


Blue Sky Cafe – Cromer – Norfolk – A149

# Into 2011

**2**011 began with a bang. I was back in London on Blackfriars Bridge, celebrating the arrival of the New Year. 2010 had been fun; I'd enjoyed enough success with photography commissions to knock kitchen life on the head. As much as I enjoyed the camaraderie, I was no longer working the tiresome shifts. Support was growing for my Roadside Britain project; after almost a year since I shot the last set of images in East Anglia, I was ready to push on, leaving English borders for fresh ground.

As April was warming up, I packed my car to head out on my longest road trip to date. My plan was to head along the A40 into Wales, and then head north, cutting back across the UK to reach Edinburgh via the northern A1. Once there, I planned to head to the tip of Scotland via the A9. The whole trip I estimated to be about 2000 miles. However, once in Wales, I decided to ditch that idea, and remain with the Welsh. The days were getting longer, the sun was shining; it was idyllic. It felt good to be back on the road, with camera, tent and supplies. More importantly, I was continuing the project as I'd imagined, free from constraints. It felt organic and fresh like the fields, which surrounded me. When I hit the A487 along the coast – it was like being reborn. The landscape was such a contrast from the flat and often bleak vistas of the East. I explored the area for about three weeks, finally heading back home via the A5. This original Roman road, then called Watling Street, stretches 260 miles from Holyhead, linking the picturesque island of Anglesey directly to the beating heart of London.

Over the course of the Summer and into the Autumn, I went on further road trips out of London in order to observe how the roadside service trade differed from elsewhere I'd been. I took a 1000km round trip to Ireland, my first ever, for a friend's wedding in Derry. Though not part of Great Britain, I couldn't miss the opportunity to investigate. The countryside was staggeringly beautiful, so raw and intriguing, with what felt like a bar at every turn. Guinness replaced tea, pubs replaced roadside cafes, and the independent diners I'd become used to seeing in England and Wales were few and far between. Instead, I noticed how, *Eddie Rocket's*, a chain of American themed diners, were prominent in the outskirts of many major cities. I wasn't disheartened however – it was an amazing trip, and a shot of Peggy's Diner, taken in County Antrim in Ulster, made it into this book.

I tracked Paul Graham's footprints along the A1 as far as Scotland, where in contrast to Wales I found few roadside services, apart from the odd service station, and a sporadic burger van now and again en route. Driving through the spectacular Highlands and along the banks of the lochs from Inverness to Fort William, I'd assumed I'd see more. However, it was November, thundering with rain with a chill in the air. Maybe my timing was wrong, but nevertheless a November trip was well worth it. Despite the rain, it was magnificent and moody.

My girlfriend accompanied me on the Scottish leg and the company was welcomed. Luckily for her we'd been together for about a year so she knew what she was getting herself into. A brooding atmosphere of dark skies and heavy rainfall followed us as we ventured deep into the Scottish heartland of myth and legend. It really was magical. I don't know what I wanted to see more – the Loch Ness Monster, a generous tot of whisky accompanied by a roaring log fire or a stunning roadside cafe or burger van. It's likely I wanted them all.

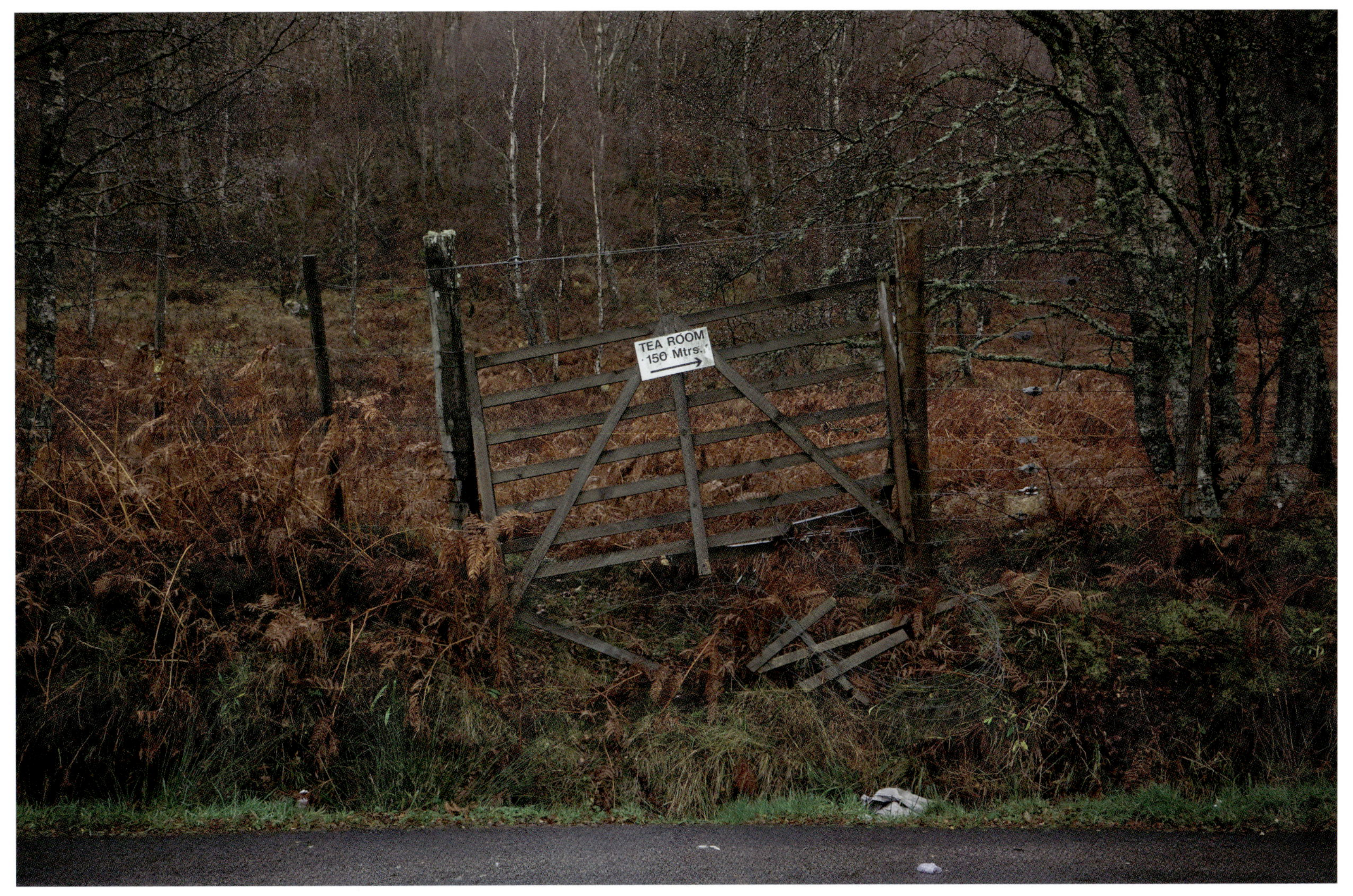


Tea Room 150 metres – Invergarry – Highlands – A82        115

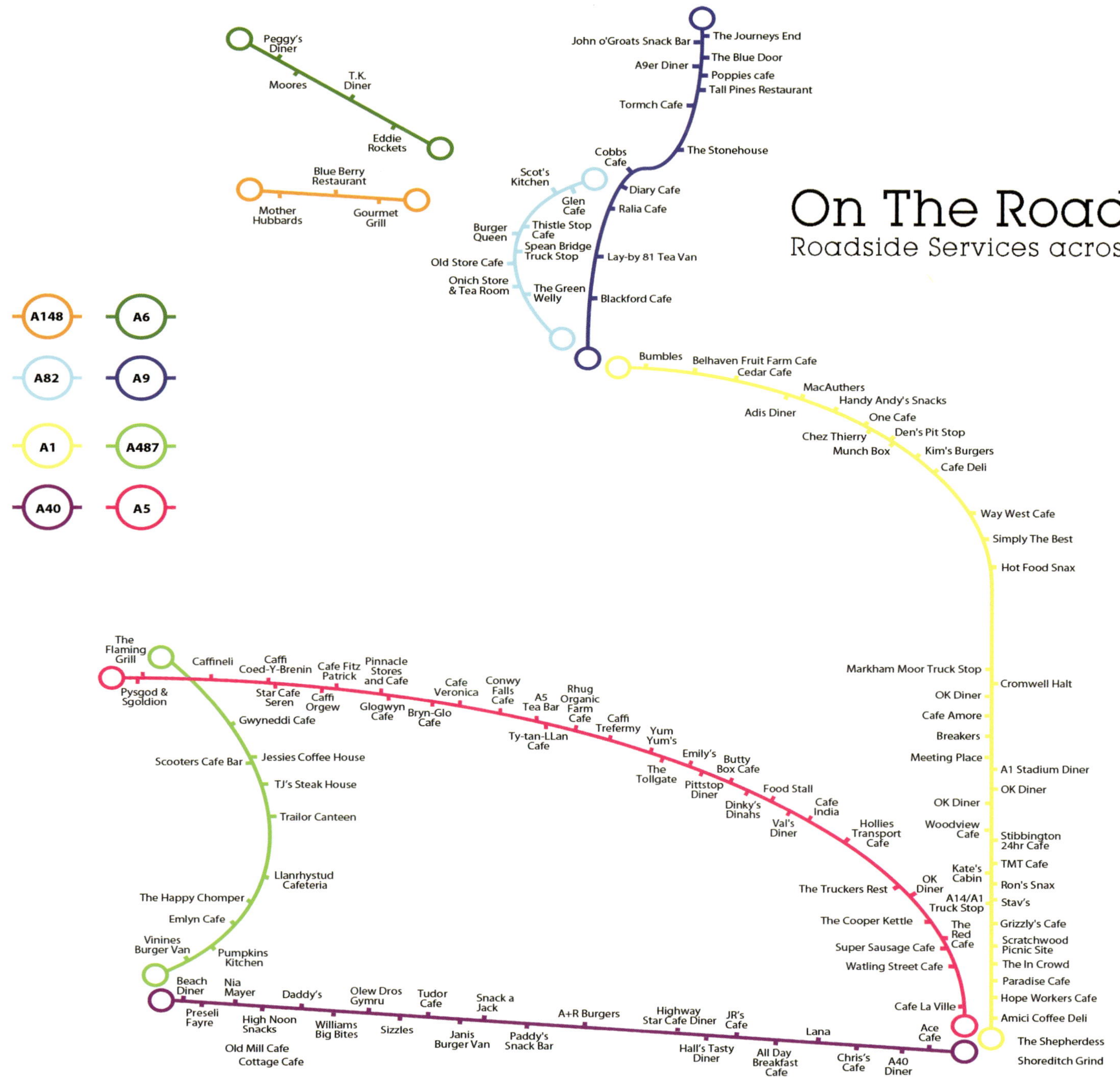

On The Road in 2011
Roadside Services across Great Britain

A148
A82
A1
A40
A6
A9
A487
A5

Peggy's Diner
Moores
T.K. Diner
Eddie Rockets

Blue Berry Restaurant
Mother Hubbards
Gourmet Grill

The Journeys End
John o'Groats Snack Bar
The Blue Door
A9er Diner
Poppies cafe
Tall Pines Restaurant
Tormch Cafe
The Stonehouse
Cobbs Cafe
Scot's Kitchen
Diary Cafe
Glen Cafe
Ralia Cafe
Burger Queen
Thistle Stop Cafe
Spean Bridge Truck Stop
Lay-by 81 Tea Van
Old Store Cafe
Onich Store & Tea Room
The Green Welly
Blackford Cafe

Bumbles
Belhaven Fruit Farm Cafe
Cedar Cafe
MacAuthers
Handy Andy's Snacks
Adis Diner
One Cafe
Den's Pit Stop
Chez Thierry
Munch Box
Kim's Burgers
Cafe Deli
Way West Cafe
Simply The Best
Hot Food Snax

Markham Moor Truck Stop
Cromwell Halt
OK Diner
Cafe Amore
Breakers
Meeting Place
A1 Stadium Diner
OK Diner
OK Diner
Woodview Cafe
Stibbington 24hr Cafe
TMT Cafe
Kate's Cabin
Ron's Snax
A14/A1 Truck Stop
Stav's
Grizzly's Cafe
Scratchwood Picnic Site
The In Crowd
Paradise Cafe
Hope Workers Cafe
Amici Coffee Deli
The Shepherdess
Shoreditch Grind

The Truckers Rest
The Cooper Kettle
Super Sausage Cafe
Watling Street Cafe
The Red Cafe
Cafe La Ville
Ace Cafe

The Flaming Grill
Caffineli
Caffi Coed-Y-Brenin
Cafe Fitz Patrick
Pinnacle Stores and Cafe
Cafe Veronica
Conwy Falls Cafe
Rhug Organic Farm Cafe
Pysgod & Sgoldion
Star Cafe Seren
Caffi Orgew
Glogwyn Cafe
Bryn-Glo Cafe
A5 Tea Bar
Caffi Trefermy
Gwyneddi Cafe
Ty-tan-LLan Cafe
Yum Yum's
Emily's
Butty Box Cafe
Scooters Cafe Bar
Jessies Coffee House
The Tollgate
Pittstop Diner
Food Stall
TJ's Steak House
Dinky's Dinahs
Cafe India
Trailor Canteen
Val's Diner
Hollies Transport Cafe
Llanrhystud Cafeteria
The Happy Chomper
Emlyn Cafe
Vinines Burger Van
Pumpkins Kitchen
Beach Diner
Nia Mayer
Daddy's
Olew Dros Gymru
Tudor Cafe
Snack a Jack
A+R Burgers
Highway Star Cafe Diner
JR's Cafe
Lana
Preseli Fayre
High Noon Snacks
Williams Big Bites
Sizzles
Janis Burger Van
Paddy's Snack Bar
Hall's Tasty Diner
All Day Breakfast Cafe
Chris's Cafe
A40 Diner
Old Mill Cafe
Cottage Cafe

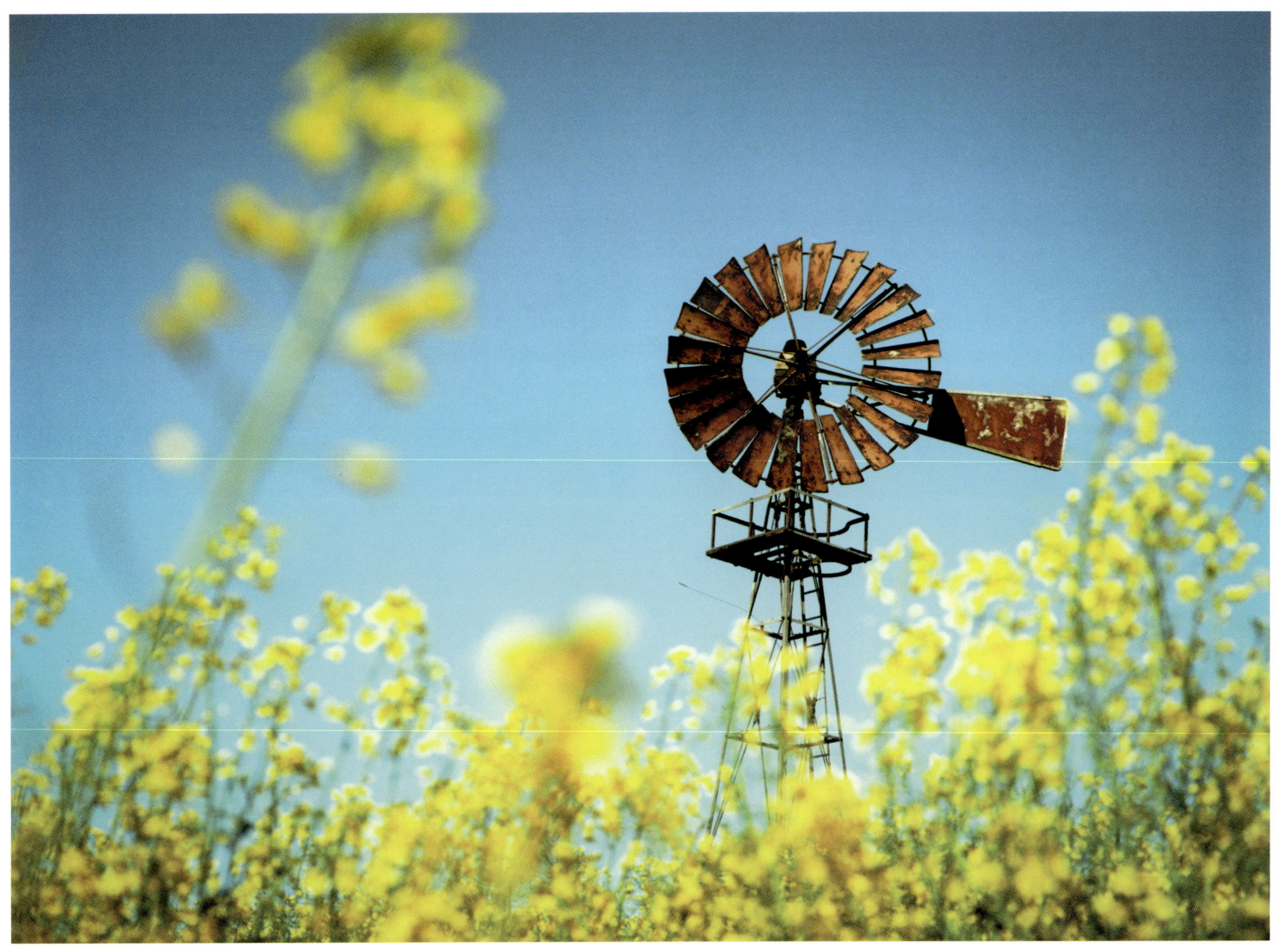

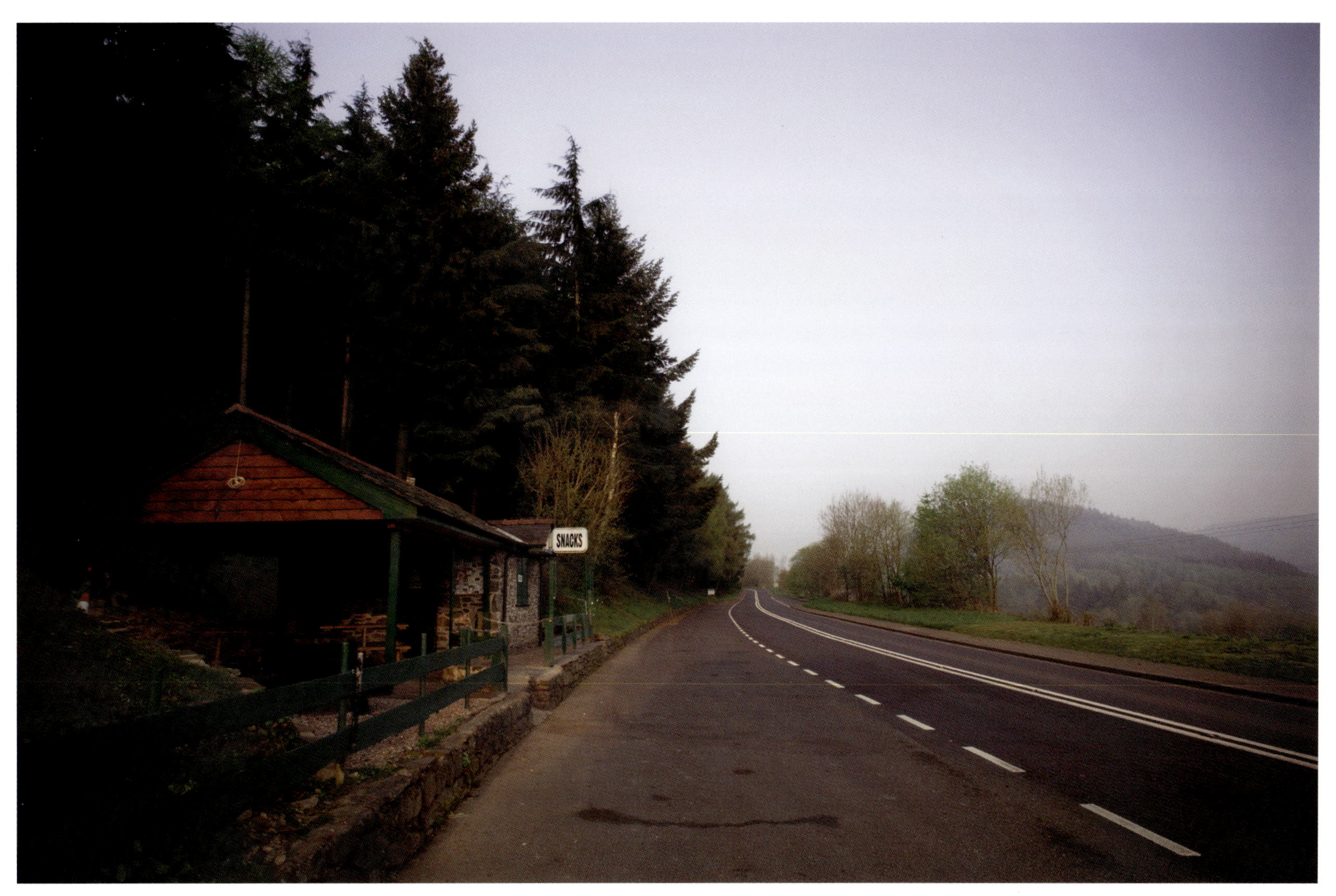



The Tollgate – Llangollen – Denbighshire – A5
Next: Ty-Tan-Llan Caffi – Cerrigydrudion – Conwy – A5

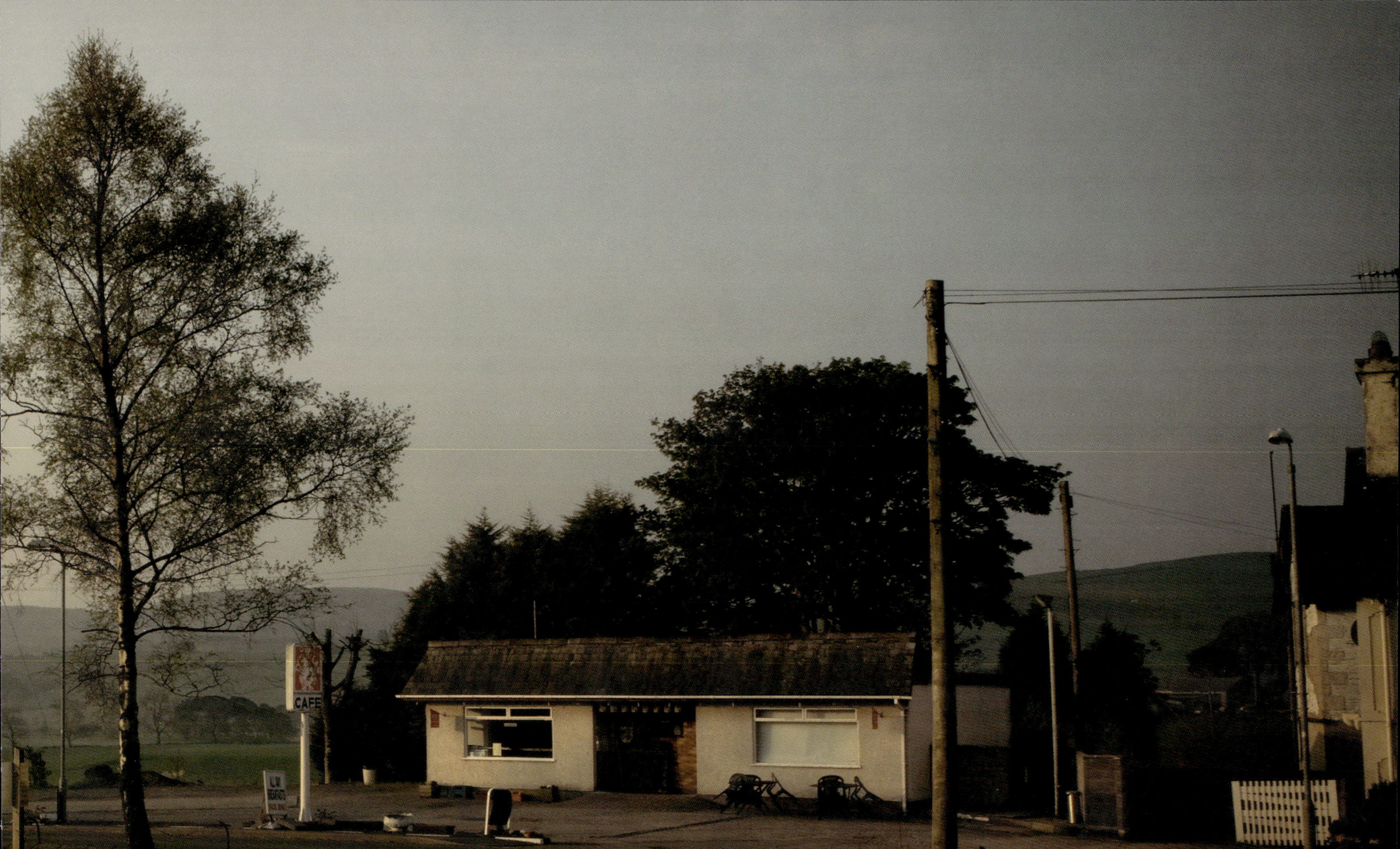
CAFE

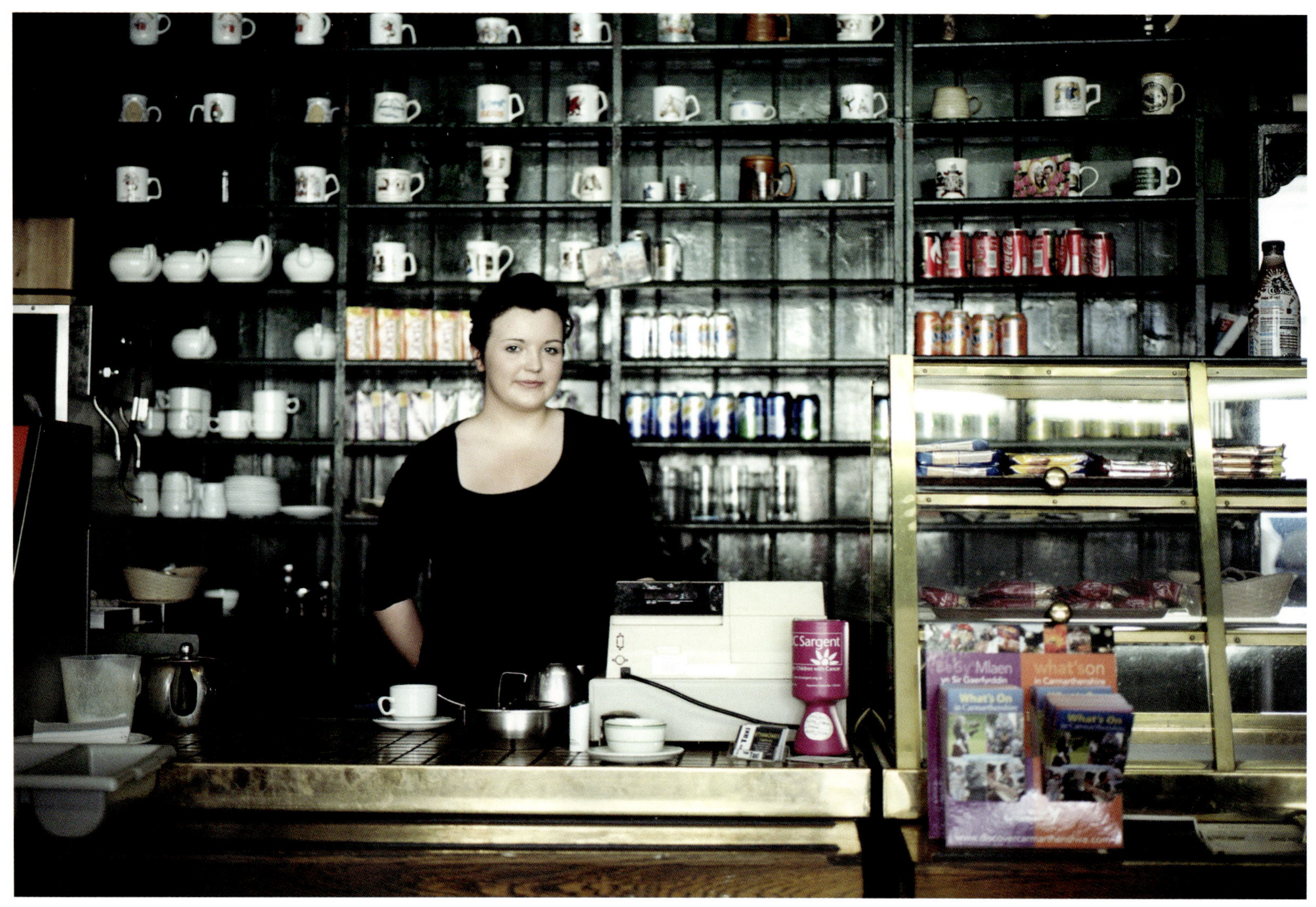

 Hannah – Tudors Cafe – Llandovery – Carmarthenshire – A40

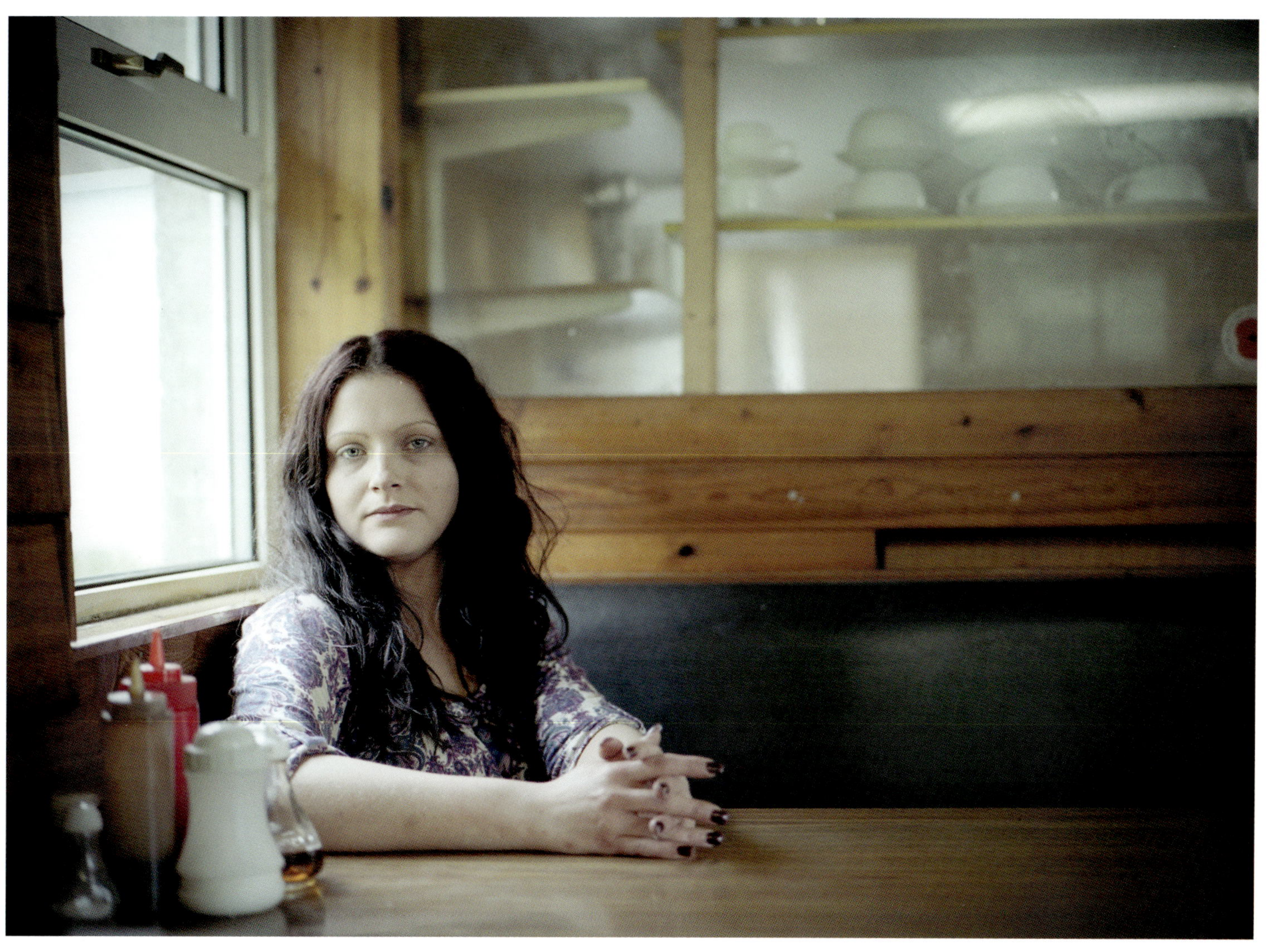

Above: Nicola Middleton – Cottage Cafe – Llanddowror – Carmarthenshire – A477
Next: Camilla and Hasi at Emily's Burger Van – Llangollen – Denbighshire – A5

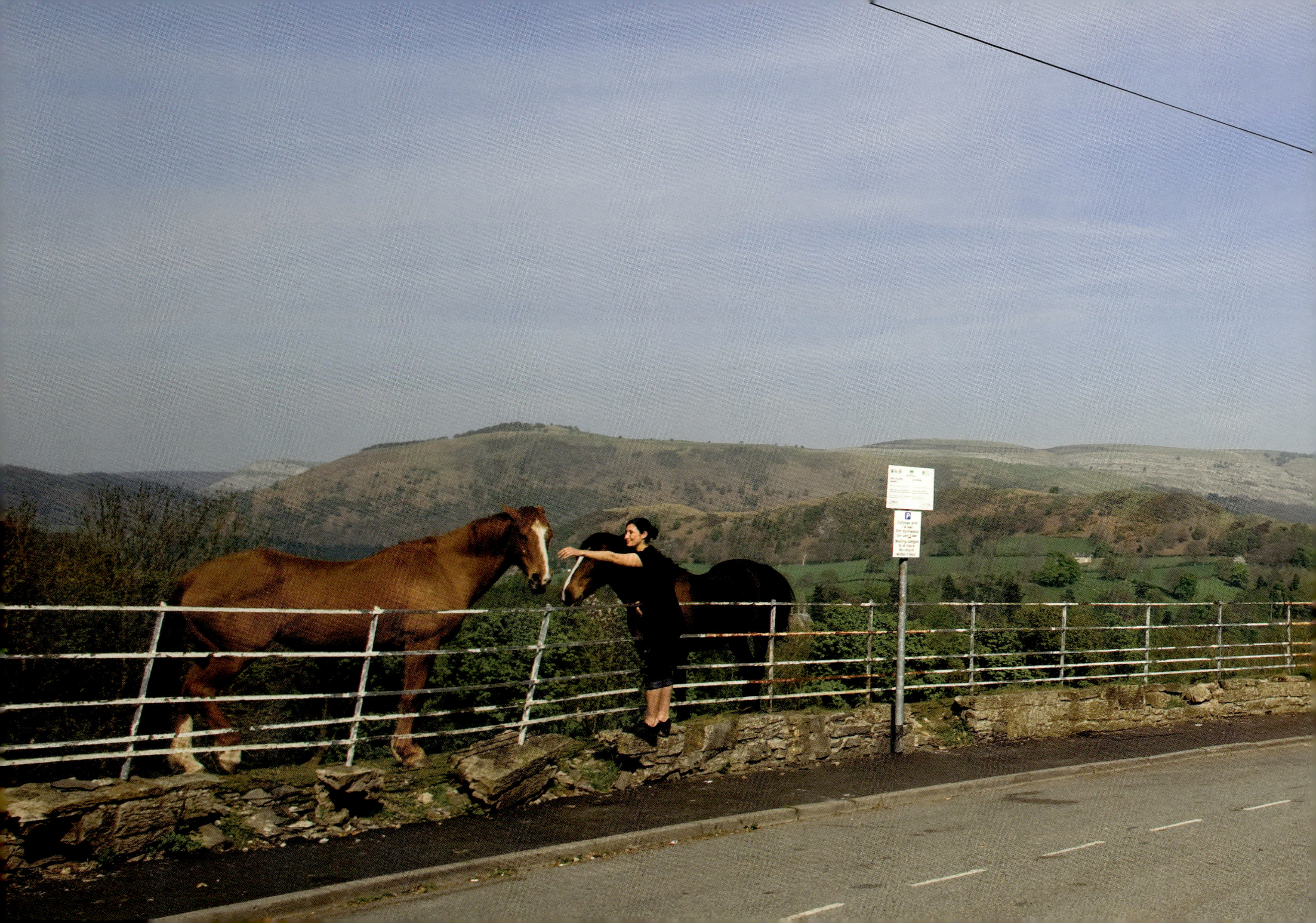

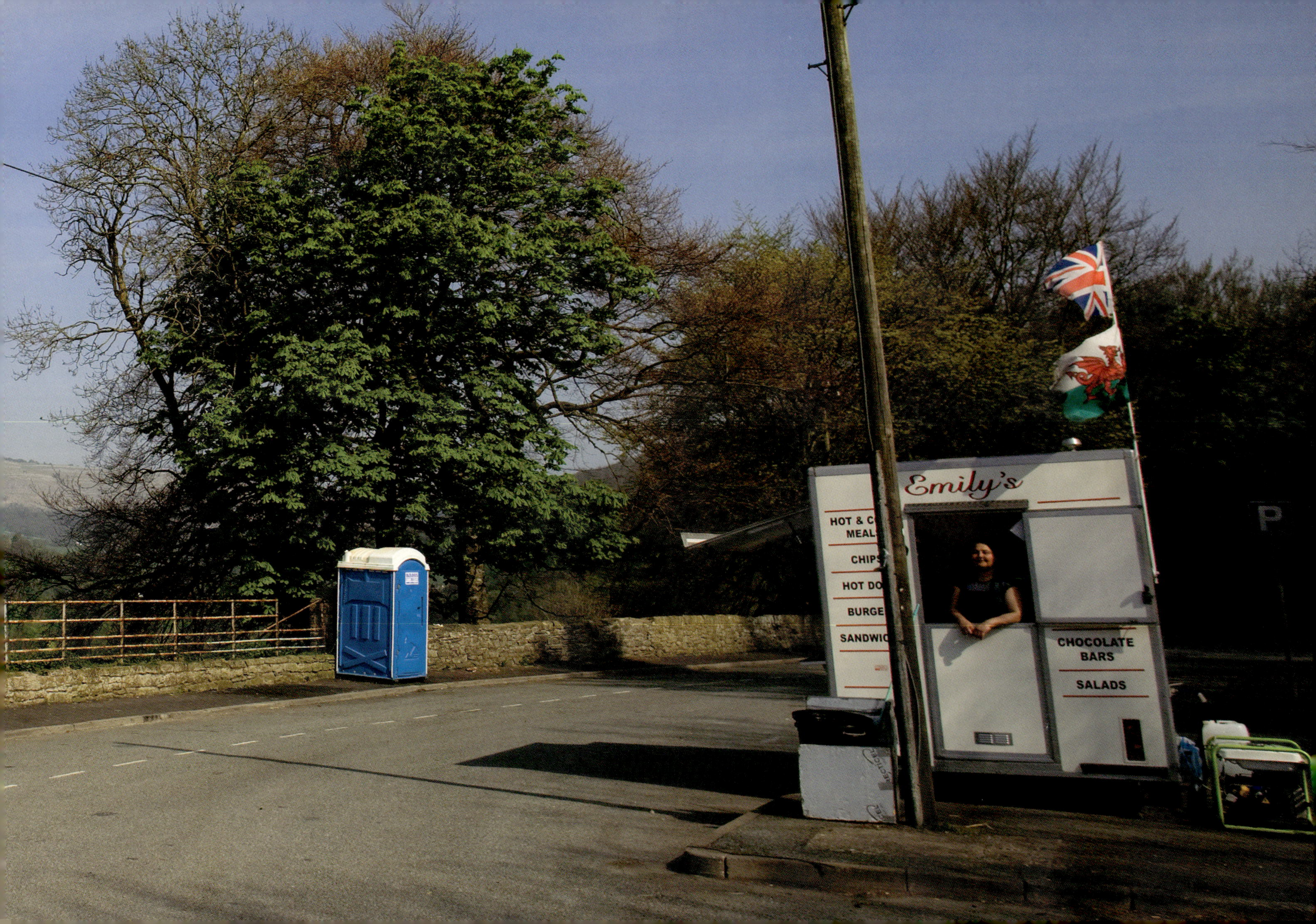
Emily's
HOT & C
MEAL
CHIPS
HOT DO
BURGE
SANDWIC
CHOCOLATE
BARS
SALADS
P

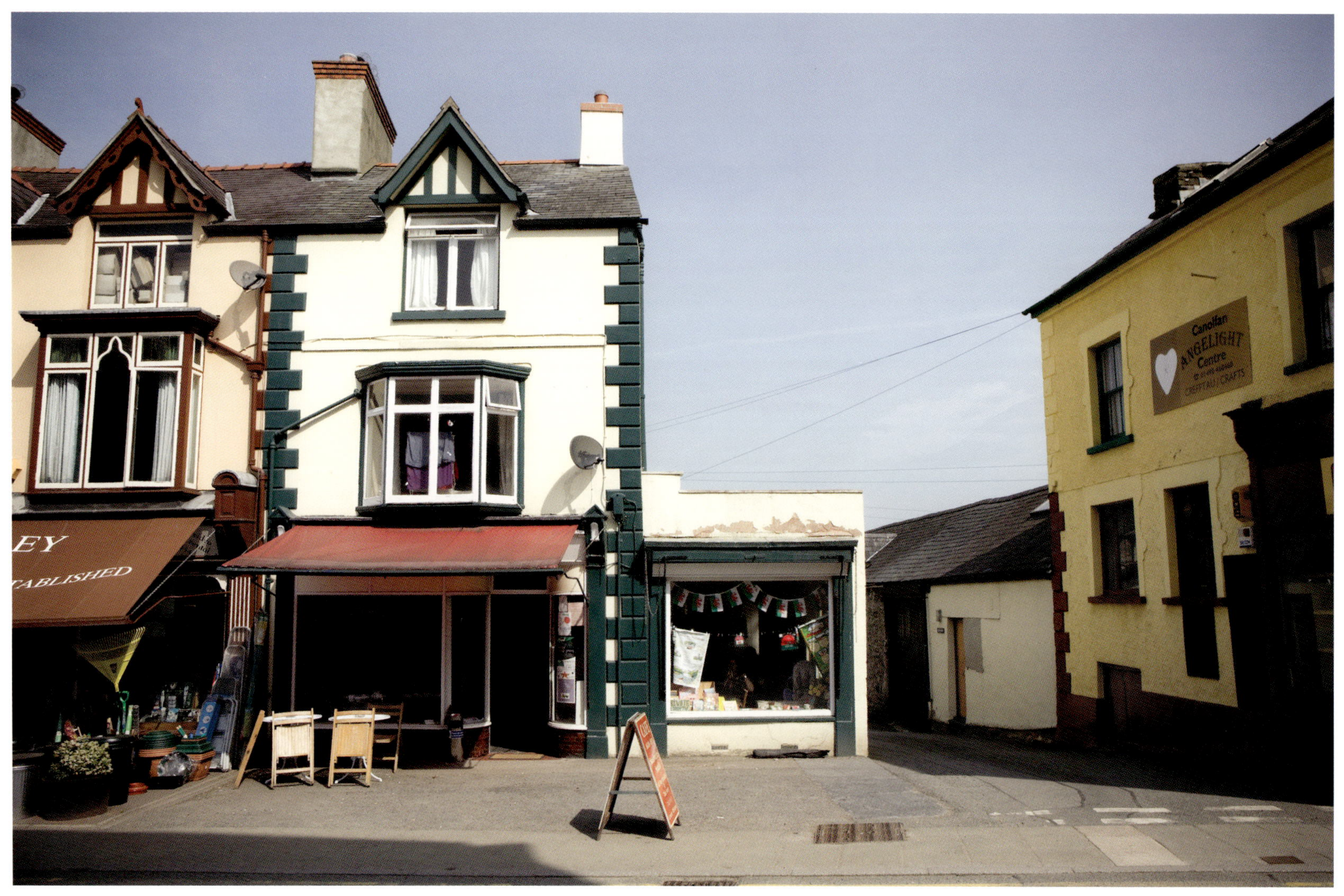



126    Caffi Treferwyn – Corwen – Denbighshire – A5

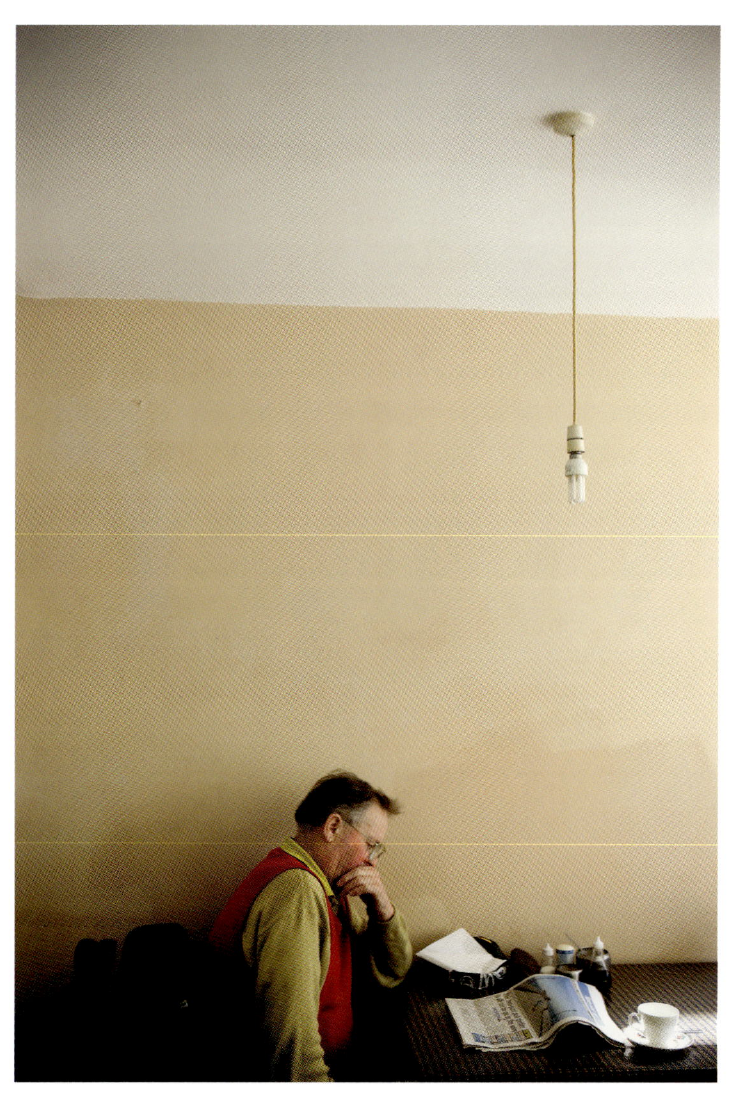

Above: Eddie – Caffi Treferwyn – Corwen – Denbighshire – A5
Next: Pinnacle Stores and Cafe – Capel Curig – Conwy – A5

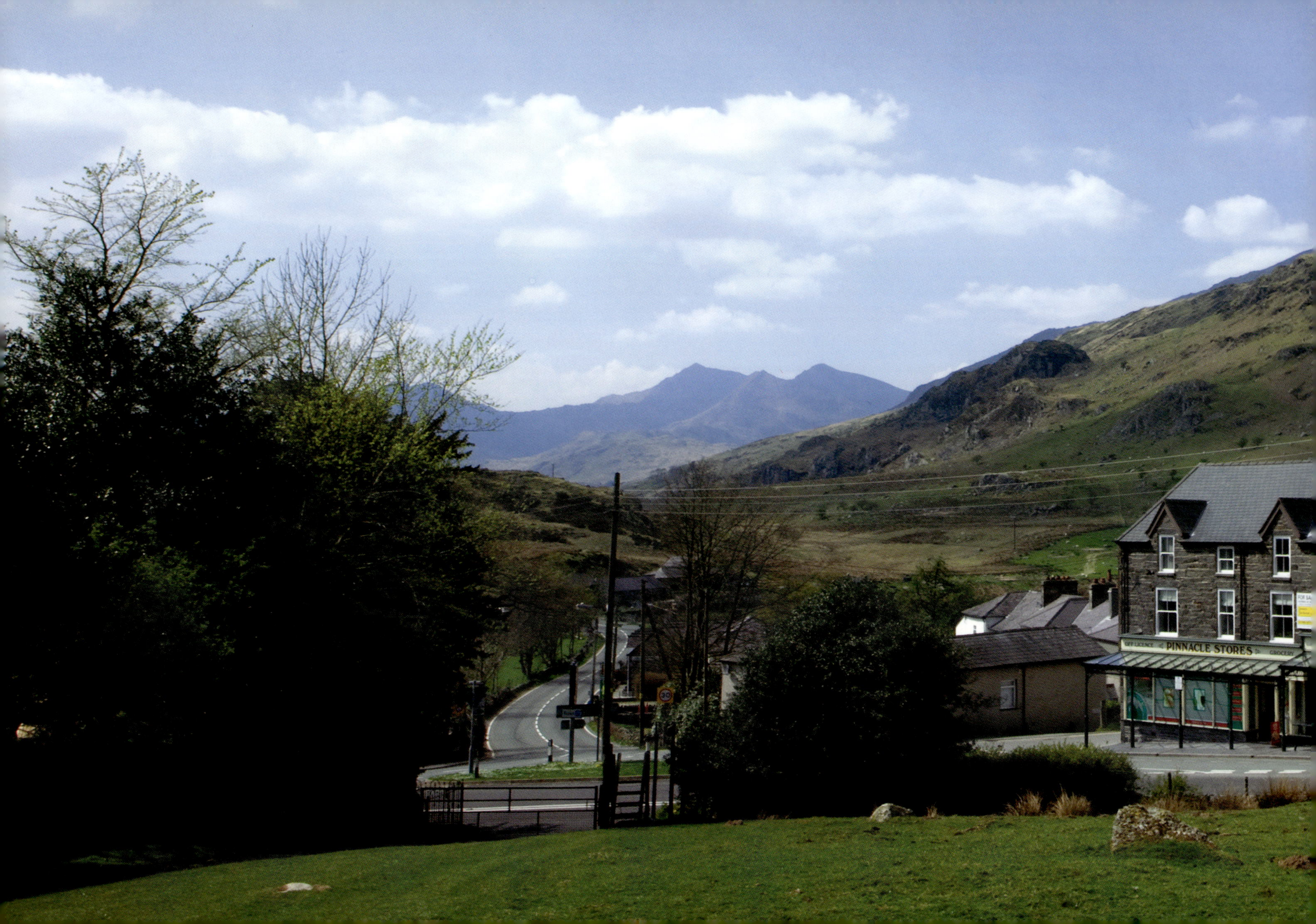

OFF LICENCE
PINNACLE STORES
GROCER

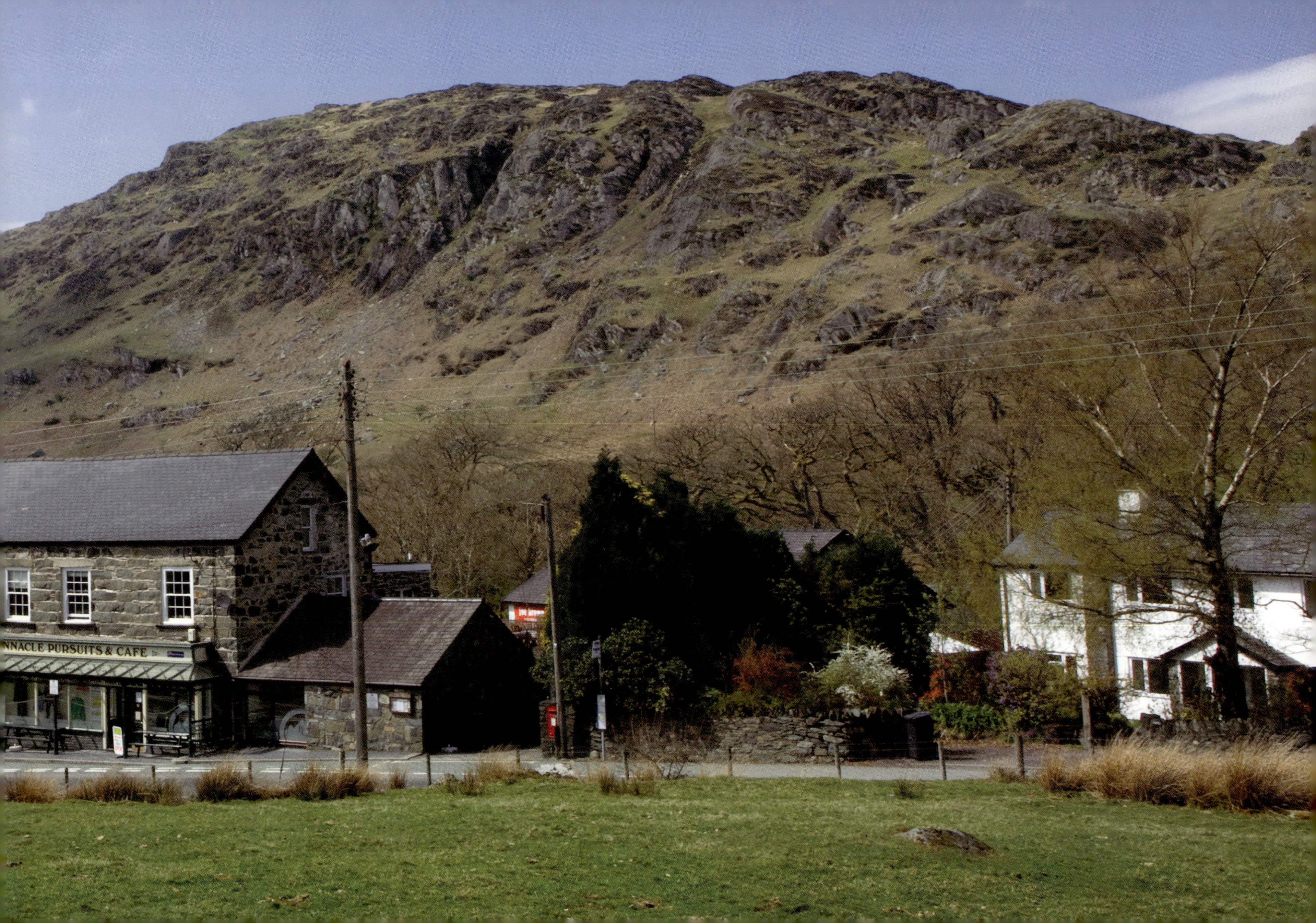
NNACLE PURSUITS & CAFE

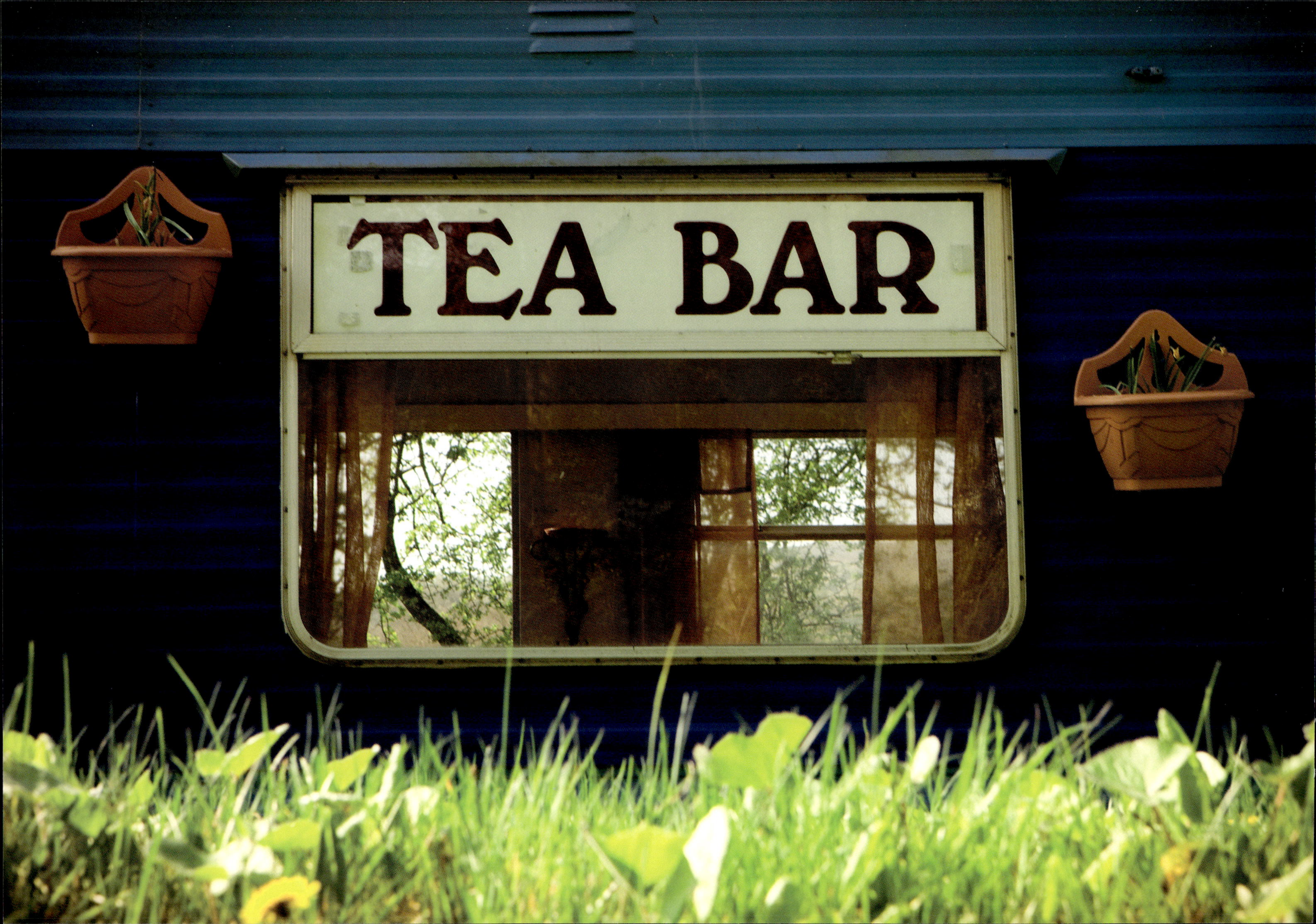
TEA BAR

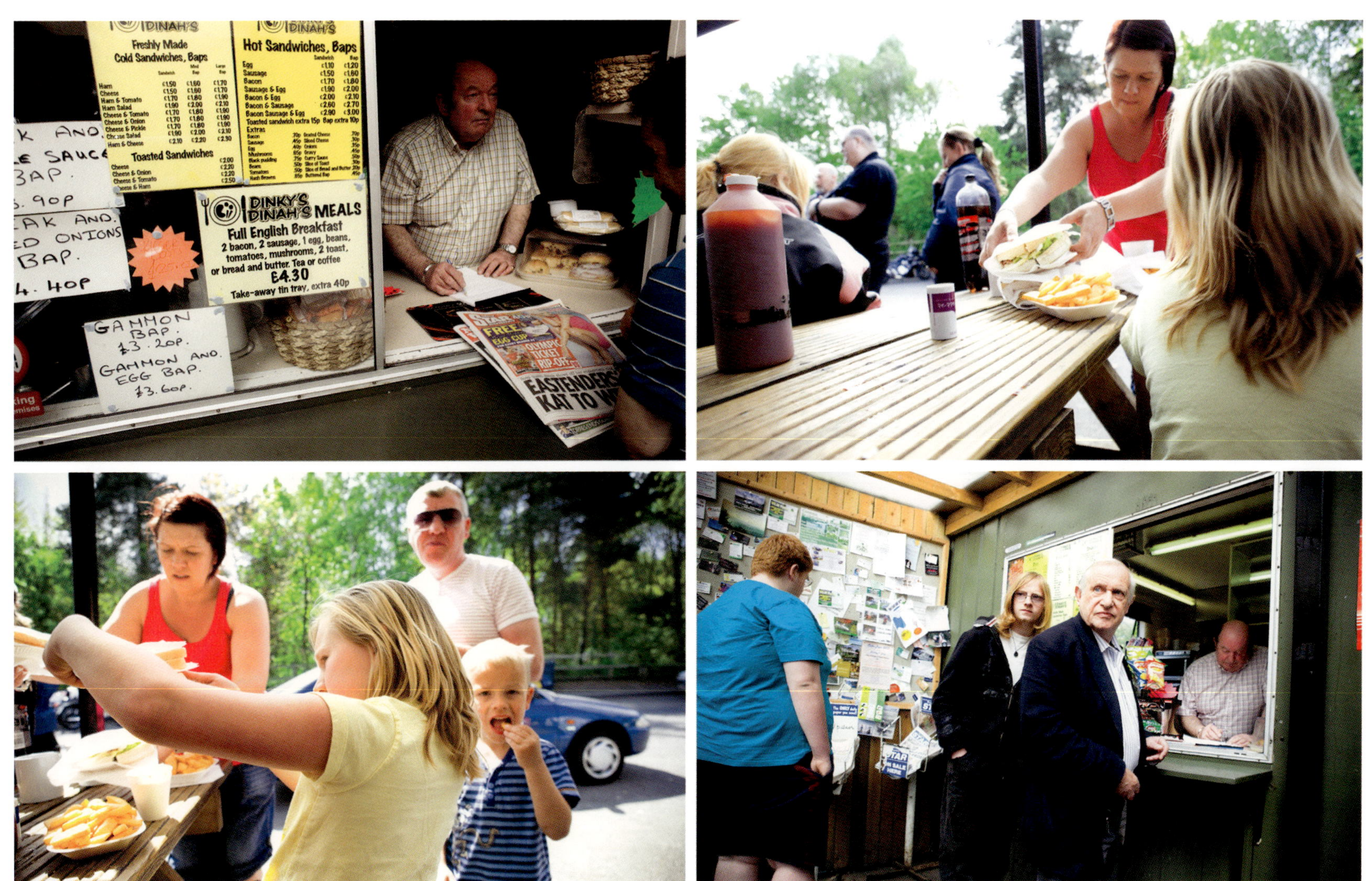

Above: Dinky Dinah – Ford – Shropshire – A458
Left: A5 Tea Bar – Betws-y-Coed – Conwy – A5

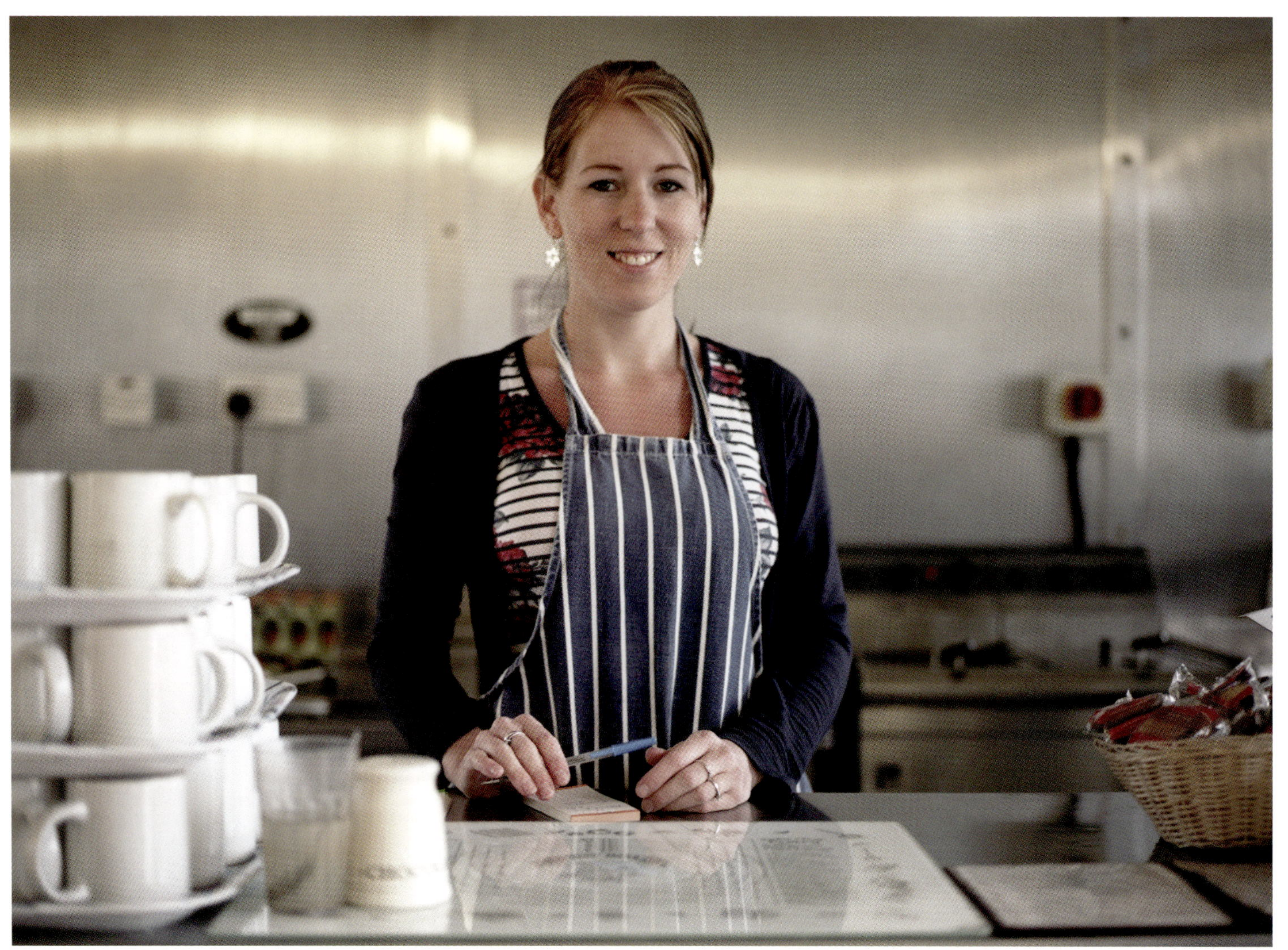

 Gemma Raynolds – Pencraig Diner 'Aleglo's Place' – Pencraig – Herefordshire – A40

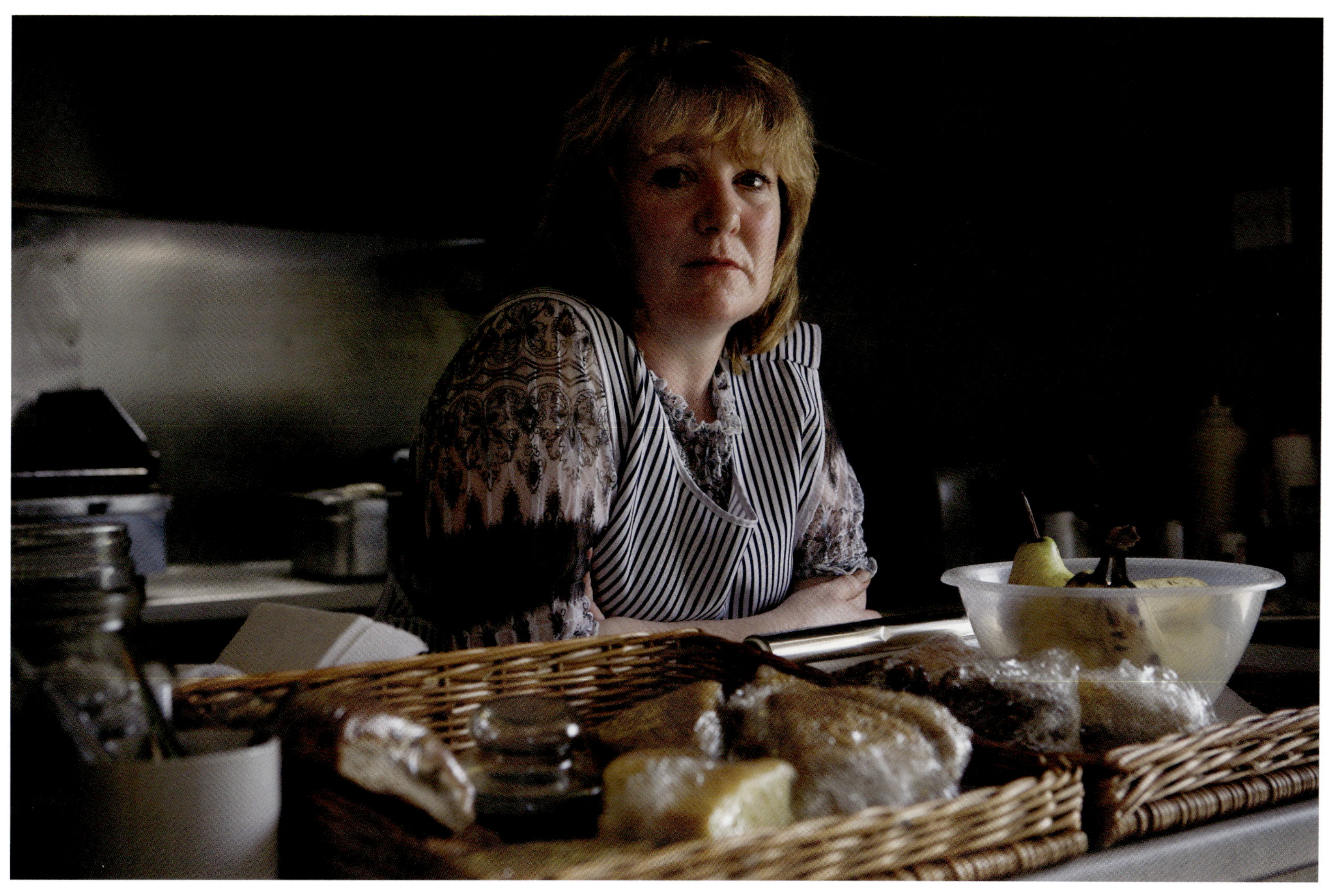

Above: Butty's Box Cafe – Shrewsbury – Shropshire – A5
Next: Belinda Kerruish with Vic Prossar and Ken Stutton – Little Britain Burger Van – Church Stretton – Shropshire – A49

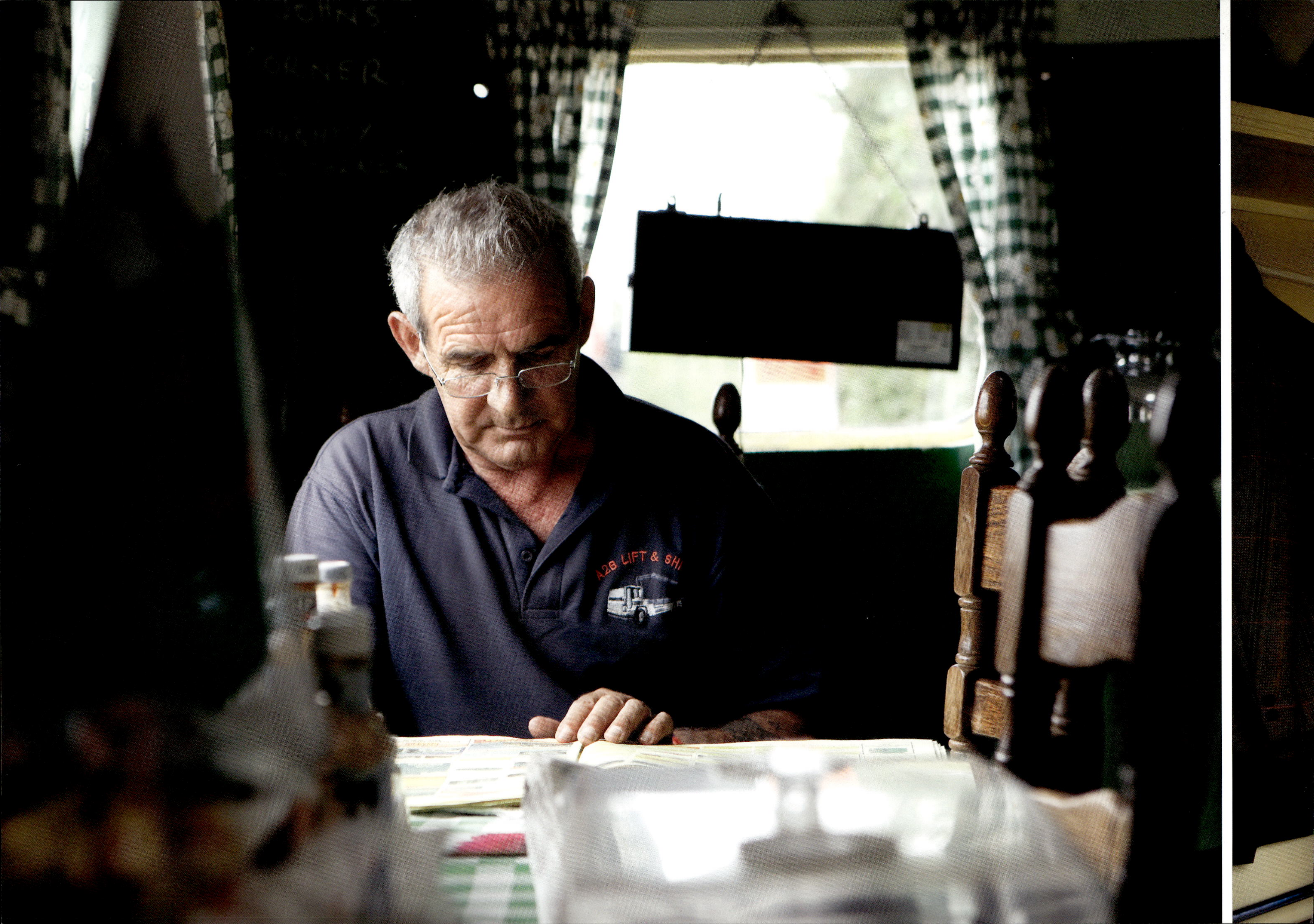

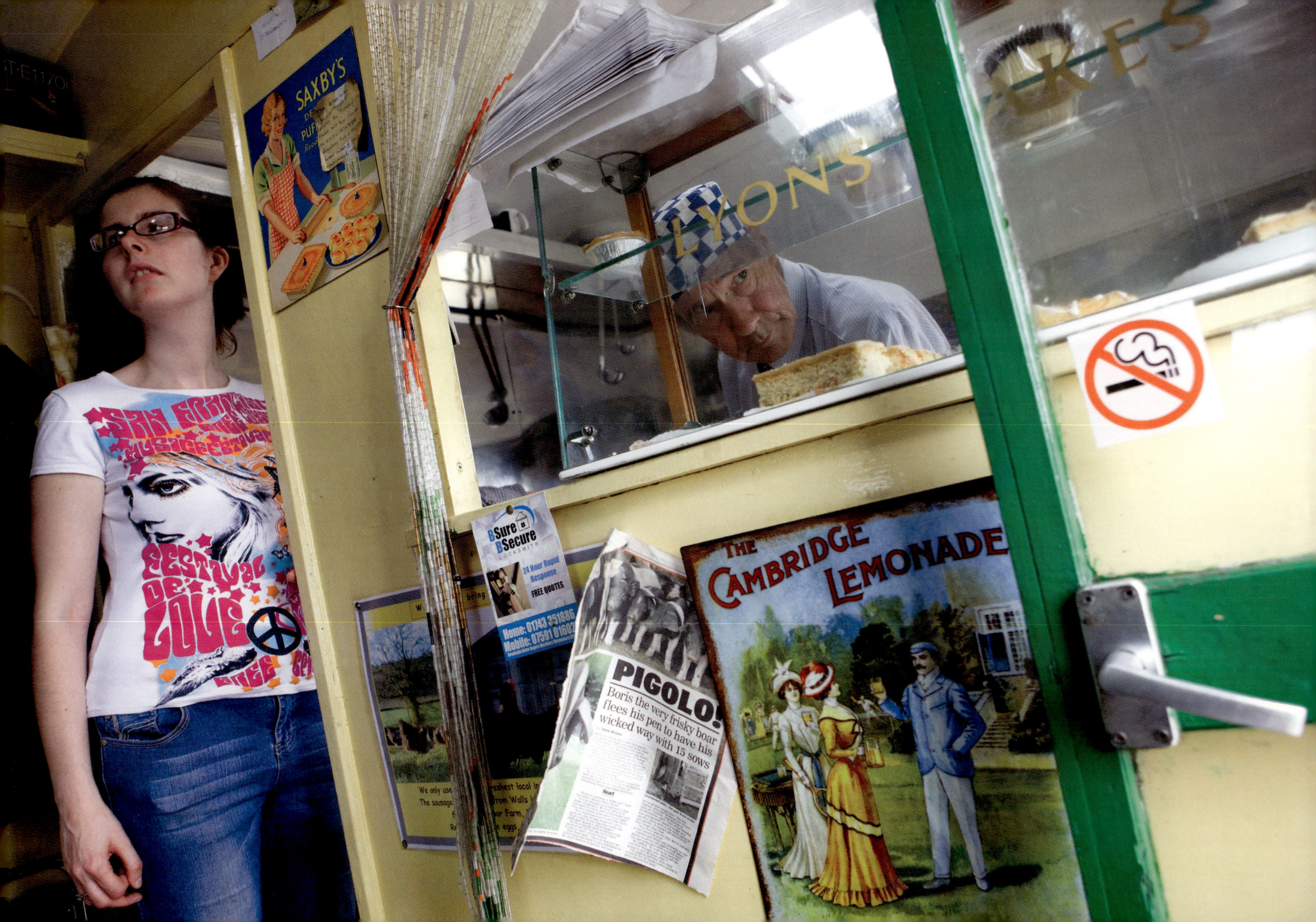
SAXBY'S
LYONS
AKES
BSure
BSecure
24 Hour Rapid Response
FREE QUOTES
Home: 07743 351886
Mobile: 07591 0160
THE CAMBRIDGE LEMONADE
PIGOLO!
Boris the very frisky boar
flees his pen to have his
wicked way with 15 sows

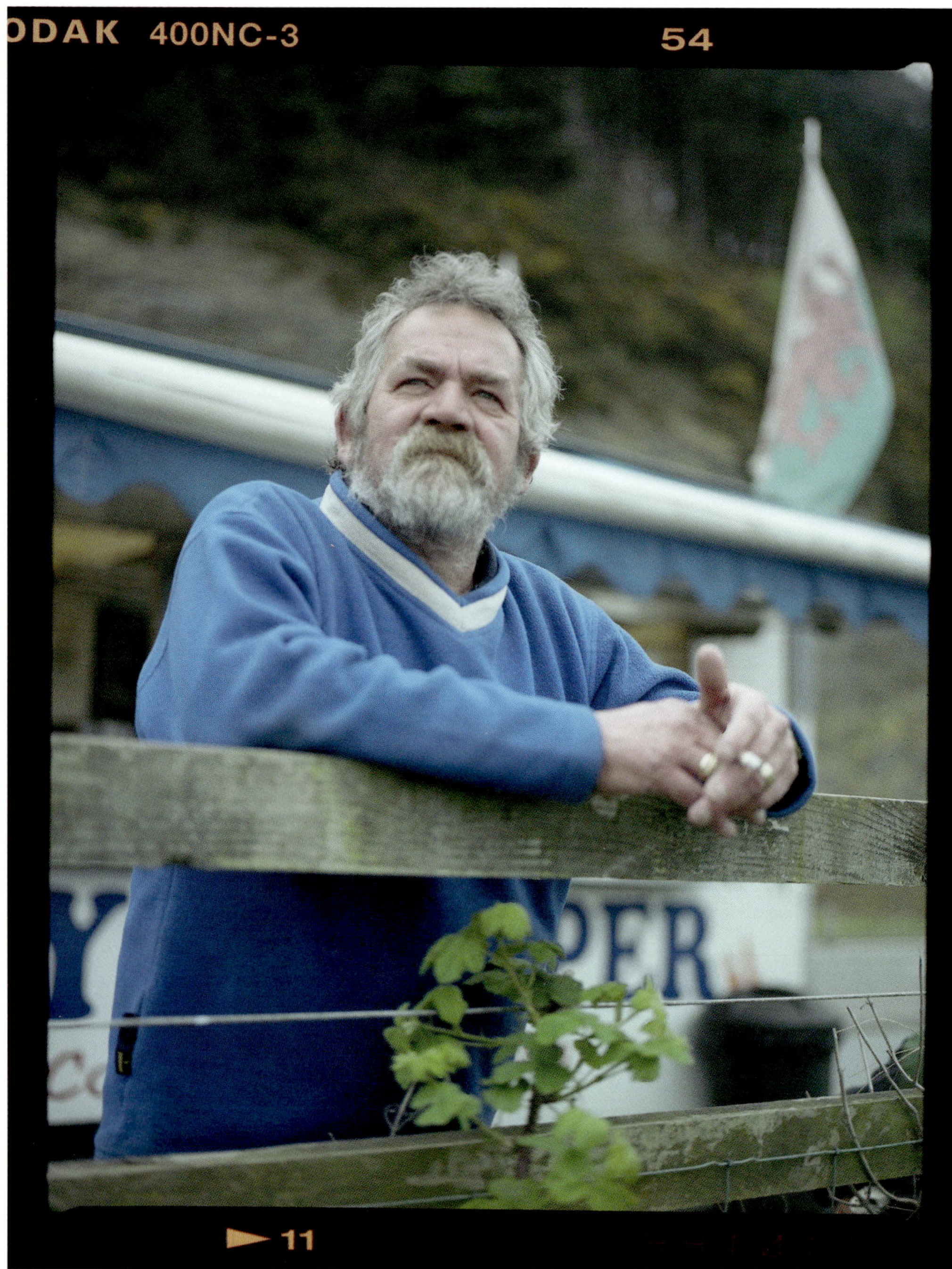
ODAK  400NC-3
54
11

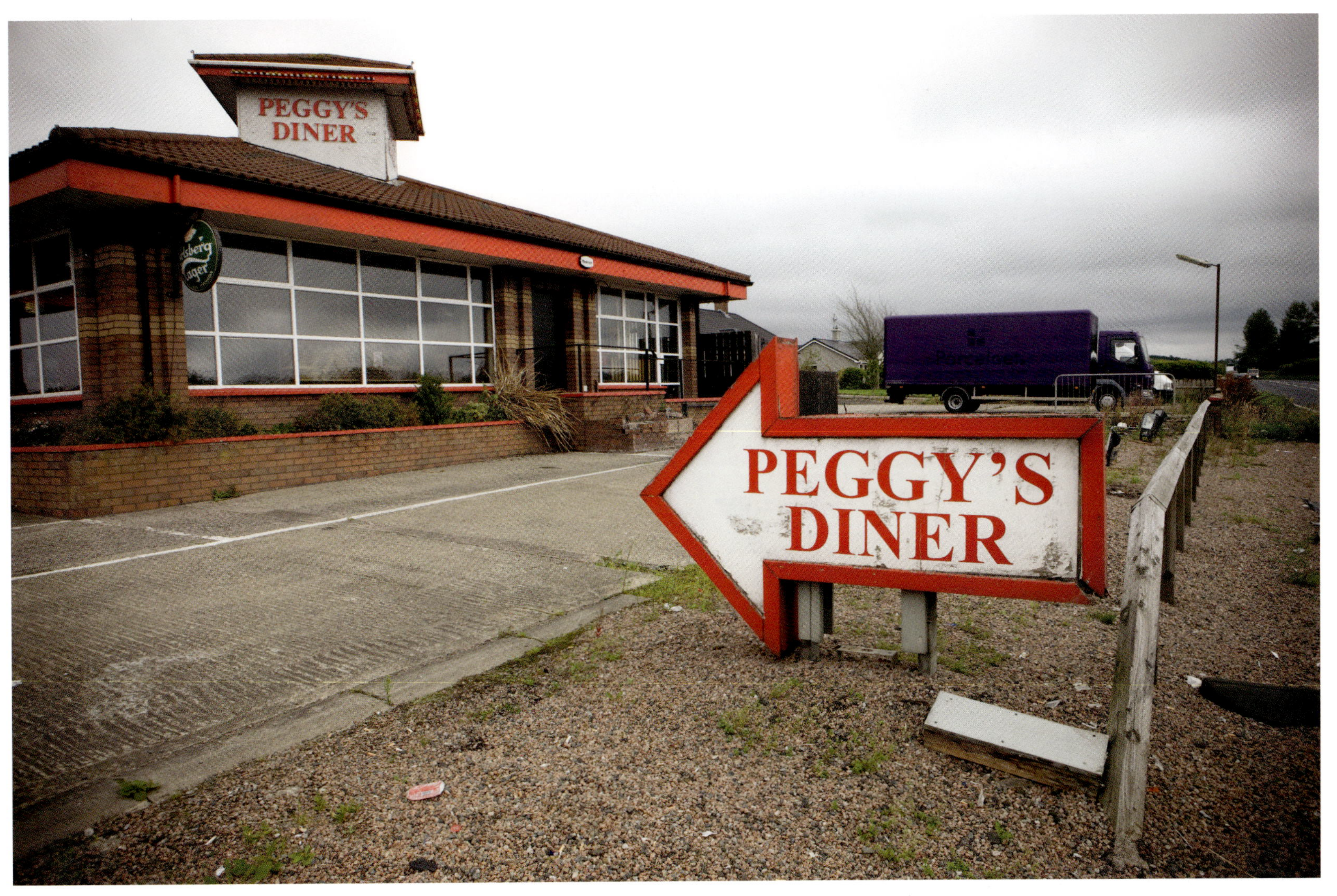

Above: Peggy's Diner – Toomebridge – Antrim – County Antrim – A5
Left: Chomper – The Happy Chomper – Aberarth – Ceredigion – A487

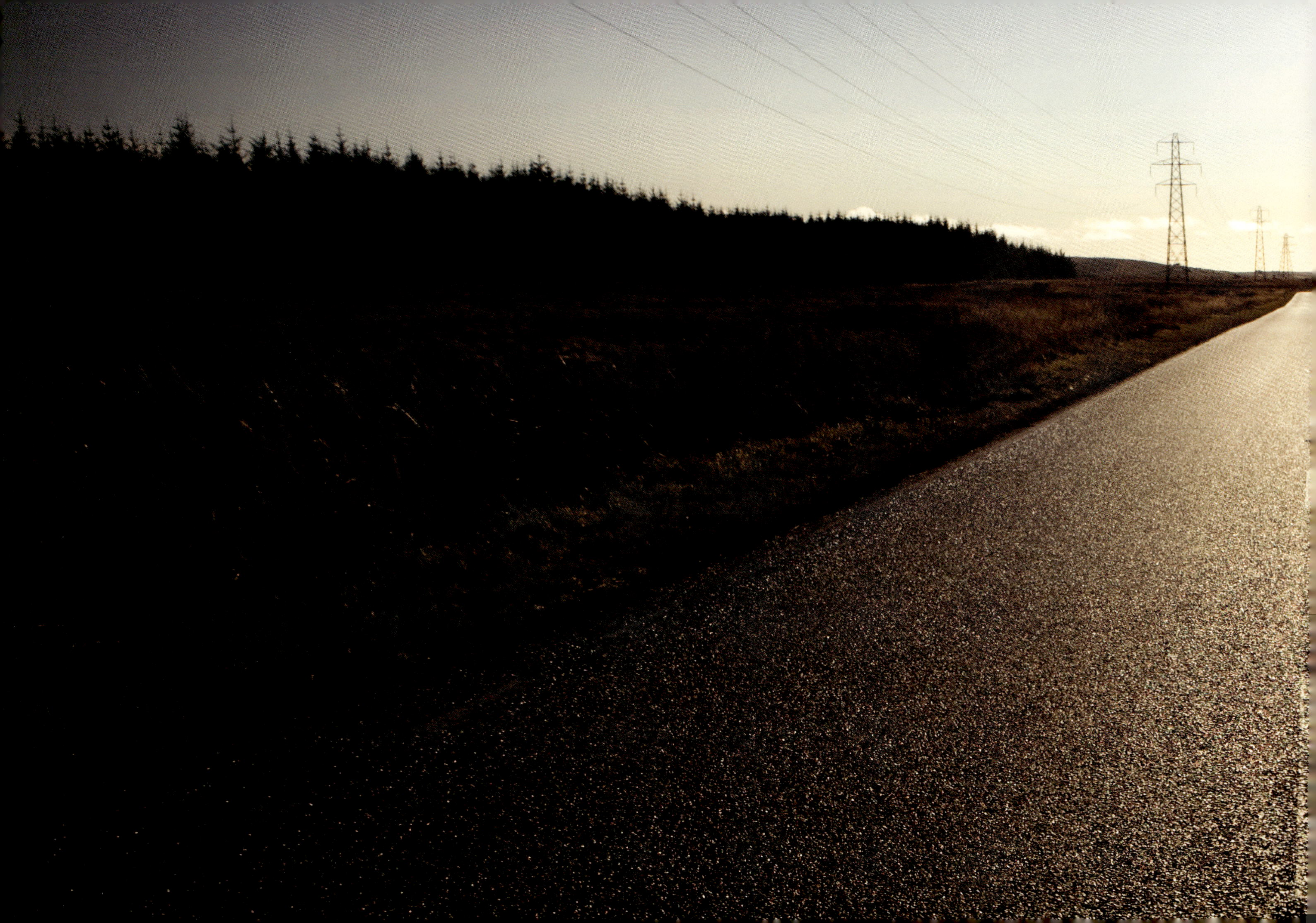

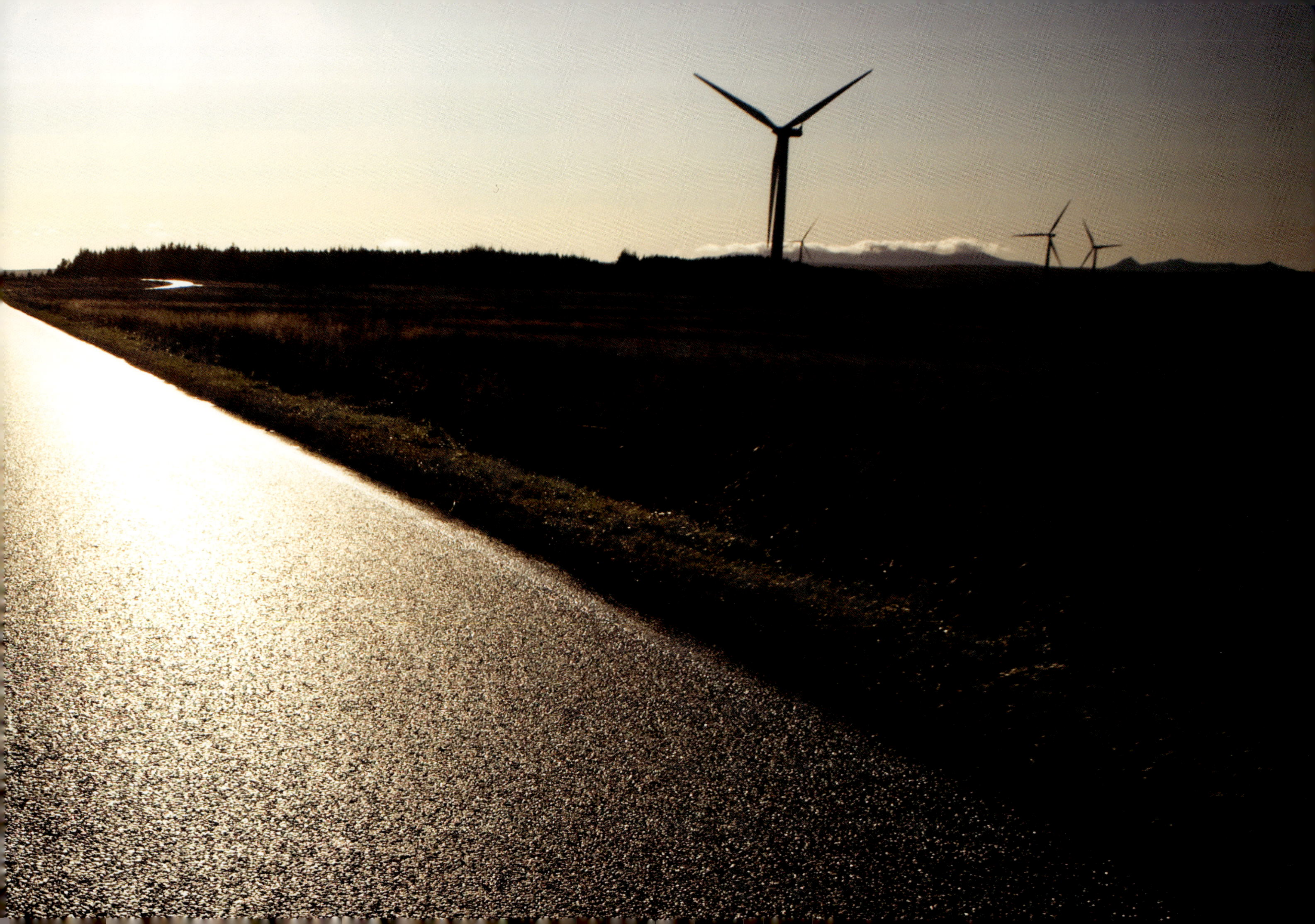

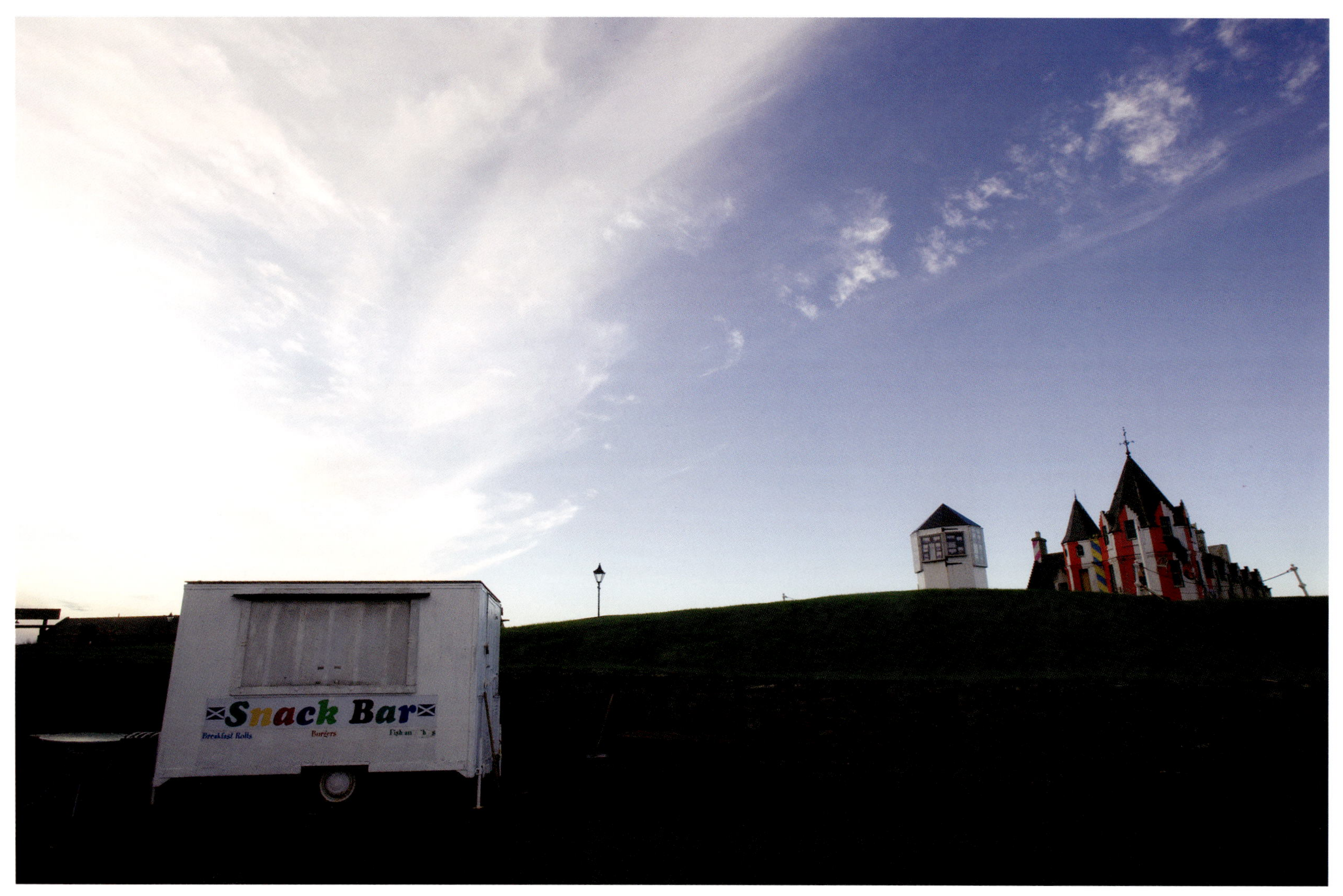

Above: Snack Bar – John o'Groats – Caithness – A9
Previous: Causeymire Wind Farm – Achkeepster – Highlands – A9

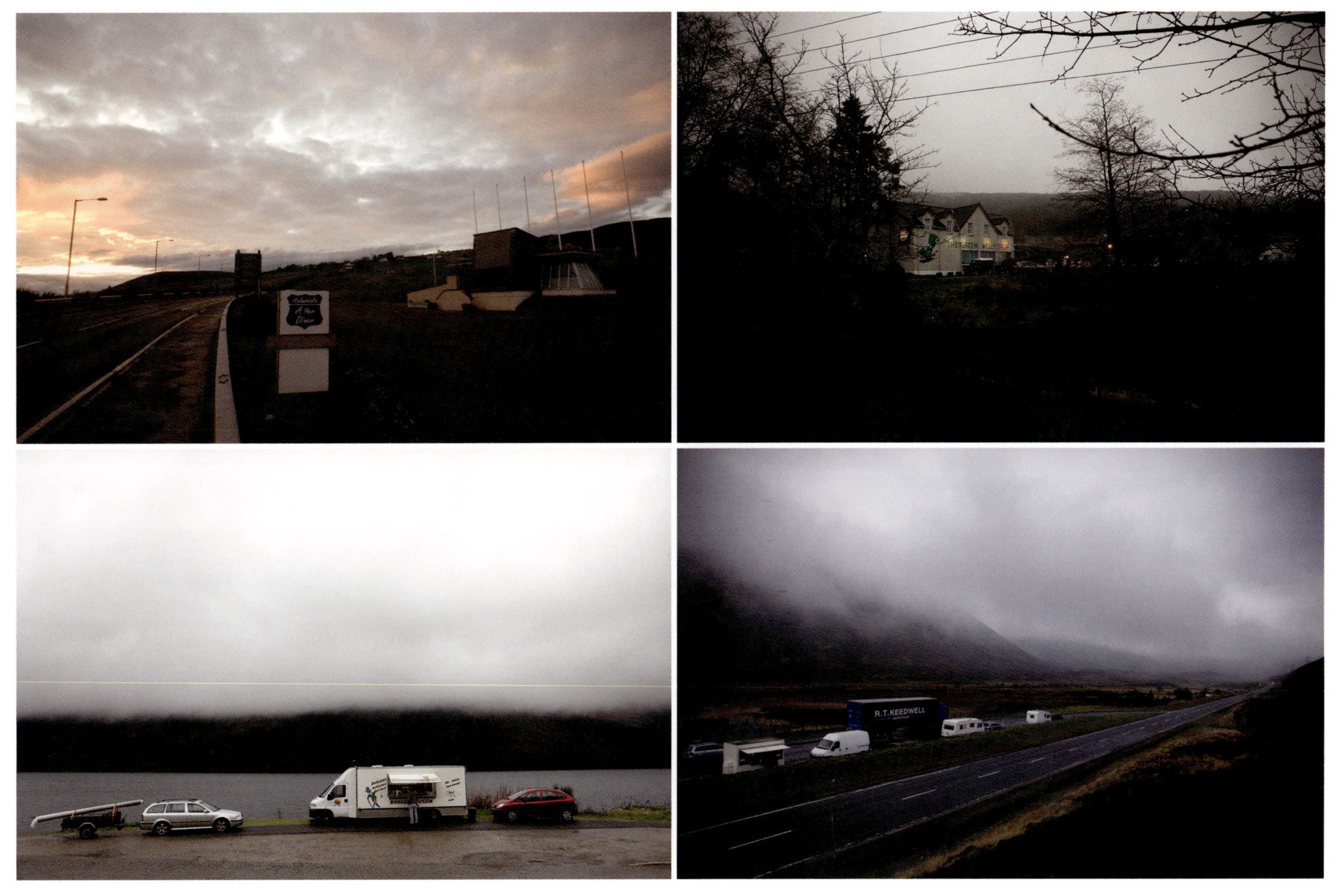

Above: On the Road in Scotland – The A9 & A82
Next: The Scottish Borders – A1

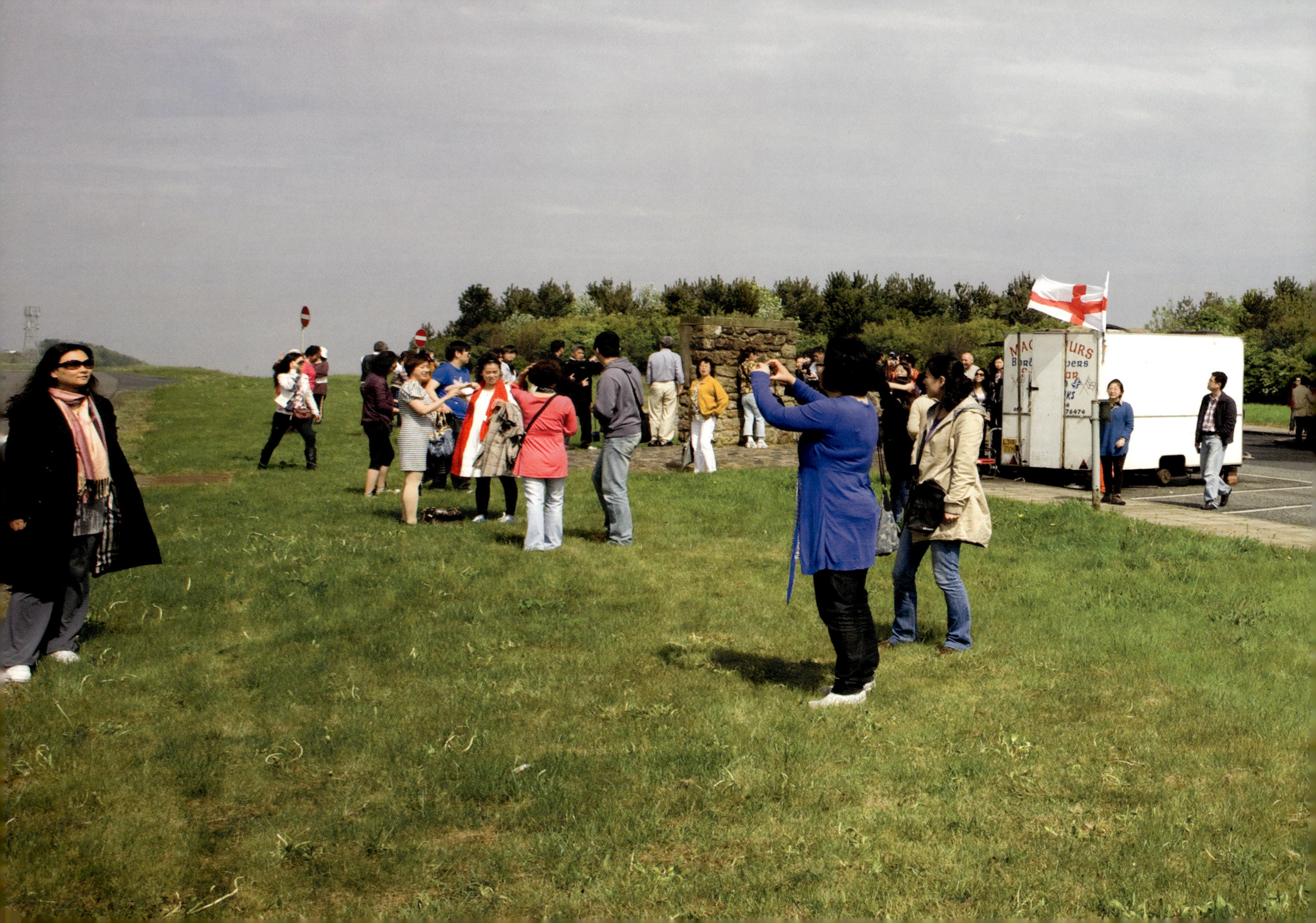

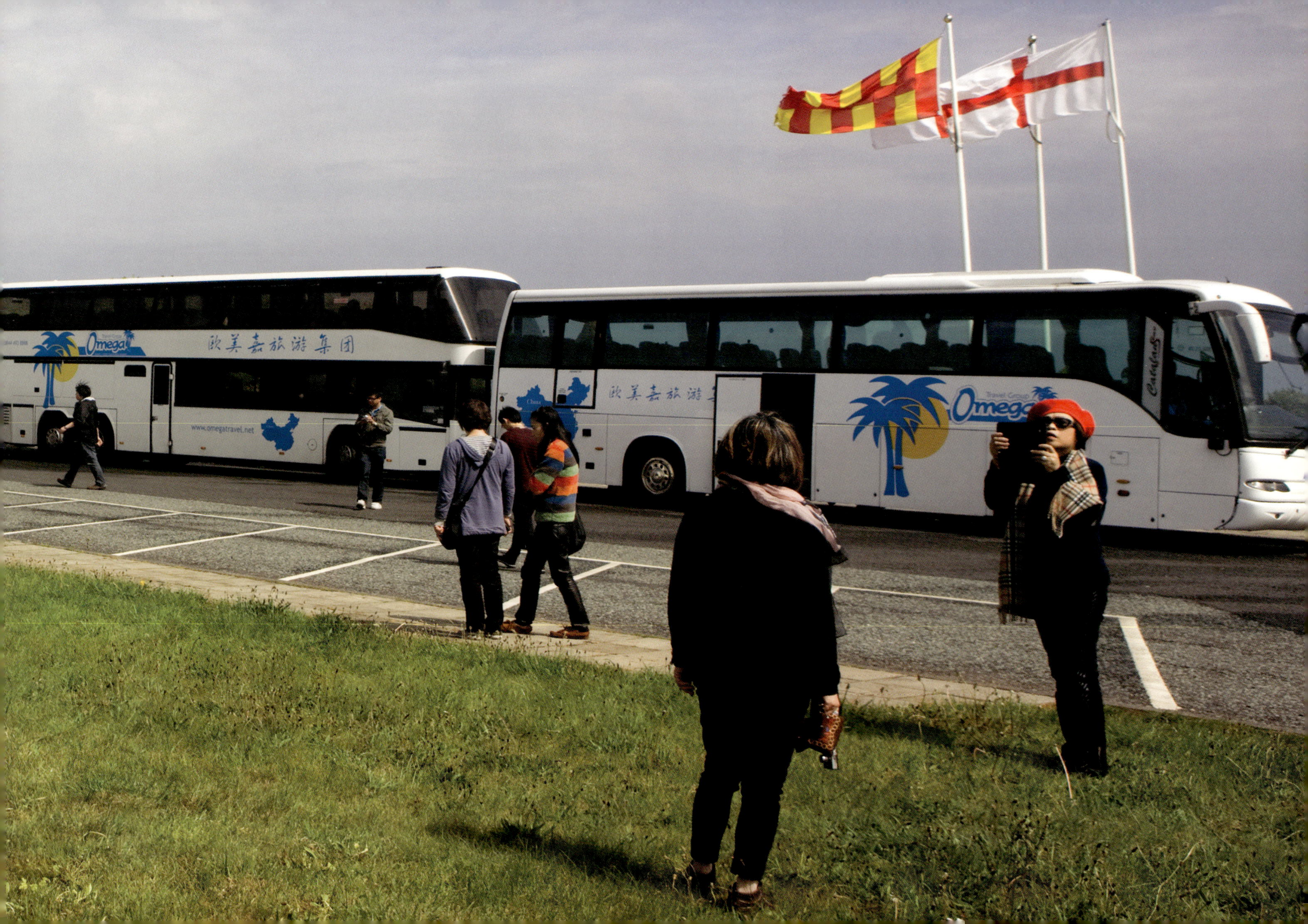

欧美嘉旅游集团
Omega
Travel Group
www.omegatravel.net
China

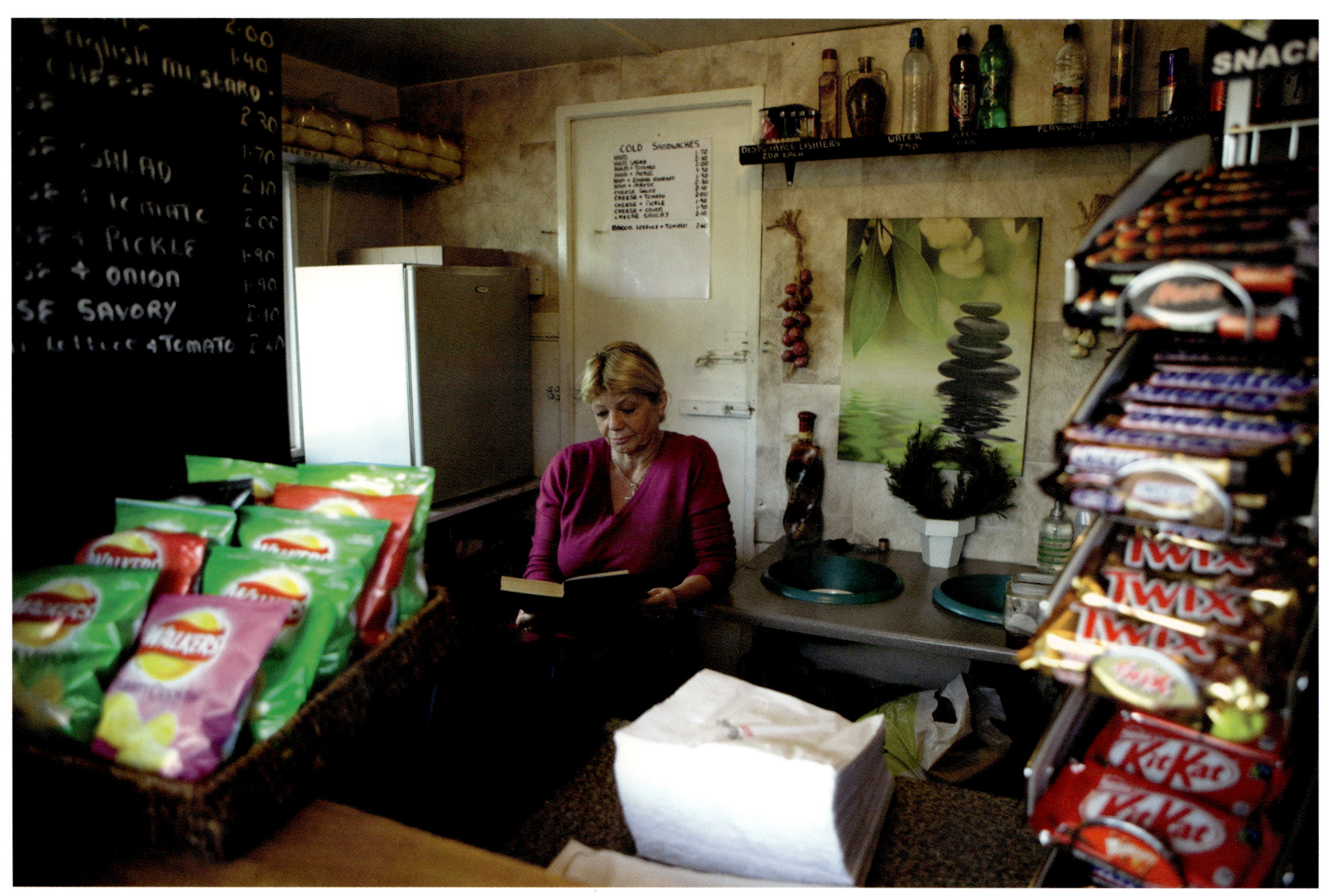



144    Kim – Kim's Burgers – Metro Centre – Gateshead – Northumberland – A1

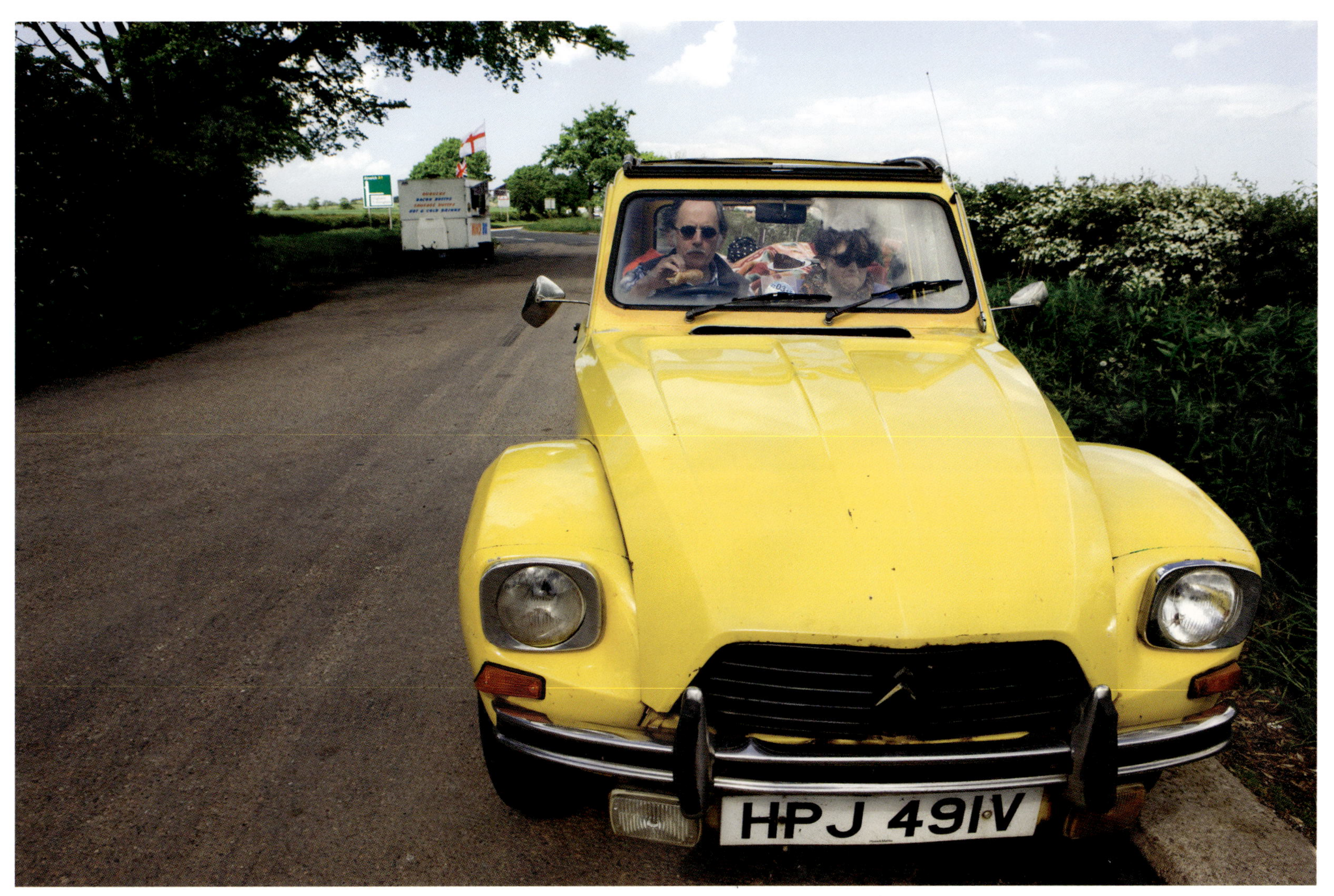



Ken & Elizabeth – Munch Box – Alnwick – Northumberland – A1

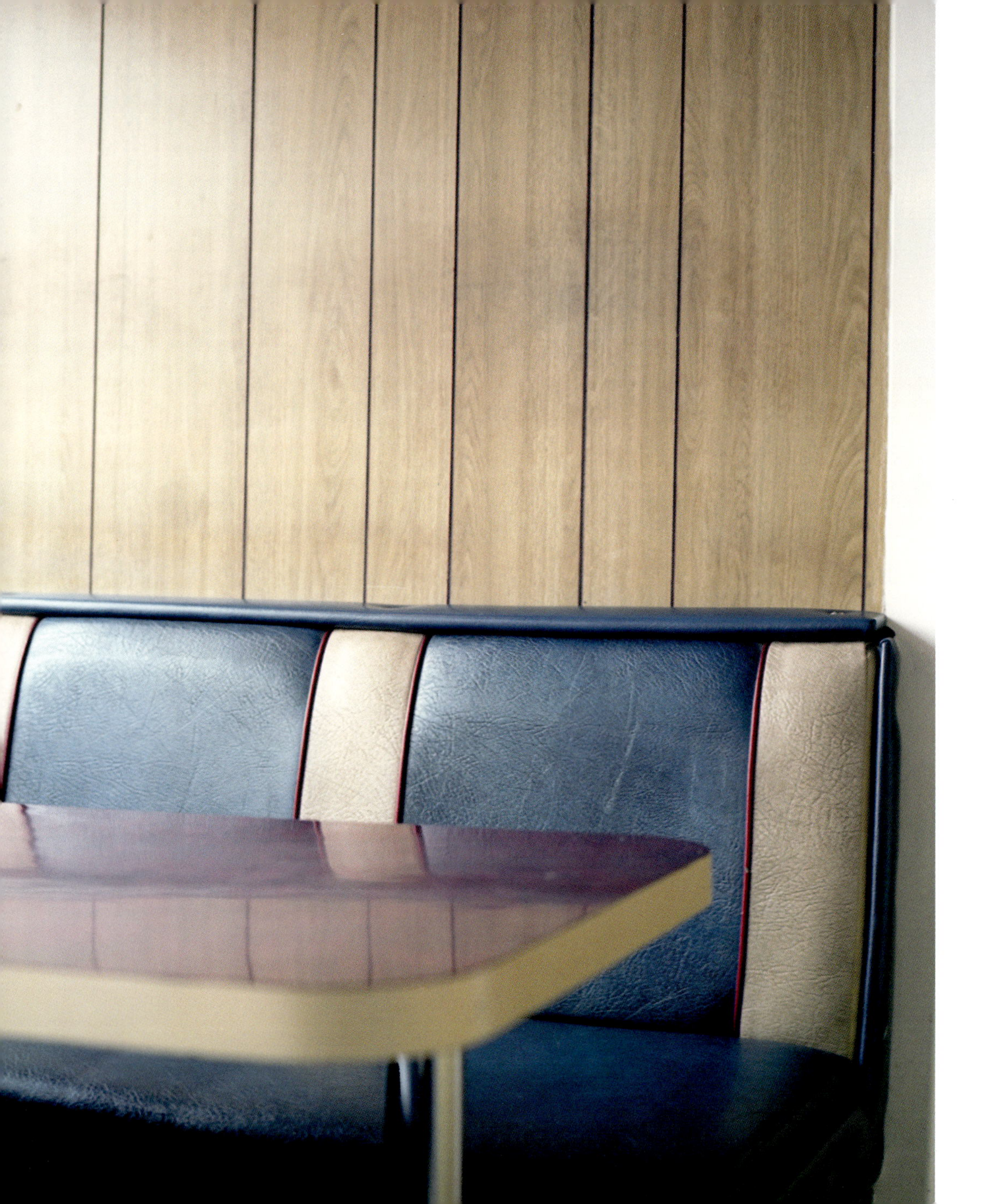

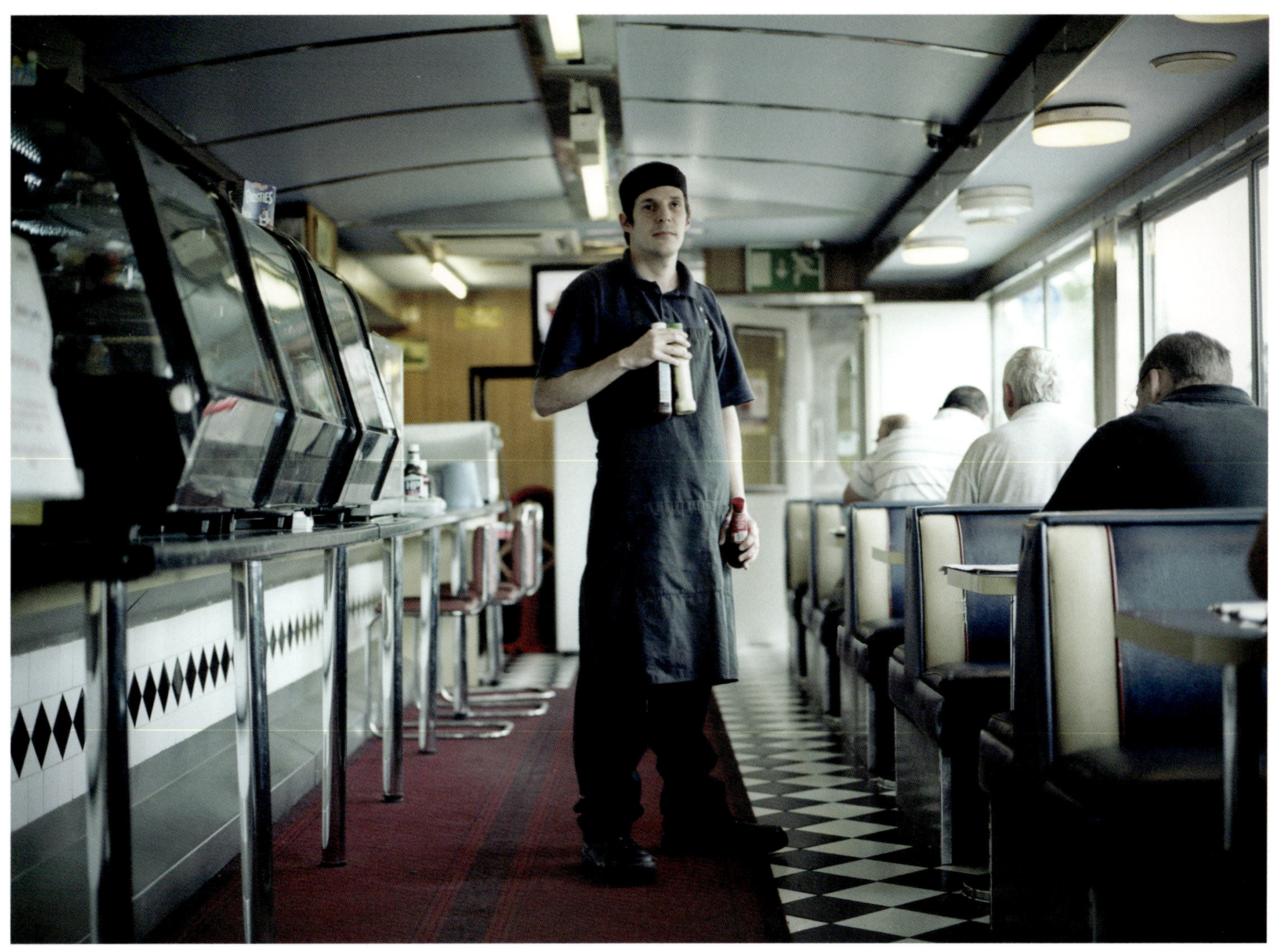

# The Romance of the Road

The romance of the open road is addictive. For me, the main draw is venturing into the unknown. The unexpected and sometimes bizarre situations I'd find myself in completely made the trips for me. Stories to tell once home, a yarn to spin over a pint.

Take, for example, my experience in a rather modest guesthouse, neatly situated next to a row of high street shops in a town which edges the A5. On arrival, one of the guests suggested I watch my belongings as the guy living in an adjacent room had a predisposition for crack and stealing. Looking back, I wonder how much truth was in his warning. At the time, with plenty of expensive equipment with me, naturally I hastily made my excuses and checked out.

Or, the hair raising, twilight camping encounter I had on what I thought was a dead end road in Anglesey, when a car skimmed past my tent, horn blaring. Shuddering my mock campsite with its passing air stream, it shocked the living daylights out of me, causing me to hastily break camp and pack up my belongings to seek a safer location, finding refuge in a nearby lay-by. Waking a few hours later, I was compensated by the most glorious views of the Britannia Bridge, Bangor; mist in the valley, sun creeping over the horizon.

Take also the over zealous Irish Traffic Officer who gleefully fined me after I'd been trailing behind a convoy of impatient drivers for what seemed like ages. Leading the cohort were an old couple bumbling along in their beat up Metro. As the rest of the clan calmly overtook the haste-free couple on an unbroken white line, I followed suit and was left 'taking one' for the anonymous team. I was handed an 80 Euro fine accompanied with a wry smile.

There was also the odd hitchhiker who got aggravated because I stopped before they wanted to; the random places I pitched a tent and the cold nights sleeping in the back of my car, with thermals and sleeping bag to warm me from the chill. I'd often wonder how Paul Graham completed his project; did he too turn his road trip into an impromptu adventure and make his home wherever he laid his hat?

Throughout the course of creating this work, I found the prospect of going into business on the roadside a daunting thought. It's ruthless. With the rise of high-street brands proliferating in the trunk road petrol stations from their motorway service station strongholds, it's becoming even harder for the independent traders to break even. One bitterly cold morning in a lay-by on the A140, the grumpy sexagenarian owner of a rather gritty run down burger van (who had previously denied me the opportunity to take photos), spilled out his heart as another brighter, bigger, and quite obviously better burger van pulled up on his patch, a lay-by of no more than 200 metres in length. It was heartbreaking.

It just goes to prove how transient roadside trade is; by its very nature, it flows and is often uncertain. By the same token, you never know who you'll meet. The roadside caff or burger van welcomes anyone who passes by, and the people who make their livelihoods are similarly disparate. Since time immemorial, travellers of all kinds have relied on the hospitality of the coach-houses, inns and public houses along their route. My sincere hope is that this trade can continue in the same entrepreneurial spirit.

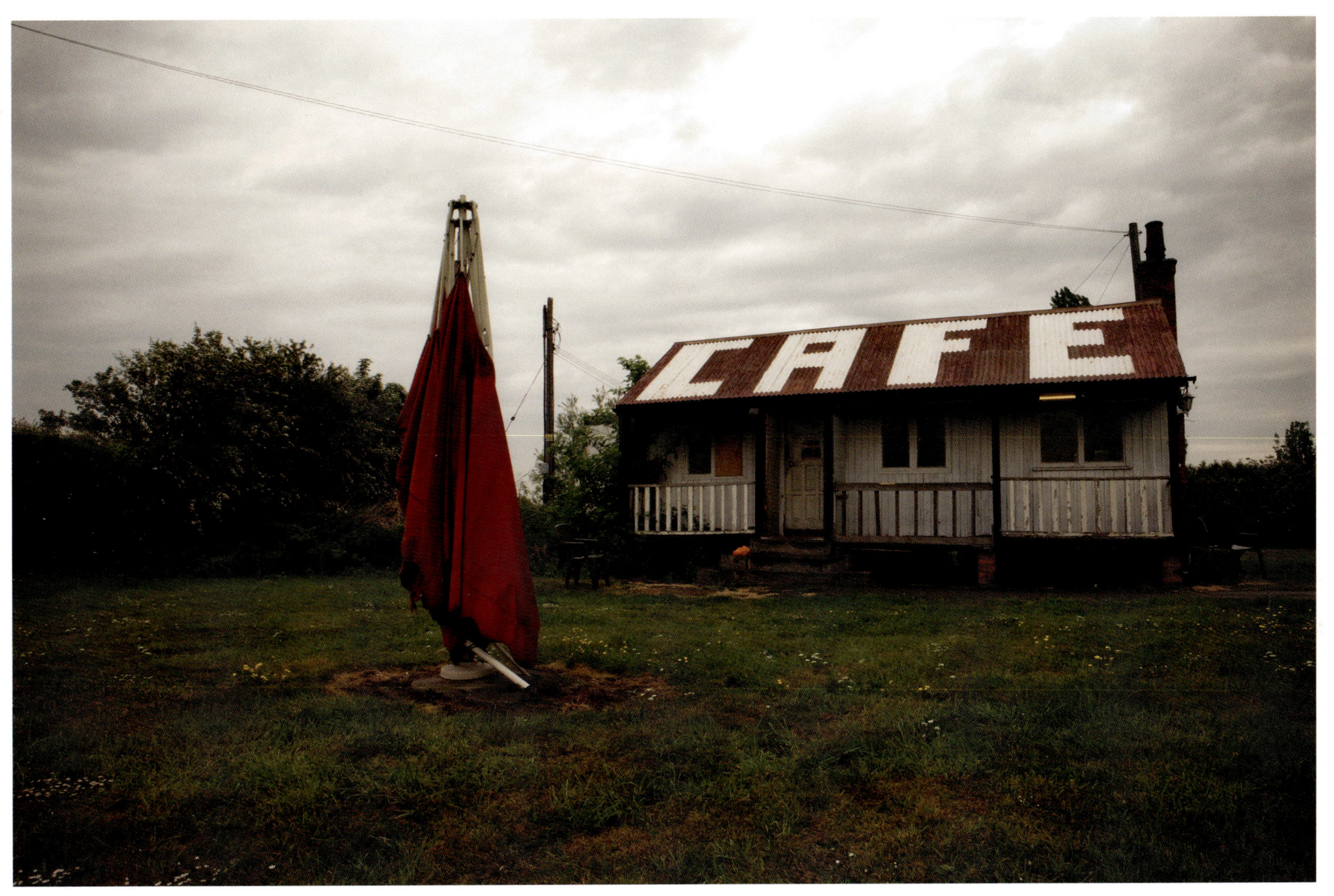


Cromwell Holt – Cromwell – Nottinghamshire – A1

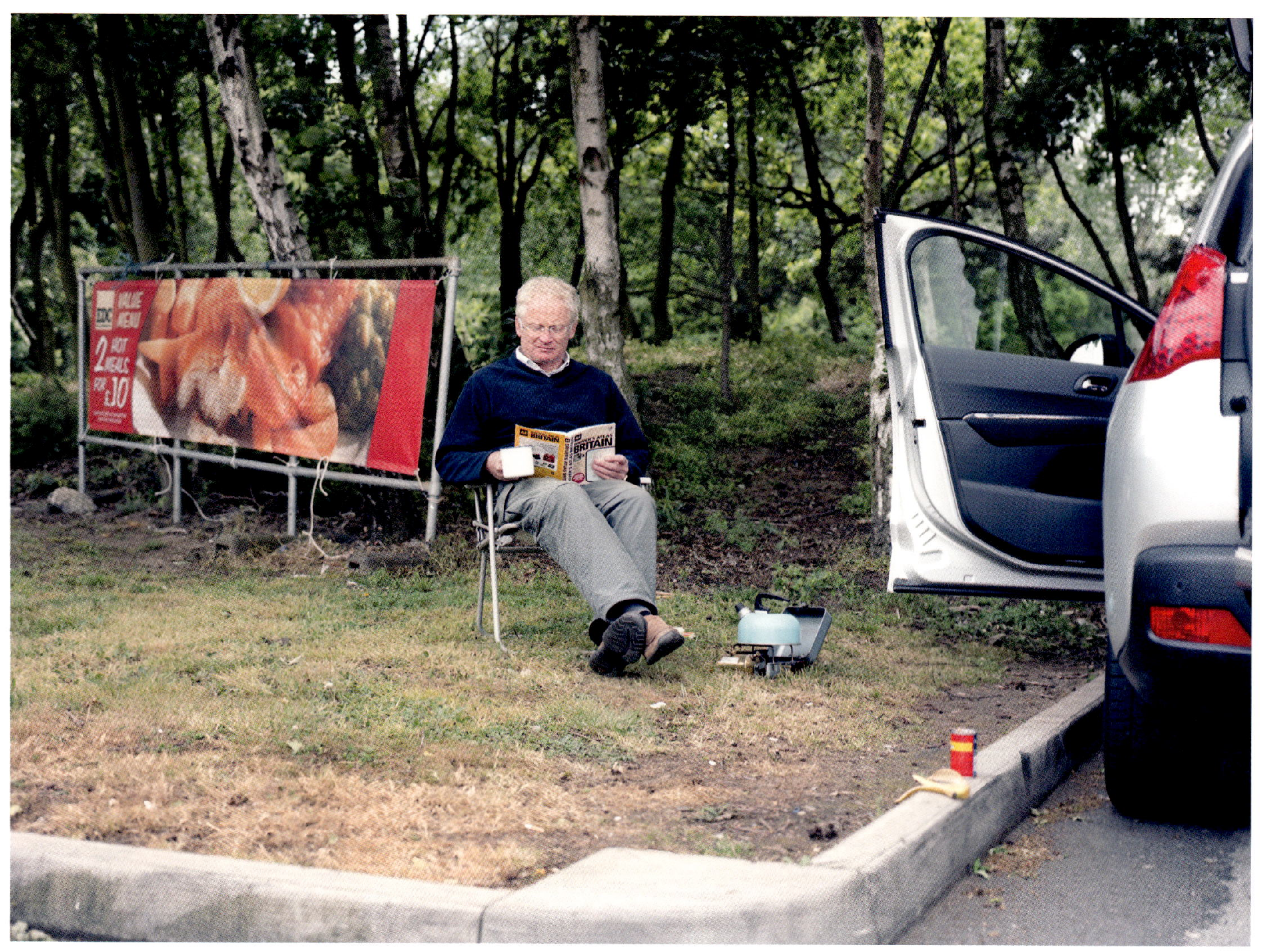


 Bob Hunt – Blyth Services – Blyth – Nottinghamshire – A1

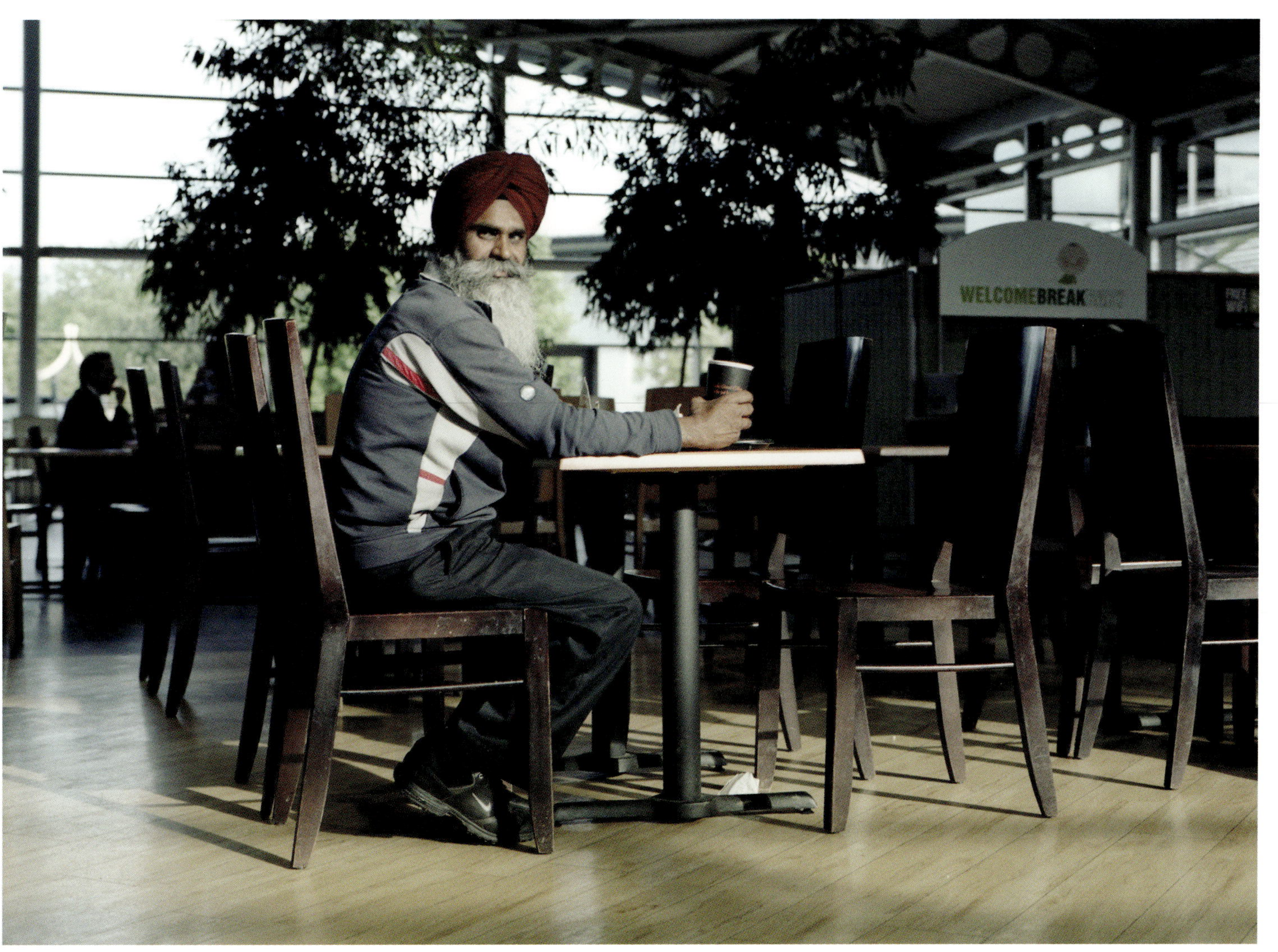

Sidu – Indian Truck Driver – South Mimms Services – Hertfordshire – A1(M)    151

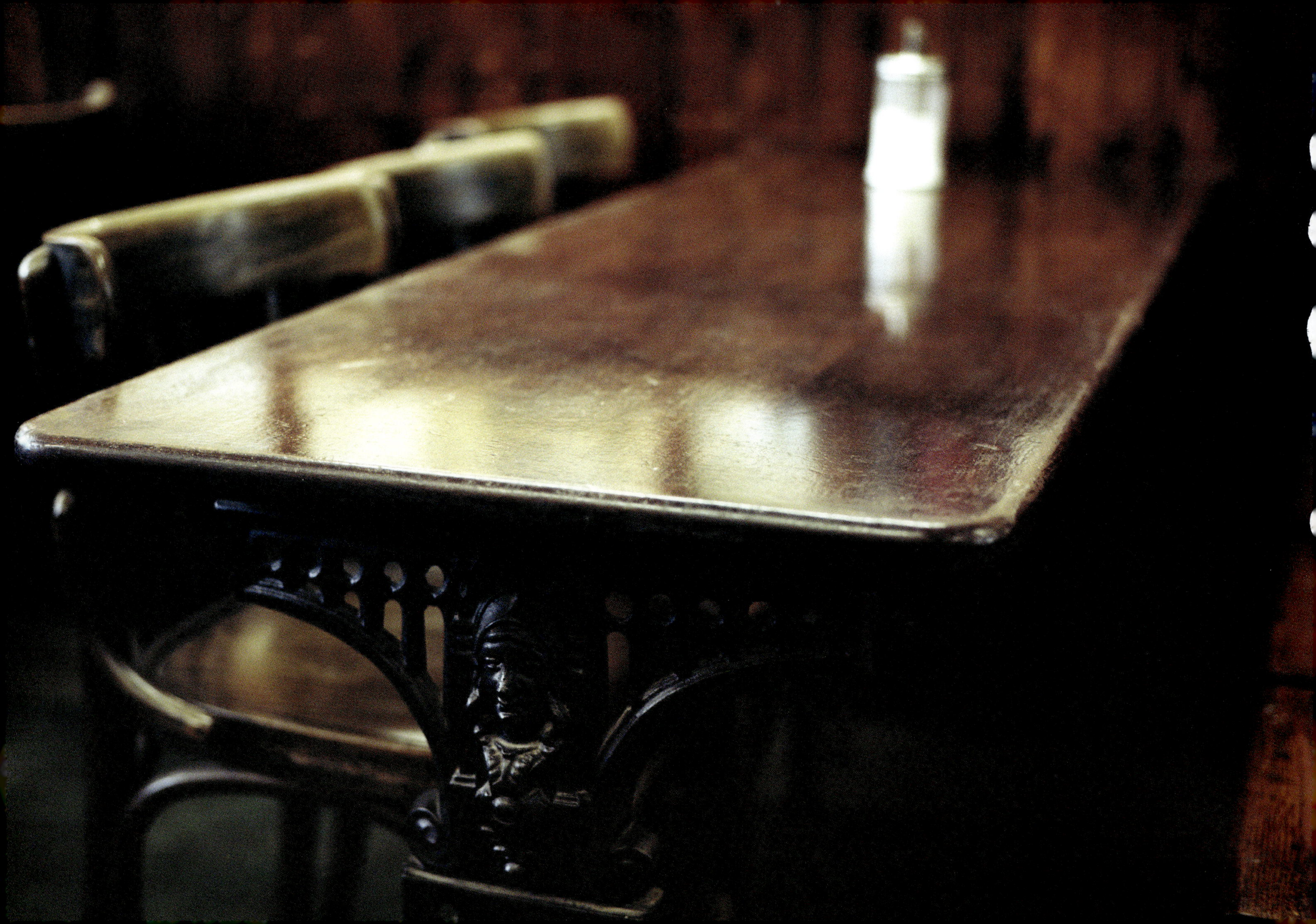

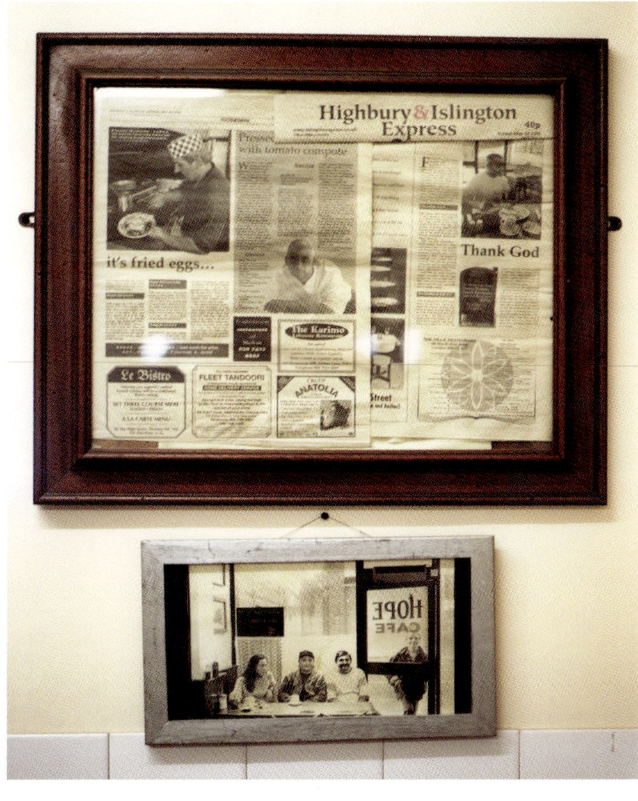

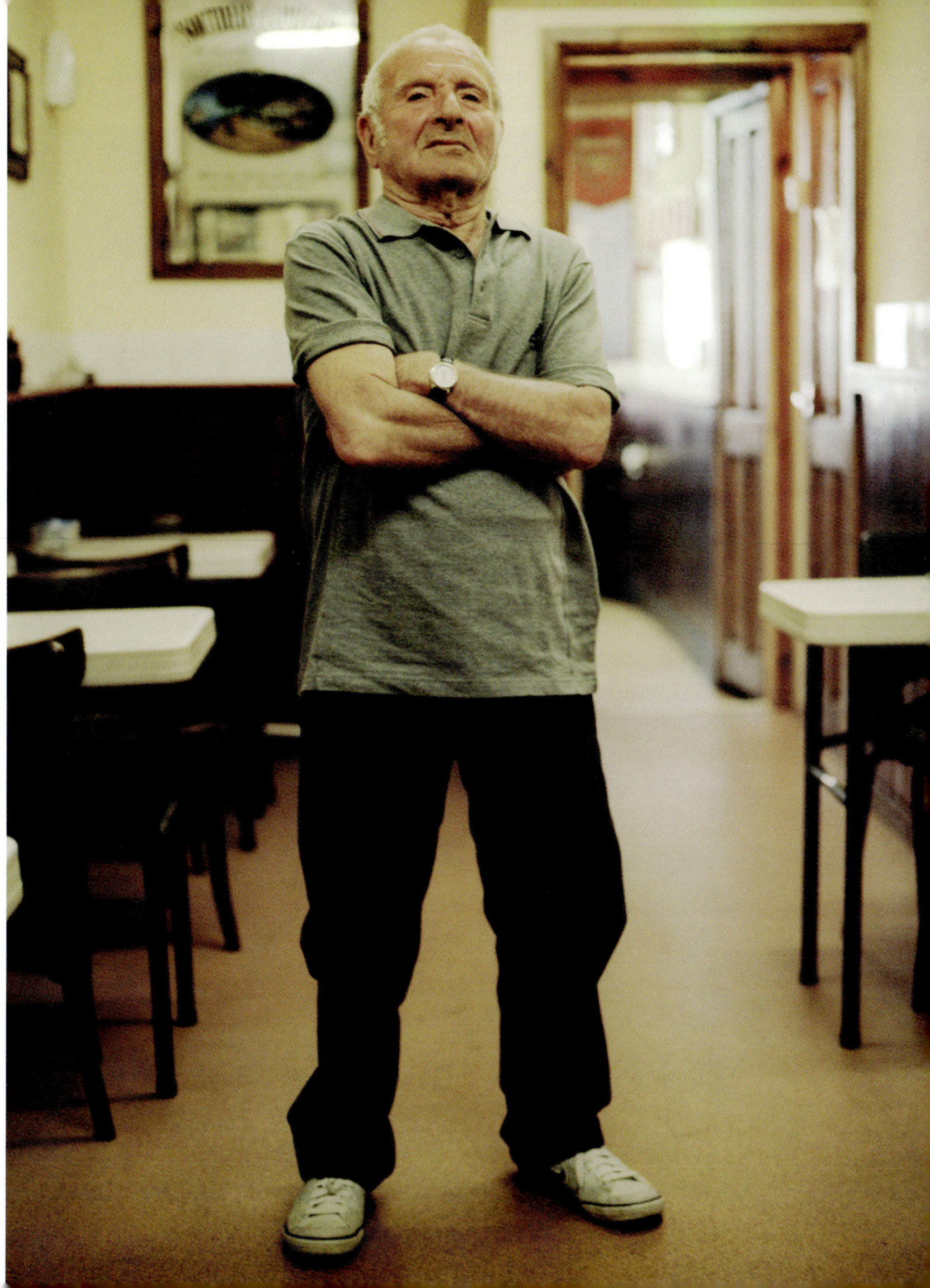

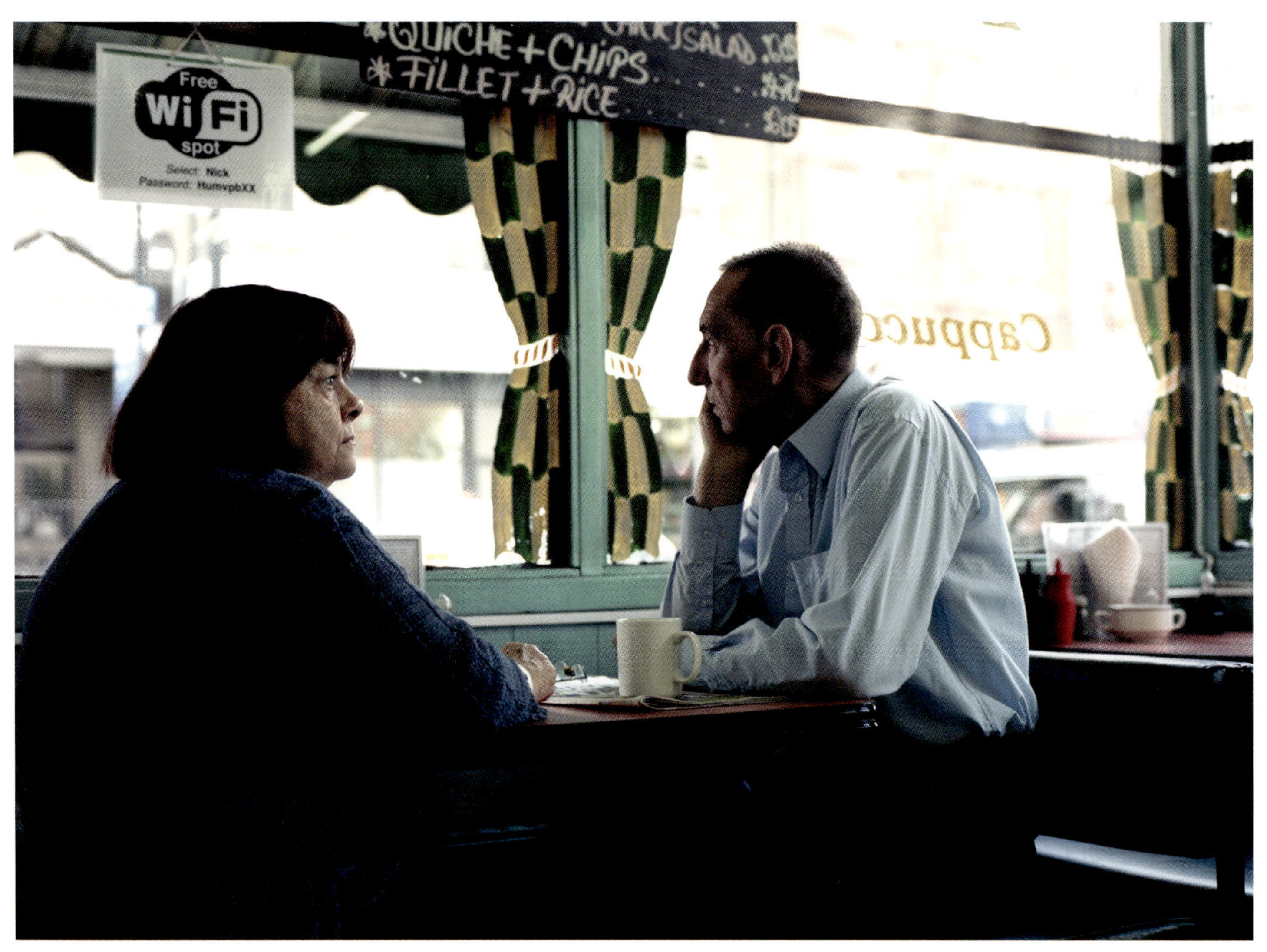


Above: The Shepherdess – City Road – City of London – Just off the A1
Previous: (George) The Hope For Workers Cafe – Holloway Road – London – A1

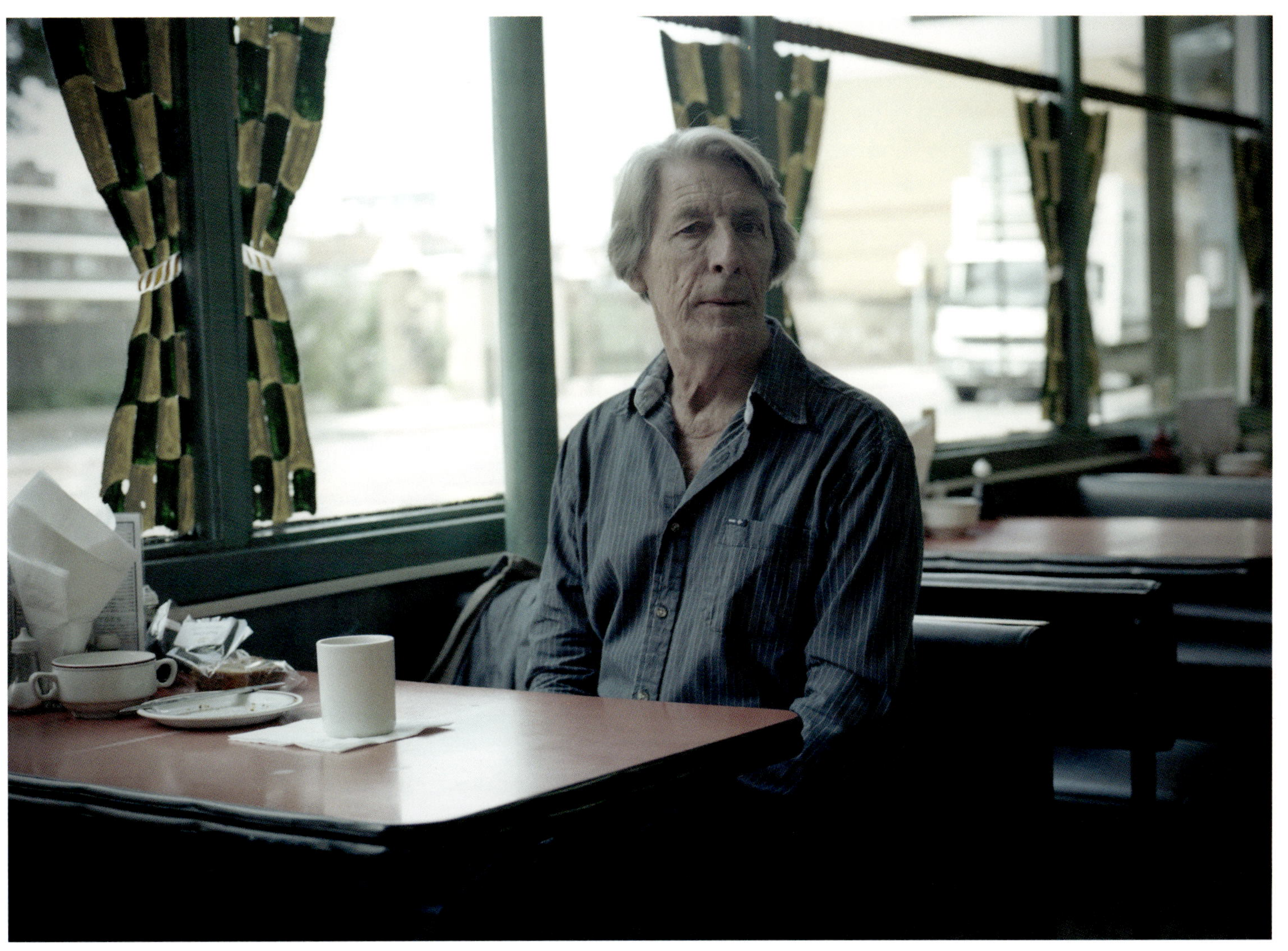

The Shepherdess – City Road – City of London – Just off the A1          155

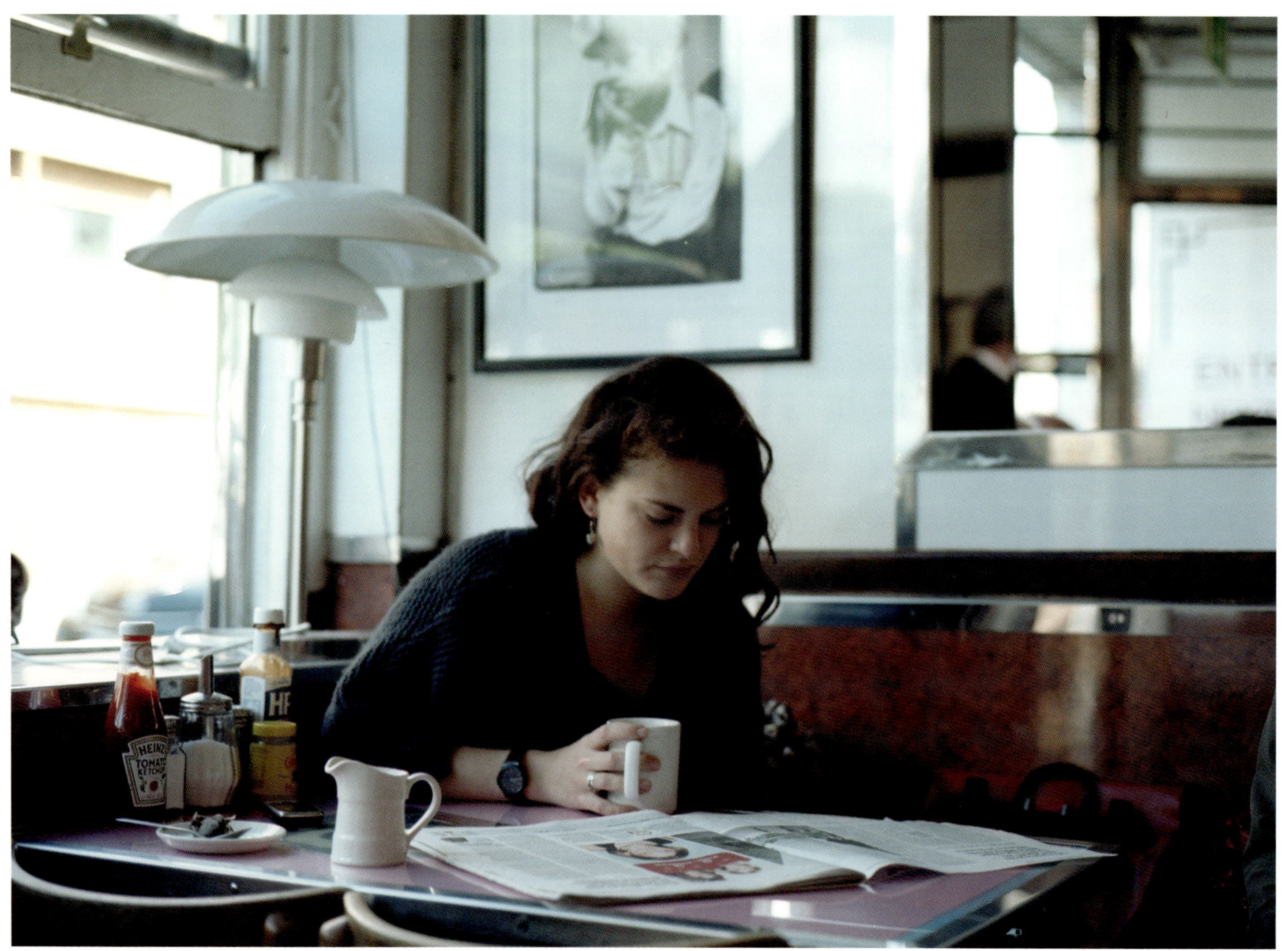

 Sausage and Mash – Essex Road – London – Just of the A1

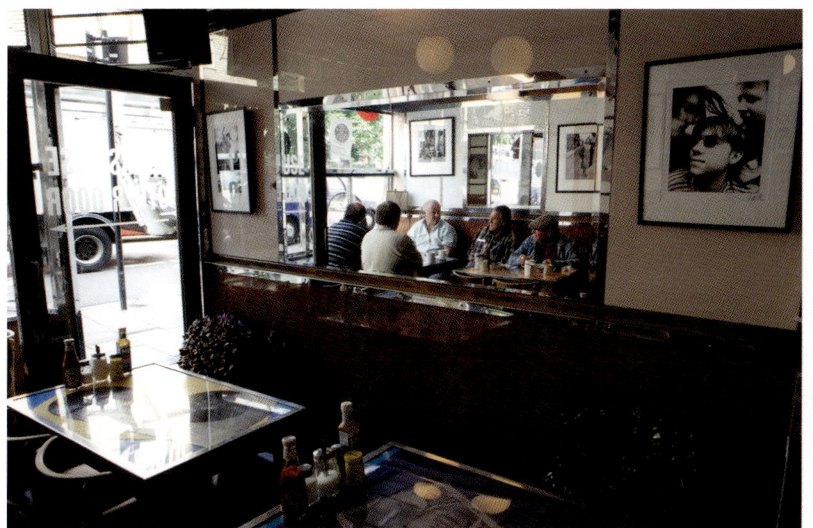
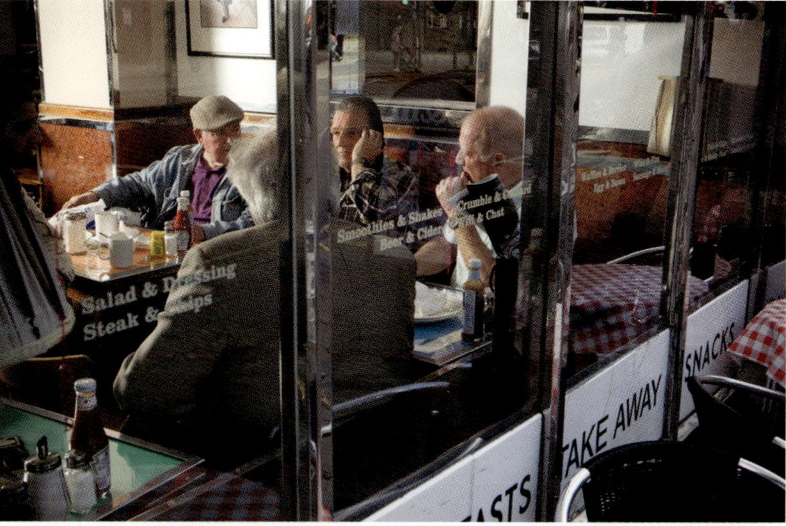
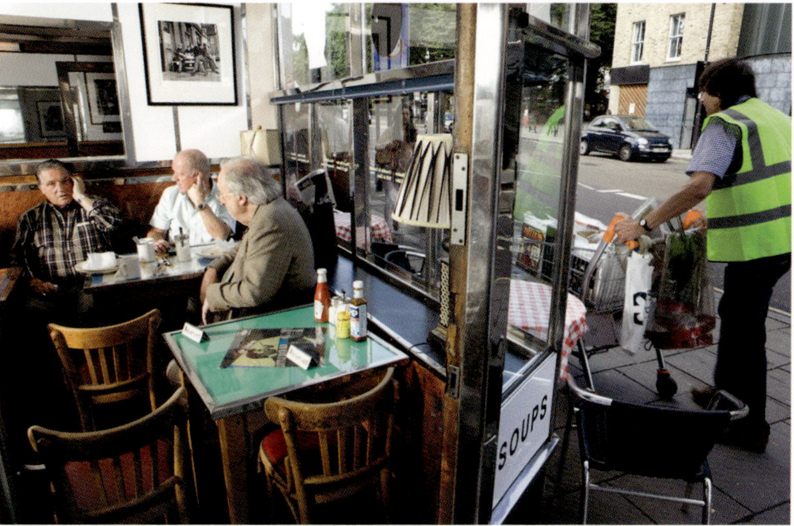
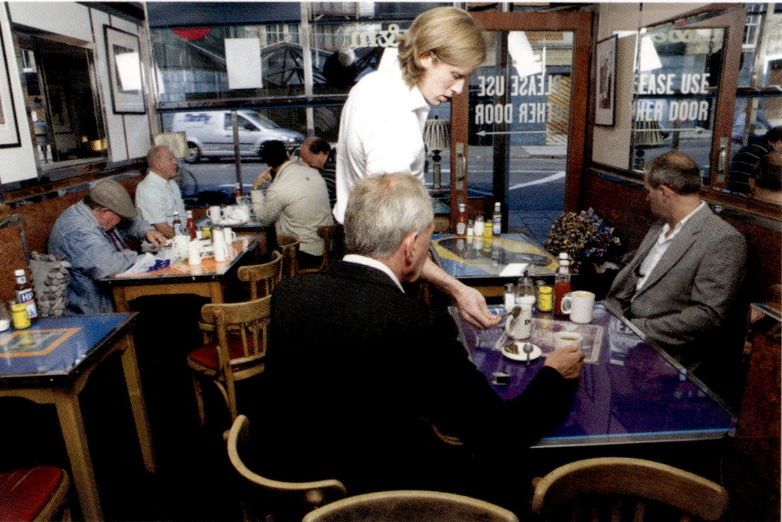

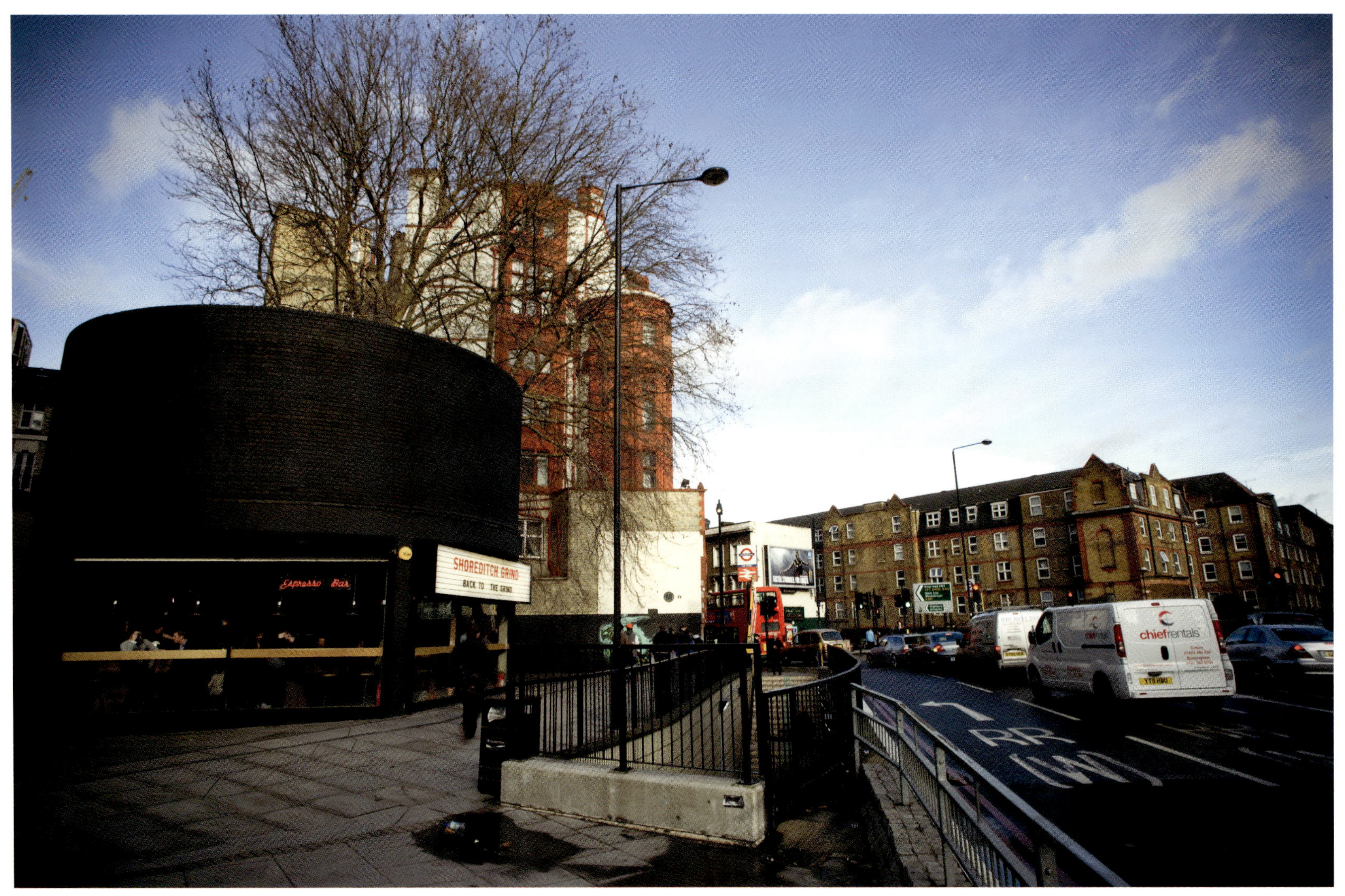

158    Shoreditch Grind – Old Street – London – A501

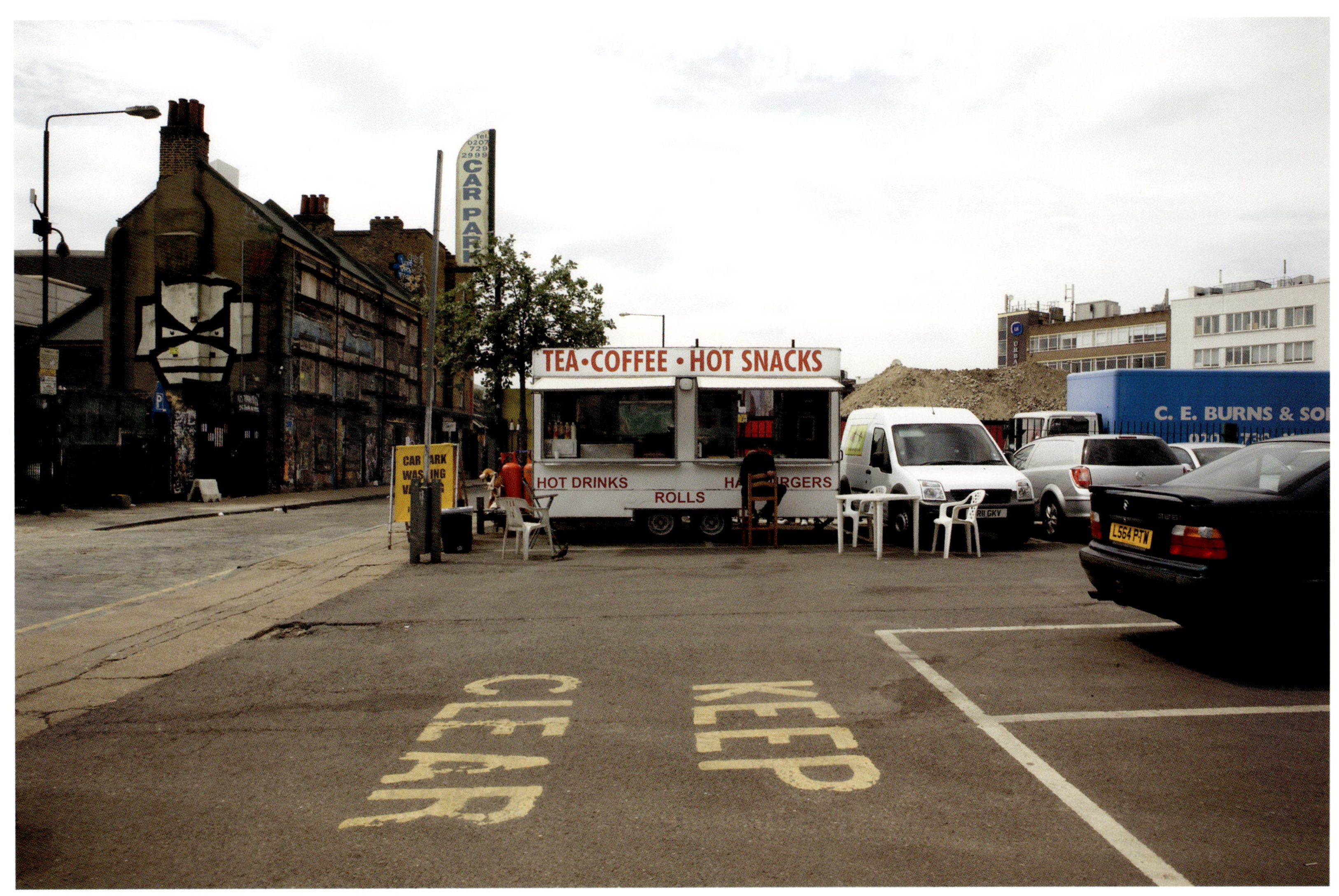


Hot Snacks – Brick Lane – London – A10

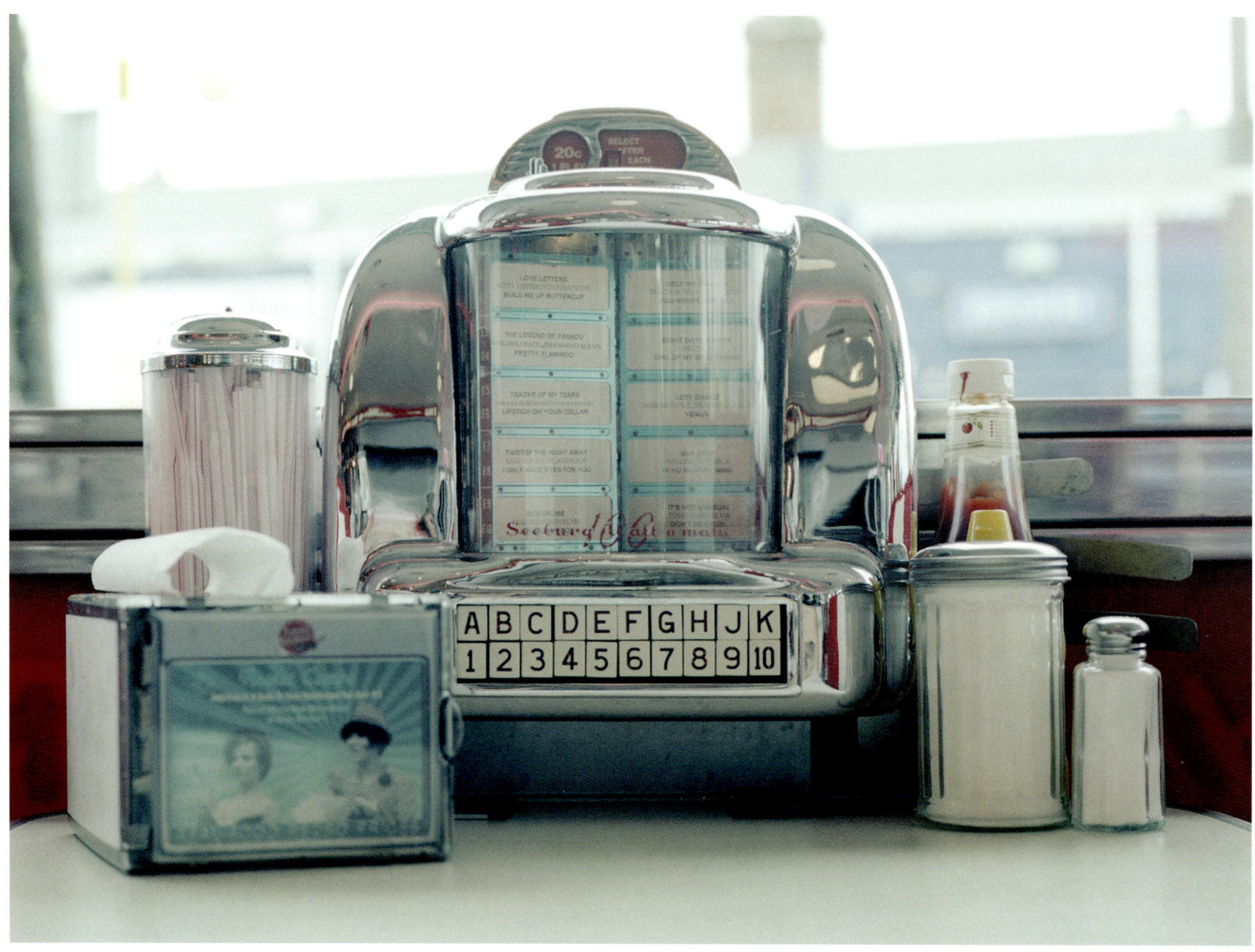

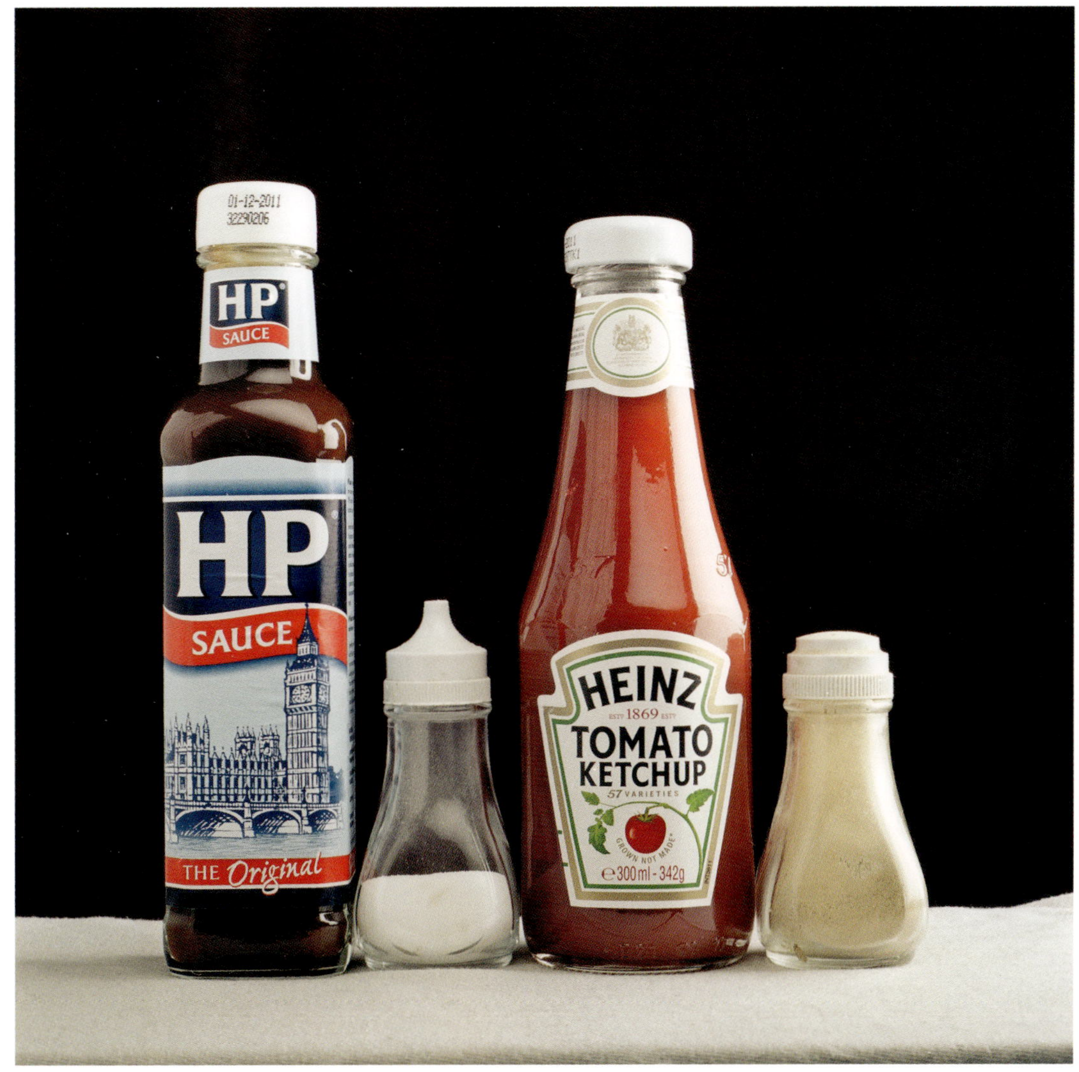
01-12-2011
32290206
HP
SAUCE
HP
SAUCE
THE Original
HEINZ
ESTD 1869 RSTD
TOMATO
KETCHUP
57 VARIETIES
GROWN NOT MADE
℮300ml - 342g

# Map & Cover Inspiration

The three roadside maps featured throughout this book and on the opposite page were inspired during the course of this project by Harry Beck's 1931 iconic underground map, designed during Beck's time working as an engineering draftsman at the London Underground Signals Office. This 'uncommissioned spare-time project' was cutting edge but was initially viewed with scepticism by those at the London Underground, although after a tentative public introduction in the form of a small pamphlet in 1933, it became instantly popular and his topological illustrations have been used ever since.  The first map, featured on page 48, was first created as a source of guidance for those visiting the Babylon Gallery during the exhibition in 2010, and later the other maps followed.

The cover image was taken at The Hope Workers Cafe, Holloway Road on the A1 in 2012. This cafe is also featured on page 13 and 152 & 153. The project photography began and finished at this very cafe.

Throughout the course of this project a combination of Kodak Portra 160 & 400 NC & VC negative as well as digital photography helped create the work. I hope you've enjoyed it.

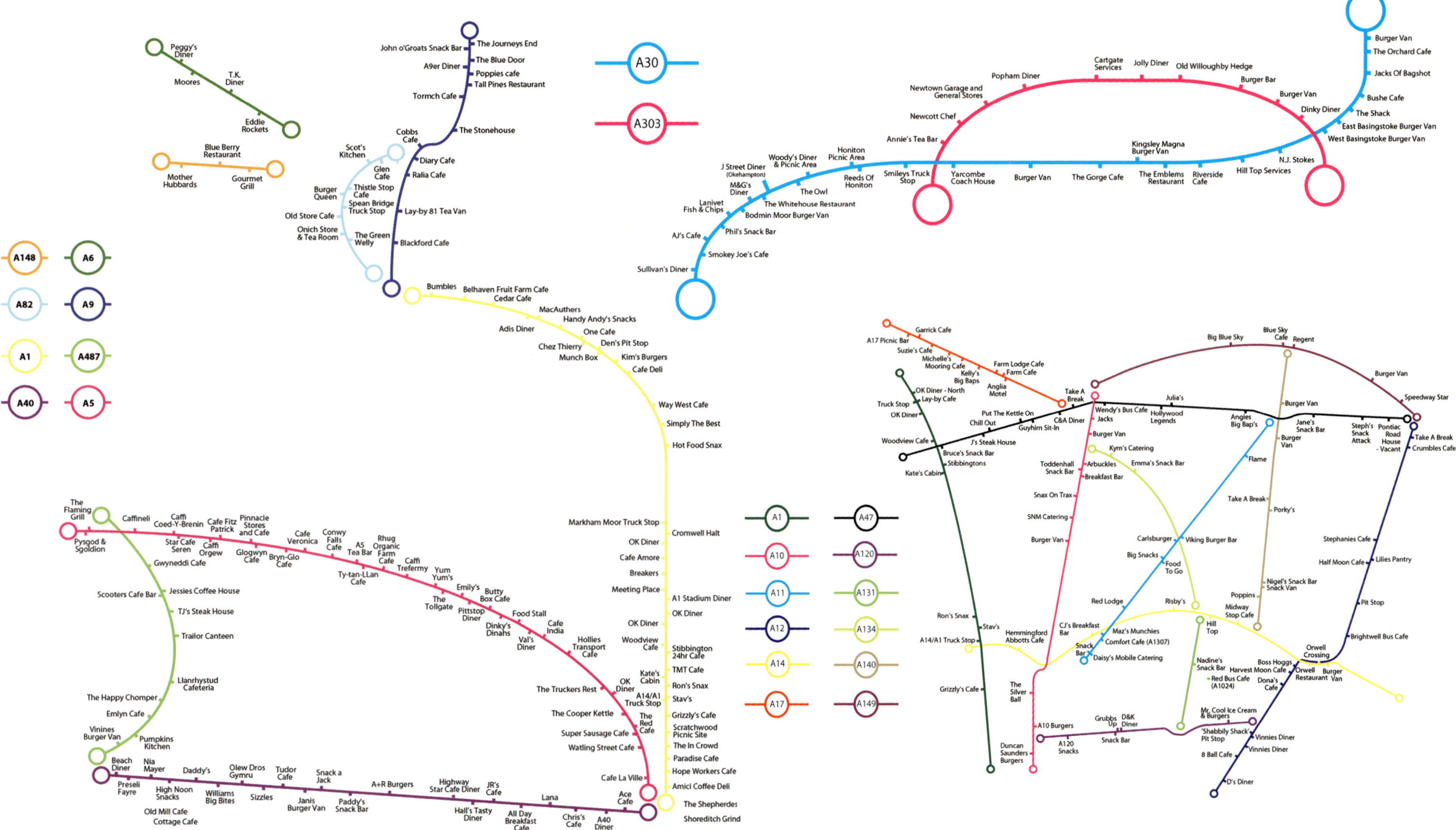


# Maps from Roadside Britain

# Thank You

Many thanks to all who supported me while creating Roadside Britain, from the countless workers, owners and customers at the many roadside services I visited, many of whom kindly provided me with complimentary cups of tea, coffee and the occasional fry up or bacon sandwich; to those who helped with the numerous exhibitions, presentations and signings of my first book titled *On The Road - London to Land's End* and to those who contributed to getting the second book ready for print.

**Thanks to the following organisations:**

University Of Westminster/Arts Council England/Babylon Gallery/ ADeC/ Ipswich & Colchester Museum Service/Host Gallery/Foto 8/ Hereford Photography Festival/Waterstones/Butter Market Studios/ Blurb/Andy's Kitchen/ Butterdesign.co.uk/Print & Design Centre/Ip-Art

**The creation of Roadside Britain wouldn't have been possible without the kind help of the following people:**

Joe Moran/Max Houghton/Katrina Vines/Zoe Davidson/Digby Chacksfield/Julia Devonshire/Emma Roodhouse/Rachel MacFarlane/ Rachel Stanley/Helena Spinney/Susie Wheeldon/Louise Fenner/ Elizabeth Magness/Serious Sam Barrett/James Young/ Paul Greene/ Rachael Palframan/Jamie Farrell/Steve Russell/Andrew Clarke/ Niav & Rafa/Eileen Fisher/ Cai Broom/Jennifer Long/Stephen Allard/ Harry Hardie/Steve "Jess The Trucker" James/Katie Thompson/Nick Butterfield/ Mum & Dad, my best friend and brother James and not forgetting the endless support from my good friends and family.

The imagery from page 47 - 113 was supported by the National Lottery through Arts Council England and first exhibited at the Babylon Gallery, Ely.

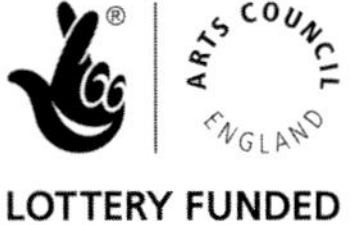

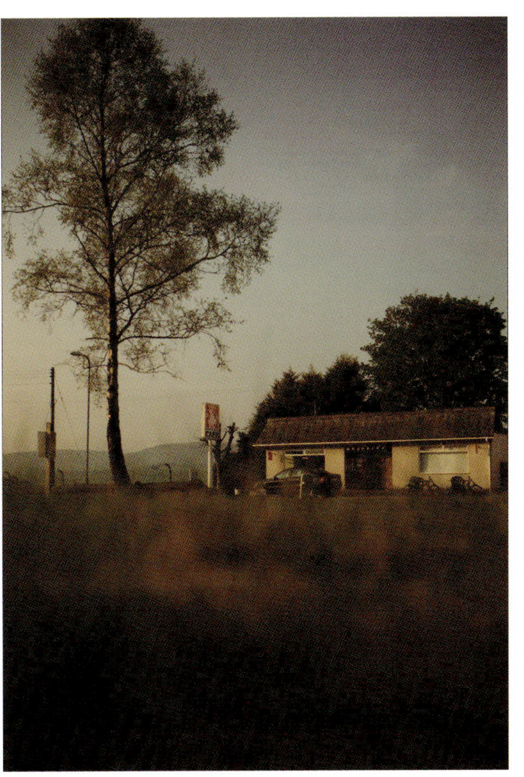

# Notes on the Authors

**S**am Mellish was born and brought up in Suffolk, UK. As a teenager, he worked throughout Europe, Asia, Africa and Australasia as a jobbing chef, later becoming a sports editorial and documentary photographer. At the age of 28 he returned to London to study for a Master of Arts in Photojournalism, and has since settled in the city, where he continues to publish and exhibit his work. *Roadside Britain* was born out of his love for the open road and a decent cup of tea.

**J**oe Moran is a social and cultural historian who writes about everyday life, especially Britain from the mid-Twentieth Century until the present day. Moran studied International History and Politics at Leeds University, before doing an MA in English Literature and a DPhil in American Studies at Sussex University. Currently, he teaches at Liverpool John Moores University, as well as writing for The Guardian, the Financial Times and other publications. He is the author of five books, including *On Roads: A Hidden History* (Profile Books 2009).

**M**ax Houghton is Course Leader of MA Photojournalism at University of Westminster. She has edited *8 Magazine* for the past six years, and writes about photographs for various international magazines and websites, including *Foam*, the BBC, the Daily Telegraph's culture hub *Telephoto*, and *Black and White Photography*.

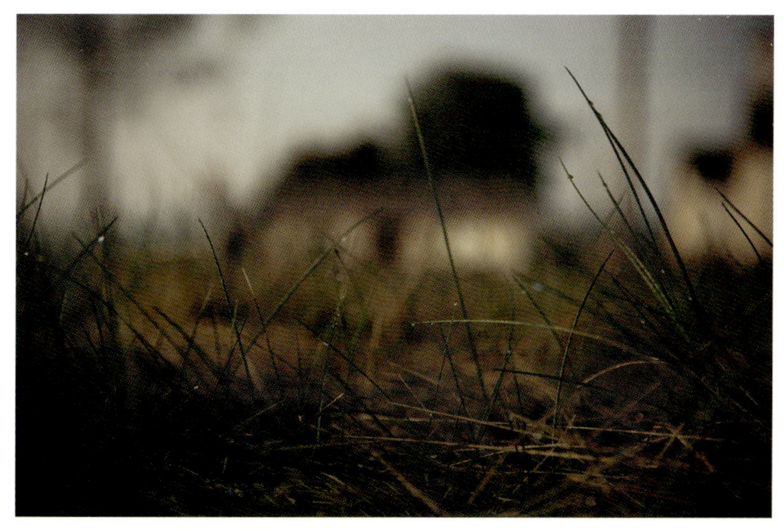

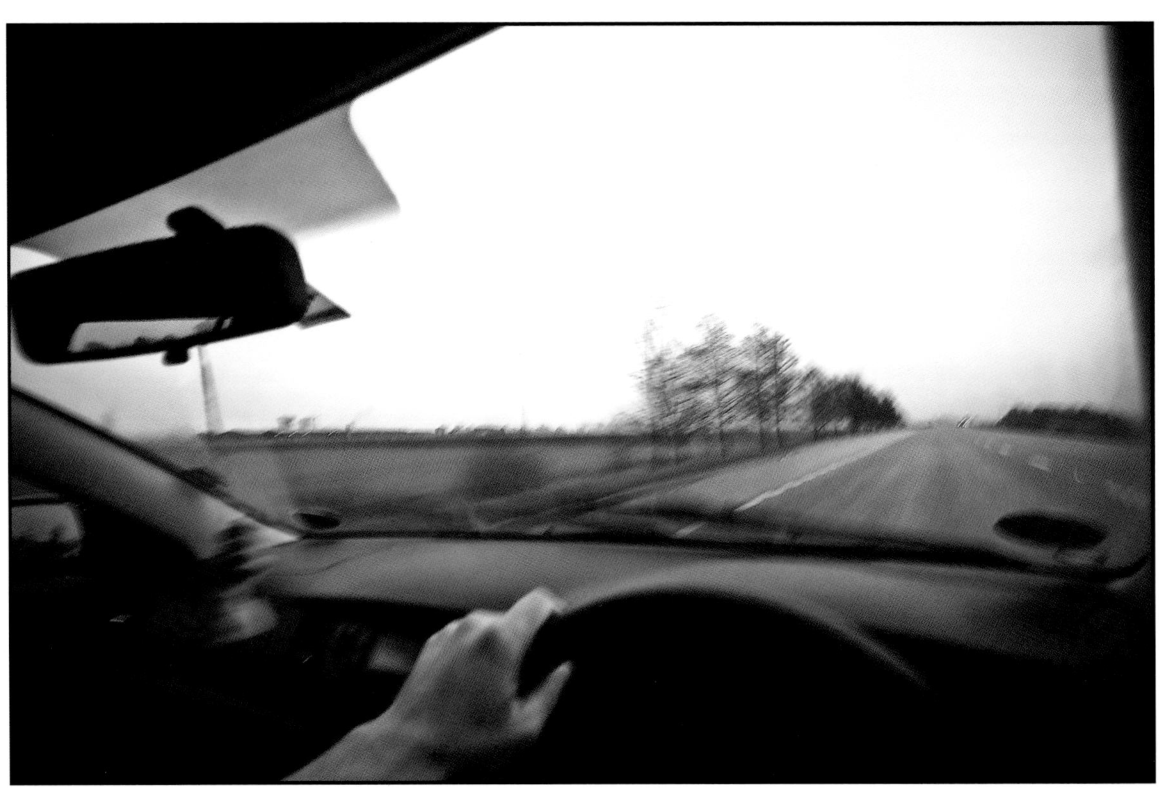